ANNALS

OF THE

PERSECUTION IN SCOTLAND

FROM THE

RESTORATION TO THE REVOLUTION.

BY JAMES AIKMAN, ESQ.,
Author of the History of Scotland, &c.

SECOND AMERICAN EDITION.

VOL. I.

PHILADELPHIA:
PRESBYTERIAN BOARD OF PUBLICATION.

Printed by
WM. S. MARTIEN.

Stereotyped by S. DOUGLAS WYETH
No. 7 Pear St., Philadelphia.

PREFACE

TO THE

AMERICAN EDITION.

THE period of church history embraced in the following volume is one of intense interest, especially to the Presbyterian reader. Scotland was the great theatre of the events here recorded; a country distinguished, from early times, for its attachment to the truth, and the singular heroism of its inhabitants in braving persecution for conscience sake. In no other period can we find a more illustrious exemplification of the true genius of Presbyterianism. Its intelligence, its abhorrence of ecclesiastical despotism, its zeal in the diffusion of knowledge, its spirituality of worship, in opposition to a religion of forms and ceremonies, its ardent love for truth, and its unflinching fortitude in adhering to principle in the face of danger and death, have all been illustrated in a manner the most impressive, in the history of our Scottish forefathers. The enemies with which it then contended were at once powerful and malignant. First with Popery, whose distinguishing trait is hostility to pure and undefiled religion, and then with its congener, Prelacy, sustained by the civil power, and abetted by a world that lieth in sin, it entered the lists, and with its sole reliance on the unfailing promises of God, it contended manfully, and although often in the fires it was not consumed, and although often in the deep waters, it was not overwhelmed. The faith of God's saints was most sorely tried, but like gold in the crucible, it stood the test and came forth purged of its dross. The record of those sufferings should never be regarded with indifference by those to whom this faith has been transmitted; nor should the memories of those men be forgotten who stood in the fore-front of the battle, that by their blood they might secure to remote generations the rights of Christian freedom and conscience, as a noble inheritance. To have such an ancestry is no common honour; to be partakers with them of a like precious faith, is a distinction more than regal.

The ancient enemies of Presbyterianism are not yet extinct. Popery and Prelacy have one common sentiment of dislike to the polity and faith which constitute its character, and in the recent revival of these powers, that dislike is daily assuming a less equivocal form. The present age is full of portents, and it would not be at all surprising if in these latter days Presbyterians should again be called to maintain their principles at the hazard of life. Against such a contingency they should be fully armed. To a cordial love for God's truth let there be added courage, and that they may derive strength from the force of example, and catch the spirit of the noble army of martyrs, let them carefully peruse these annals of past persecution.

EDITOR OF THE BOARD OF PUBLICATION.

CONTENTS.

BOOK IX. A.D. 1674—1676.

BOOK X. A.D. 1676—1677.

INTRODUCTION.

THE first annunciation of the gospel in Eden to fallen man, was accompanied with an assurance of persecution:—"I will put enmity between thee and the woman, and between thy seed and her seed: it shall bruise thy head, and thou shalt bruise his heel." And the same was explicitly renewed under the New Testament dispensation, where it is declared with peculiar emphasis—"Yea, all that will live godly in Christ Jesus shall suffer persecution." But, like "the primal curse, 'tis softened into mercy;" nay more, it is transformed into a blessing—"Blessed are ye when men shall revile you and persecute you, and shall say all manner of evil against you falsely for my sake: rejoice and be exceeding glad; for great is your reward in heaven." That these promises have been made good, the history of the Church in all ages bears testimony; and there is no testimony stronger than that of the Church in Scotland, whether we consider the fiery trials she has gone through, or the noble records her martyrs have left to the truth and faithfulness of God.

Christianity appears to have been introduced at a very early period, and never to have been wholly extinguished by the idolatries of Rome, in the south-western districts, where the Lollards of Kyle arose as harbingers of the Reformation, some time towards the end of the fourteenth century. In the year 1407, James Resby, an English presbyter, and a disciple of Wickliffe, was burned for Lollardism in Scotland, especially for interspersing these most dangerous dogmas in his sermons, "that a Pope was not in fact the vicar of Christ; nor could any Pope be so, unless he was holy;" besides forty other similar or worse conclusions: and his tenets spread widely. He was followed, 1431, by Paul Craw, "deprehendit," says Knox, "in the Universitie of Sanct Androis, and accusit of Heresie before suche as wer called Doctors of Theologie," and sent to expiate his errors in the flames. At his execution, they put "ane ball of bras in his mouthe to the end that he sould not gif confession of his faythe to the pepill, neyther yit that thai sould understand the defence which he hade agains thair unjust accusation and condemnation."

The political anarchy and confusion which prevailed in Scotland at this time, and in which the priests took an active share, seem to have diverted their attention for a while from prosecuting their schemes against the new obnoxious opinions; but when Luther shook the papacy, and his doctrines gaining ground on every side, had stirred up their slumbering hatred, the renovated warfare was announced by the martyrdom of Mr. Patrick Hamilton and of "the Scottish John Baptist," as Mr. George Wishart has been styled. But the prelates, who had shut their eyes to the signs of the times, grievously miscalculated.

The ministry of these two eminent men had produced on the already prepared population, a disposition not only to profess the truth themselves, but also to endeavour a national reformation; and their martyrdom hastened the crisis. Instead of terrifying, it enraged the people against the superstition which could require for its support the perpetration of such deadly crime.

During the nominal reign of the unfortunate Mary, but more especially after her flight into England, the cause rapidly progressed; and the Regents, however different in character, were obliged by the circumstances of the times in which they were placed, to aid in its furtherance. The absurd constitution of Scotland, that allowed a child unfit for governing himself to assume the power of governing a nation, occasioned various changes. After the accession of James VI., till previously to his marriage, he acquiesced in the presbyterial government, which, upon his return from Denmark with his queen, he declared in presence of the General Assembly to be "the purest kirk upon earth," and promised to defend it "against all deadly"—a promise he soon forgot, and forced upon his reluctant subjects a mongrel Episcopacy. This was followed up by his son Charles, who, after some preliminary encroachments, sent down a liturgy with an order to adopt it.

July 23, 1637, was the remarkable day on which the Bishop of Edinburgh, robed in his canonicals, attempted to introduce it in the High Church; but no sooner had he opened the service-book, than an old woman, Janet

Geddes by name, threw her stool at his head, which was quickly followed by a number of others, the whole congregation meanwhile crying out—"A Pope! a Pope!" and both the bishop and dean were forced out of the church, and driven home amid a shower of stones, hardly escaping with their lives. Commotions followed, till a free General Assembly met at Glasgow, November 21, 1638, where the Presbyterian form of church government was declared and acted upon as the government of the church, most agreeable to the gospel and the law of the land, which was acknowledged by the king at the treaty of Dunselaw, June 18, 1639.

When the civil war broke out, the English parliament convened an Assembly of Divines at Westminster, to which the General Assembly of the Kirk of Scotland sent four of their chief ministers, not less distinguished for their talents, than revered for their piety—Alexander Henderson, Samuel Rutherford, George Gillespie, and Robert Baillie, accompanied by Lord Maitland, afterwards Duke of Lauderdale, "a man of excellent parts, had they been blessed and improven; but as then his reputation was entire." The Confession of Faith, Catechisms, and Directory for Worship, which were here agreed upon, were received and sanctioned in their session 1648, and ratified by the Scottish parliament. For defending these, the persecutions narrated in the following pages were endured.

ANNALS OF THE PERSECUTION.

BOOK I.

A. D. 1604.—A. D. 1660.

Presbytery, the favourite form of religion in Scotland with the people, opposed by James VI.—At first opposed, afterwards sanctioned by Charles I.—Solemn League and Covenant—Confession of Faith—Defeat of the Duke of Hamilton and death of Charles —State of the Church—Charles II. crowned—Divisions among the Presbyterians—Resolutioners—Remonstrators—Protectorate of Cromwell—State of religion during that period—Restoration—Sharpe sent to London—Religious parties in Scotland—Sharpe's double dealing—Sudden change of manners—Rejoicings—Fears of the Remonstrators—Difference with the Resolutioners—First measures of the King—Promotes the enemies and persecutes the friends of the Covenant—Proceedings of the Committee of Estates, urged on by Sharpe—King's letter to the Edinburgh ministers—Exultation of the Resolutioners—Persecute their brethren—Committee of Estates order Lex Rex, &c. to be burned—Proclamation against the Remonstrants—Interference with regard to elections—Proclamation for a meeting of Parliament.

Ever since the days of the Reformation, Scotland has been distinguished by the attachment of her inhabitants to simplicity in the forms of their religious worship, and a dislike to pomp or lordly power in their ministers. Presbytery, of which these are the prominent features, has in consequence always been the favoured mode of ecclesiastical polity with the people; unfortunately her monarchs, previous to the Revolution of 1688, were as decidedly averse to it; and their tyrannical attempts to substitute a hated hierarchy in its place, involved the country, for three generations, in contention and bloodshed, persecution and distress, till the struggle issued in the final expulsion of the Stuarts from the throne.

James VI., after having given the Presbyterian church the royal sanction, and paid it the highest encomiums as the "purest kirk upon earth," and having repeatedly promised and vowed "to support it against all deadly," spent the greater part of his life in endeavours to overturn it. He succeeded in forcing upon an unwilling people a kind of mongrel prelacy, and left to his son the hazardous task of finishing his designed uniformity in religious worship between the two kingdoms.

Charles proceeded with more violence; and, by attempting to obtrude a detested liturgy, he destroyed the fabric it had cost his father so much king-craft to rear, and led to the remarkable renewing of the National Covenant, which, early in the year 1638, was subscribed with enthusiastic fervour by all ranks throughout the land. A free General Assembly convened at Glasgow in that year, November 21, accomplished what has usually been termed the second glorious Reformation, by restoring Presbytery to its primitive simplicity, and sweeping away all the innovations against which they had so long struggled. The proceedings of this assembly were afterwards solemnly confirmed by the estates; and Scotland for a short period enjoyed a hollow peace, while the king was contesting with his English parliament. Afraid, however, if the king overcame in the contest, that they would hold their own liberties by a very feeble tenure, they entered into a solemn league and covenant with the parliament for the mutual preservation of their religion and liberty, for promoting uniformity in worship and doctrine between the two nations, and for exterminating popery, prelacy, and schism: their weight decided the fate of the war.

When the English hierarchy had fallen, and the king's power was reduced, an assembly of the most learned divines that perhaps ever met in Britain, was called by authority of the English parliament. Assisted by commissioners from Scotland, they drew up the admirable Confession of Faith, with the Larger and Shorter Catechisms, still the standards of our church; but they differed on the Directory for Worship, against which some of the most learned of the Independents dissented—a prelude to more serious differences.

After Charles had been beaten out of the field, and was intriguing in a variety of ways with the army and with the English parliament, a majority in the Scottish estates, headed by the Duke of Hamilton, rashly "engaged" by a secret treaty to attempt his rescue. The church opposed war with England, as Charles would give only an equivocal pledge for supporting the establishment of Presbytery in that country; and they feared his duplicity in case he regained unrestricted power; and the minority in the estates also "protested" against it. The engagers being defeated at Preston, the protesters, whose leader was the Marquis of Argyle, came into power, and Scotland separated into two parties. Shortly after the defeat of the Scots, the king was brought to trial and executed, in spite of their remonstrances, which, now that they were divided among themselves, and had no army to back them, were little regarded.

At this time the Church of Scotland reached her greatest pitch of splendour. "For though," says a contemporary historian, "alwayes since the assembly at Glasgow the work of the gospel hade prospered, judicatories being reformed, godly ministers entered, and holy constitutions and rules daily brought into the Church; yet now, after Duke Hamilton's defeat, and in the interval betwixt the two kings, religion advanced the greatest step it had made for many years: now the ministrie was notably purified, the magistracy altered, and the people strangely refined. It is true, at this time hardly the fifth part of the lords of Scotland were admitted to sit in parliament; but those that did sit were esteemed truly godly men; so were all the rest of the commissioners in parliament elected of the most pious of every corporation. Also godly men were employed in all offices, both civil and military; and about this time the General Assembly, by sending abroad visiters into the country, made almost ane entire change upon the ministry in several places of the nation, purgeing out the scandalous and insufficient, and planting in their place a sort of godly young men, whose ministry the Lord sealed with ane eminent blessing of success, as they themselves sealed it with a seal of heavy sufferings; but so they made full proof of their ministry.

"Scotland hath been even by emulous foreigners called Philadelphia; and now she seemed to be in her flower. Every minister was to be tried five times a-year, both for his personal and ministerial behaviour; every congregation was to be visited by the Presbytery, that they might see how the vine flowrished and the pomegranate budded. And there was no case nor question in the meanest family in Scotland but it might become the object of the deliberation of the General Assembly; for the congregational session's book was tried by the presbytery, the presbytery's by the synod, and the synod's by the General Assembly. Likeways, as the bands of the Scottish Church were strong, so her beauty was bright; no error so much as named; the people were not only sound in the faith, but innocently ignorant of unsound doctrine; no scandalous person could live; no scandal could be concealed in all Scotland, so strict a correspondence there was between ministers and congregations. The General Assembly seemed to be the priest with Urim and Thumim; and there were not ane hundreth persons in all Scotland to oppose their conclusions: all submitted, all learned, all prayed; most part were really godly, or at least counterfeited themselves Jews. Than was Scotland a heap of wheat set about with lillies, uniform, or a palace of silver beautifully proportioned; and this seems to me to have been Scotland's high noon. The only complaint of profane people was, that the government was so strict they hade not liberty enough to sin."

"But this season lasted not long." The Presbyterians, who were averse to the ruling party in England, as sectarians in religion and republicans in politics, immediately proclaimed Charles II.; and commissioners were sent to the Hague, where he was subsisting on the bounty of his sister, to invite him upon conditions to assume the government. During the negotiations, while the terms were discussing, he authorized Montrose, already too well known for his cruelties, to attempt his unconditional restoration by force; and it was not till he heard of his failure, that he consented to take the oaths and become the covenanted king of Scotland.

His arrival, however, instead of uniting, occasioned deep and irreconcilable dissensions among the Scots—between those who distrusted, and those who affected to believe, his professions; yet as the church continued to maintain the ascendancy, they were kept within bounds till after the fatal battle of Dunbar. But when it became necessary to supply the loss occasioned by that disaster, they became apparent. The king required that all those who had hitherto been excluded as malignants, who had favoured the engagement, and were understood to be friendly to his unlimited power, should be restored to offices of trust both in the army and state: this was resisted by the strictest and most devout of the Presbyterians, who, considering them as enemies to the church, dreaded their admission into the king's councils, while he himself was suspected. The virtues of the king, and his inimitable improvement in adversity, were deemed sufficient answer, and resolutions favourable to their claims having been obtained by surprise from the major part of the commission, a schism took place by the minority protesting against the concession.

From this date the Presbyterians separated into two parties, who distracted the country for several years by their violent contentions; those who arrogated to themselves the praise of liberality and loyalty—their superior regard for the decrees of the church and the letter of the covenant—ranging under the name of resolutioners; while those esteemed the most holy, indefatigable, and laborious ministers, who preferred the spirit to the form of their religious constitution, were numbered among the protesters. They were likewise called remonstrators, from having followed up their protest by a remonstrance. Meanwhile Charles was crowned at Scone with great solemnity, the Marquis of Argyle, who was attached to the resolutioners, putting the crown upon his head; but the divisions continued till Cromwell obtained the supreme power, who granted free toleration to all sects, and liberty to the Presbyterians in every thing, except permitting the General Assembly to meet, which some of the more pious considered no bad service.

This period, down to the Restoration, has ever been considered as that in the Scottish Church most remarkably distinguished for the prevalence of real personal religion; and it was evident that God was preparing a people in this land for a day of hot and fiery trial. "I verily believe," says Kirkton, "there were more souls converted to Christ in that short period of time than in any season since the Reformation, though of treeple its duration. Nor was there ever greater purity and plenty of the means of grace than was in their time. Ministers were painful, people were diligent; and if a man hade seen one of their solemn communions, where many congregations mett in great multitudes—some dozens of ministers used to preach, and the people continued as it were in a sort of trance (so serious were they in spiritual exercises) for three dayes at least—he would have thought it a solemnity unknown to the rest of the world. Besides, the ministers, after some years, began to look at the questions about which they had divided, as inconsiderable; also it was found error made no great progress, the genius of the people being neither very curious nor easily changed."

The numbers who stood the test and suffered to the death, bear witness that the religious state of the country at the Restoration, as given by him, must be substantially true; as the numbers who apostatized make it evident that many must have dissembled. "There be in Scotland some nine hundred paroches."* "At the king's return every paroch had a minister, every village had a school, every family almost had a Bible; yea, in most of the country, all the children of age could read the Scriptures, and were provided of Bibles either by their parents or their ministers. Every minister was a very full professor of the reformed religion, according to the large Confession of Faith, framed at Westminster by the divines of both nations. Every minister was obliged to preach thrice a-week, to lecture and catechise once, besides other private duties, wherein they abounded according to their proportion of faithfulness and abilities. None of them might be scandalous in their conversation or negligent in their office, so long as a presbyterie stood; and among them were many holy in conversation and eminent in gifts. The dispensation of the ministry being fallen from the noise of waters and sound of trumpets, to the melody of harpers, which is alace the last messe in the banquet. Nor did a minister satisfy himself except his ministry had the seal of divine approbation, as might witness him to be really sent from God."

"Indeed, in many places the Spirit seemed to be poured out with the word, both by the multitudes of sincere converts, and also by the common work of reformation upon many who never came the length of a communion; there were no fewer than sixty aged people, men and women, who went to school, that even then they might be able to read the Scriptures with their own eyes. I have lived many years in a paroch where I never heard an oath; and

* These were divided into sixty-eight presbyteries, which were again cantoned into fourteen synods, out of all which, by a solemn legation of commissioners from every presbytery, they used to constitute a national assembly.

you might have ridde many miles before you heard any: also, you could not for a great part of the country have lodged in a family where the Lord was not worshipped by reading, singing, and public prayer. Nobody complained more of our Church-government than our taverners, whose ordinary lamentation was, their trade was broke, people were become so sober."*

Such was the delightful picture drawn by an eye-witness; and to render it perfect and permanent, the Presbyterians longed with desire for the restoration of their king, whose presence alone they believed would remove the only spots that in their eyes dimmed its lustre—the suspension of their General Assemblies, and the late sinful toleration. As soon as there was the least prospect of the desirable event, several ministers in Edinburgh—resolutioners—despatched Mr. James Sharpe to London, with instructions to watch over the interests of the Church, particularly of their own party; and as they knew that the king had a strong antipathy against the remon strants, who, during his stay in Scotland, had been assiduous in their upright though ungrateful endeavours for his conversion, and incurred his displeasure and that of his confidants by their uncourtly reproofs

* Kirkton mentions that the English often offered the protesters the government of the nation, which they refused, till Cromwell, "weary with their scrupulosity, and being highly caressed by Mr. (afterwards Archbishop) Sharpe, his large proffers in behalf of the resolutioners, was forced to allow them equal liberty, and so they continued in a balance till after his death."—*Hist. of the Church of Scotland*, pp. 48—56.—Law, in his Memorials, has a similar statement. "It is not to be forgotten, that from the year 1652 to the year 1660, there was great good done by the preaching of the gospel in the west of Scotland, more than was observed to have been for twenty or thirty years before; a great many brought into Christ Jesus by a saving work of conversion, which was occasioned through ministers preaching nothing all that tyme but the gospell, and had left off to preach up parliaments, armies, leagues, resolutions, and remonstrance, which was much in use before, from the year 1638 till that time 52, which occasioned a great number of hypocrytes in the Church, who, out of hope of preferment, honour, riches, and worldly credit, tooke on the form of godliness but wanted the power of it." P. 7

and uncompromising adherence to their principles, they were anxious to separate themselves from this the honestest portion of their brethren, and directed their agent carefully to remind his majesty of the difference between them and their more uncomplying opponents.

During the protectorate, as no persecution had been allowed on account of religious opinions, a few in Scotland seem to have adopted the tolerant maxims of the decried usurper; and although sectaries never flourished in that soil, they seem to have been sufficiently numerous to have excited the fears of the resolutioners, who, insensible to the benefits they enjoyed under the toleration of Cromwell, and eager to secure the liberties of their own kirk from the oppression of the prelatists, were equally anxious to guard against any freedom being allowed to those whom they termed fanatics.*

There was, besides, a third party, who, although previously discernible to those who understood the signs of the times, sprang up at once upon the afflicted vision of the resolutioners, when the rays of royalty again beamed above the horizon—a new race, who, having never been acquainted with the work of reformation, nor with the just proceedings of the nation, but weary of Presbyterian strictness, were ready to condemn the covenant and all the loyal and honest acting of the covenanters. These, consisting

* Mr. Robert Douglas writes to Mr. Sharpe, May 8, 1660:—"Your great errand will be for this kirk. I am confident the king will not wrong our liberties whereunto he himself is engaged. He needs not declare any liberty to tender consciences here, because the generality of the people and whole ministry have embraced the established religion by law with his majesty's consent. It is known that in all the times of the prevailing of the late party in England, none here petitioned for toleration, except some inconsiderable naughty men." And the ministers of Edinburgh, *i. e.* resolutioners, in a letter, May 10, to the Earl of Rothes, who was going to meet the king at Breda, used the following remarkable expressions: "He [the king] knows likewise how much the people adhere to the establishment of the Church; so that there is no pretext for an indulgence to such as shall recede from it, but many inconveniences would ensue upon the granting it." Correspondence between Messrs Douglas, Dickson, &c. with Sharpe.—*Wodrow's Introd.*

chiefly of young men of rank, were prepared for any change, and were supposed, in general, to be rather favourable to Episcopacy. A knowledge of this circumstance, and the frequent representations of the alarming fact by his correspondents, seem early to have influenced Sharpe to desert his employers and go over to the enemy.

In May, he went upon an embassage to Charles at Breda, and there was confirmed in the treachery which he completed shortly after the king's landing in England. His villanous hypocrisy in managing the overturn of the polity he was despatched to support, was consummate; yet now, when we know the part he played, it is not difficult to perceive, in his most specious letters, an overacting which must have betrayed him to men less confiding than his employers.* Besides preventing all access to the king, and representing the chief leaders in Scotland as favourable to prelacy, he dissuaded his friends from addressing against it, and cruelly widened the breach between them and the protesters. His ambition was stimulated by his revenge; he wished to gratify his private resentment against the most eminent of the latter—Samuel Rutherford, James Guthrie, and Lord Warriston. Yet, however much we may detest the traitor, it is matter of high gratulation that his mission failed; for, had he acted faithfully and succeeded, he would have procured for Scotland an iron yoke of political presbytery, which might indeed have preserved the beloved polity secured by acts of parliament, by prohibitions, and by every civil pain and penalty by which churchmen support their power; but he would have destroyed religious liberty, and delivered the nation over to a thraldom which would have been worse, as it would probably have been more permanent, than the prelacy that ensued—it would, it is likely, have been

* "I profess," says Mr. Douglas, "I did not suspect Mr. Sharpe in reference to prelacy more than I did myself, nor more than the apostles did Judas before his treachery was discovered."—*Wodrow's Introd.*

more moral, but it might not have been less oppressively severe.*

When Charles was at last restored to the wishes and prayers of his people, as if some enchanter's wand had touched the frame of society, the whole kingdom in an instant changed, and, from a state of grave seriousness and exemplary decency, burst out into one disorderly scene of riot and revelry; and the day of thanksgiving for this happy event was celebrated in Edinburgh in a manner that had been very unusual in that capital for at least a quarter of a century. After sermon, the magistrates proceeded to the cross, on which was a table covered with sweetmeats, and the well ran with wine; there, amid the flourishing of trumpets and the beating of drums, the royal healths were drunk, and three hundred dozen of glasses broken in honour of the day! On the Castle Hill, fireworks were exhibited, the principal figures in which were Cromwell and the Devil, who, after diverting the multitude with a flight and pursuit, exploded and disappeared amid shouts of applause.

The considerate part of the community viewed the unconditional recall of the king with very different sensations; but these, in that frantic hour, were few in number, and chiefly consisted of the remonstrators, whose dark forebodings were deemed the offspring of their own guilty consciences accusing them of their former disloyalty. In vain did they ask for evidence of his being changed from what he was, before they could trust their liberties into his hands without security. They had all along been

* There is much retribution in this world, although it be not the place of final account. Here especially God punishes his own people. The wicked may prosper in their wickedness—" he sees their day is coming"—but the Lord will never suffer his children to sin with impunity. This was remarkably exemplified in the case of these good men, who were now so anxious to prevent their brethren from enjoying liberty of conscience, in order that they themselves might engross the royal favour and the chief places in the Church; their own agent betrayed them; and the very means they were using to accomplish their improper and selfish aims, were turned against them, and became the instruments of their correction.

jealous of Sharpe, and their suspicions had been heightened by some surmises of his transactions at London; but all their advances towards their brethren had been repulsed by the resolutioners, who put the most unbounded confidence in that traitor's assurances of the king's friendly countenance towards themselves, and his intended vengeance upon them. The first measures of Charles, however, put an end to the differences of the truly pious among both parties, who were soon undeceived, and sent to the furnace to be refined together.

All the high offices of Scotland were disposed of to men either of no religion, or of that very accommodating kind which is always found on the side of interest and power. Middleton, a soldier of fortune, created an Earl, was appointed commissioner to hold the next parliament; the Earls Glencairn had the chancellorship — Crawford, the treasury — Rothes, president of the council—and Lauderdale, secretary of state, and one of the gentlemen of the bedchamber, (the only Scottishman admitted to this honour;) Sir Archibald Primson was clerk-register; and Sir John Fletcher, king's advocate. Meanwhile those who were esteemed the leaders of the covenanters, although they had ever sturdily maintained their loyalty, after the greater part of the others had yielded, were thrown into prison and threatened with prosecutions for treason. The Marquis of Argyle was seized at London, whither he had gone to congratulate the king, and sent to the tower; and orders were forwarded to Scotland, to Major-General Morgan, commander-in-chief, to secure Sir James Stewart, provost of Edinburgh; Sir Archibald Johnstoun, Lord Warriston; and Sir John Christy of Carswell. Warriston escaped for the time; but the other two were arrested in a somewhat ludicrous manner. The General having heard that Christy was in town upon private business, waited upon the Provost, and required him in virtue of his office, to apprehend Sir John and carry him to the Castle; which his lordship having done, when he was about to take leave, with many expressions of regret, he was informed "that it behoved him to bear his friend company;" nor did he obtain a release till about ten years after.

Until the meeting of a new parliament, the administration of Scottish affairs was entrusted to the surviving members of the committee of estates, nominated by the last Scottish parliament; and as they had all concurred with the king in swearing the National and Solemn League and Covenant, it was expected that they would at least be favourable to the established religion of the land; but it very soon appeared how little confidence can be placed in the professions or even oaths of public men, when the stream runs in an opposite direction. Their first meeting, at which the chancellor presided, was held in Edinburgh, August 23, and their first act was a proper prelude to the tyranny about to be inflicted on their country.

On that day, a few of the protestors, who had in vain endeavoured to convince their brethren of the critical situation in which the Presbyterian church stood, met at Edinburgh to draw up a humble address and supplication to the king, suited to the emergency. They were in all nine ministers, of whom the chief were Mr. James Guthrie of Stirling, and Messrs. Traill, and John Stirling of Edinburgh, with two ruling elders. As the meeting and its object were no secrets, the chancellor and committee dispatched messengers, who seized their papers, containing a scroll of their supplication, with copies of some letters to their brethren in Glasgow, requesting a full meeting for considering the subject; and immediately after issued a warrant for imprisoning in Edinburgh Castle the whole of those who had been present at the unlawful conventicle—terms about to become of frequent use and of fearful import.

The scroll consisted of declarations of their abhorrence of the murder of his majesty's royal father, and the actings of the late usurping power—of thankfulness for the Lord's preservation of his own sacred person, and for his quiet restoration without the effusion of Christian blood—professions of zeal for the glory of God, the good of the church, and faithful and loyal tenders of all the duties of honour, subjection, and obedience, due from humble and loving subjects to their native and lawful sovereign; but they expressed their fears of the popish prelatical and malignant party, of their attempting the overthrow of the pure religion as established, and the re-introduction of all the corruptions which were formerly cast out;* and they reminded his majesty of his and their solemn engagements to God, of the Lord's mercy to him and them, and their mutual obligations to faithfulness in the performance of their vows.

They were therefore charged with proceedings expressly derogatory to his majesty's royal prerogative, and tending to the disturbance of the present peace of his majesty's dominions; and next day the

* These excellent men, for such undoubtedly they were, who had enjoyed undisturbed liberty of conscience and freedom of religious worship under Cromwell, thus adverted to that period, and thus would have requited their protectors.—" Neither are we less apprehensive of the endeavours of the spirit of error that possesseth sectaries in these nations, which as it did at first promote the practice of a vast toleration in things religious, and afterwards proceeded unto the framing of the mischief thereof into a law, so we doubt not but it will still be active unto the promoting and procuring the same under the specious pretence of *Liberty for tender consciences*. The effects whereof have, in a few years past, been so dreadful, that we cannot think of the continuing of it, but with much trembling and fear." Then follows a text upon which the whole annals of the persecution will form a most striking and instructive commentary. " Therefore, knowing that to kings, princes, rulers, and magistrates appertains the conservation and purgation of religion, and that unity and peace be preserved in the church, and that the truth of God be kept pure and entire, that all blasphemies and heresies be suppressed, all corruptions or abuses in discipline and worship prevented or reformed, and all the ordinances of God duly settled, administered, and observed, We, your majesty's most humble subjects, do, with bowed knees and bended affections, humbly supplicate your majesty that you would employ your royal power unto the preservation of the reformed religion in the church of Scotland, in doctrine, worship, discipline, and government, and unto the carrying on of the work of uniformity in religion in the churches of God in the three kingdoms, in one confession of faith, form of church-government, directory for worship and catechising; and to the extirpation of popery, prelacy, superstition, heresy, schism, profaneness, and whatever shall be found contrary to sound doctrine," &c.

committee of estates prohibited, by proclamation, all unlawful and unwarrantable meetings and conventicles in any place within the kingdoms of Scotland without his majesty's special authority; and likewise all seditious petitions and remonstrances under what pretext soever, which might tend to the disturbance of the peace of the kingdom, or alienating or diminishing the affections of his majesty's subjects from their due obedience to his majesty's lawful authority, and that under the highest pains. Sheriffs and magistrates of burghs were ordered to be careful within their respective bounds, that no such pernicious or dangerous meetings should be permitted, but that they should be prevented, hindered, and made known to the executive. These proceedings were ostensibly directed against the remonstrants alone, but were intended to answer the double purpose of overawing the elections for the ensuing parliament, and paving the way for the complete overturn of freedom in the state, and presbytery in the church.

Mr. Sharpe on his arrival from London, gave a keener edge to the proceedings of the committee, and, by his duplicity, prevented the good men among the resolutioners from taking any steps, either for their own security or the relief of their oppressed brethren. In answer to an epistle from his employers to the king, entreating his favour and countenance for their church, he brought the following, addressed to Mr. Robert Douglas, Minister, Edinburgh, to be by him communicated to the presbytery:—

"Charles R., trusty and well beloved, we greet you well. By the letters you sent to us with this bearer, Mr. James Sharpe, and by the account he gave of the state of *our church* there, we have received full information of your sense of our sufferings and of your constant affection and loyalty to our person and authority: And therefore we will detain him here no longer—of whose good services we are very sensible—nor will we delay to let you know by him our gracious acceptance of your address, and how well we are satisfied with your carriage, and with the generality of the ministers of Scotland in this time of trial, whilst some, under specious pretences, swerved from that duty and allegiance they owed to us. And because such, who by the countenance of usurpers have disturbed the peace of that our church, may also labour to create jealousies in the minds of well-meaning people, we have thought fit by this to assure you, that, by the grace of God, we resolve to discountenance profanity and all contemners and opposers of the ordinances of the gospel. We do also resolve to protect and preserve the government of the church of Scotland as it is settled by law, without violation, and to countenance in the due exercise of their function all such ministers who shall behave themselves dutifully and peaceably as becomes men of their calling. We will also take care that the authority and acts of the General Assembly at St. Andrew's and Dundee, 1651,* be owned and stand in force until we shall call another General Assembly, which we purpose to do as soon as our affairs will permit. And we do intend to send for Mr. Robert Douglas, and some other ministers, that we may speak with them in what may further concern the affairs of that church. And as we are very well satisfied with your resolution not to meddle without your sphere, so we do expect that church judicatories in Scotland and ministers there will keep within the compass of their station, meddling only with matters ecclesiastick, and promoting our authority and interest with our subjects against all opposers: and that they will take special notice of such who, by preaching, or private conventicles, or any other way, trangress the limits of their calling by endeavouring to corrupt the people, or sow seeds of disaffection to us or our government. This you shall make known to the several presbyteries within that our kingdom. And as we do give assurance of our favour and encouragement to you, and to all honest,

* The acts of these Assemblies were almost entirely levelled against the remonstrators.

deserving ministers there, so we earnestly recommend it to you that you be earnest in your prayers, publick and private, to Almighty God, who is our Rock and our Deliverer, both for us and for our government, that we may have fresh and constant supplies of his grace, and the right improvement of all his mercies and deliverances to the honour of his great name, and the peace, safety, and benefit of all our kingdoms; and so we bid you heartily farewell."

Delighted with this most gracious epistle, the Edinburgh presbytery printed and caused it to be transmitted to all the Presbyteries in Scotland, praised it from their pulpits, and procured a silver box to preserve the precious original. It was not to be supposed that, under language so explicitly guaranteeing the government of the Church of Scotland, as settled by law, that, by any lurking inuendo, Episcopacy could be meant; the resolutioners therefore considered the day as their own, and, with premature speed, hastened to chant their victory. They warmly thanked his majesty for his letter, which they told him in their address they had received upon a day formerly devoted by them to mourning, September 3,* which had revived their spirits, and excited them to bless the Lord who had put such a purpose in his royal heart to preserve and protect the government of the Church without violation; nor was the "choice of such an able and faithful person," as Lauderdale, "for the weighty employment of secretary less an object of gratulation!" But while we look back with pity upon the speedy dissipation of all the good men's hopes and anticipations, it is impossible not to feel that they in some measure merited them for the facility with which they allowed themselves to become

* The anniversary of the battles of Dunbar and Worcester—an ominous coincidence as it turned out. Another was remarked at the time. "It was a sad observation, that that very day of the month being the 23d of August, on which the protesters were apprehended, was the very same day whereon one hundred years before the Popish religion had been abolished, and the true religion established in parliament; and some feared this might be the turning of the tide backwards."—*Kirkton*, p. 73.

the dupes and the tools, in persecuting their own brethren, of these very men by whom they themselves were afterwards persecuted.

Sharpe, whose composition the letter was, followed out his plan of dividing the ministers. He was well aware that the remonstrators were the most acute and least liable to be imposed upon of the Presbyterians; he knew also that they suspected him, and he hated them; he therefore, by an insinuation in it, pointed them out as persons who, under specious pretences, had swerved from their duty during the usurpation; and the Church judicatories hastened to inflict punishment upon them for this indefinite crime;—"Our synods after this," says Kirkton, "doing little other thing than censuring and laying aside those of that way. And though the preceding harvest before the king's return all the synods of Scotland hade agreed to bury by-past differences, yet, upon the receipt of this blessed letter, the old wounds opened; and wherever the public resolution-men were the plurality, the protesters were censured upon the burried differences. In the synod of Merse, they laid aside five ministers; in Lothian, many were laid aside both in Lithgow and Biggar presbyteries; so it was in Perth and in the north: and the truth is, had not the course of synods been interrupted by the introduction of bishops, few had keeped their places who were afterwards ejected by that infamous proclamation at Glasgow in the year 1662."

Nor was the committee idle; Mr. Patrick Gillespie, principal of Glasgow College, was brought prisoner to Edinburgh Castle, and Mr. Robert Row, minister of Abercorn, and W. Wiseheart of Kinniel, were confined to their chambers in the town. Having forbid any meetings for petitioning, they proceeded to display their antipathy to those principles of freedom, for which their fathers had contended, by emitting a proclamation against Rutherford's Lex Rex—a work which was held in high estimation by the covenanters, as it advocated the cause of liberty and the legitimate limitations on power, with an energy and clearness the enemies of freedom could not bear; and another work, supposed to be written by Mr. James Guthrie, entitled "The Causes of God's Wrath against Scotland," which enumerated the sins of the land, princes, priests, and people, with a faithfulness that was intolerable. They declared these two books to be full of seditious and treasonable matter, animating his majesty's good subjects to rise up in rebellion against their lawful prince and sovereign, and poisoning their hearts with many seditious and rebellious principles, prejudicial to his royal person and authority, and to the peace of the kingdom. All, therefore, possessed of copies of the obnoxious publications were required to deliver them up to the king's solicitor within a certain time, under pain of being considered enemies to his majesty's authority, and liable to be punished accordingly. They were both burnt at the cross—a favourite, if not a very convincing, mode of answering such like productions. With revolting meanness, they at the same time caused the inscriptions to be effaced from the tombs of Alexander Henderson in Edinburgh, and George Gillespie at Kirkaldie—men who needed not the frail remembrance of a monumental stone to make their memories live in the recollection of their country, and whose services have more lasting record than a graving-iron could bestow.

Some few days after, they made a still more explicit disclosure of their aversion to the "good old cause"—a sneering form of expression became fashionable among the courtiers—by another proclamation directed against the remonstrants and their adherents, not only forbidding meetings for consultation, which were still legal, but likewise any adverting, in their sermons or otherwise, to the state of the Church, or the danger to be apprehended from the introduction of the exploded and hated prelatical offices and forms; and, as they knew the effect of popular preaching, they appear to have been most anxious at once to suppress all pulpit opposition to the course they were about to pursue.

Of the watchmen upon the Scottish Zion, the remonstrants had been the most wakeful and most jealous of encroachments upon the established covenanted constitution of the Church and state, and the committee were assured, that when they apprehended danger, they would not be silent; they therefore expressly commanded that none, in sermons, preachings, declamations, or speeches, should presume to reflect on the conduct of his majesty or his progenitors, misconstrue his proceedings, or meddle in his affairs or estate, present, bygone, or in time coming, under the highest penalties; and if any who heard what could be construed into slander against the king did not reveal it, they were to be liable to the same punishment as principals. This proclamation, the anti-type of so many furious attacks upon the liberty of the lieges, was calculated to ensnare those who, being accustomed openly to speak their sentiments, were not prepared at once to renounce all mention of public affairs in common conversation or public discourses, whether ministers, elders, or private gentlemen; and numbers of each description were immediately made to feel its oppressive weight.

Had a free election been allowed, notwithstanding the loyal frenzy of many, and the hypocritical pretensions of more, there might some troublesome members have procured admission to the estates; but those whose influence and opposition were most dreaded, being by this proclamation placed in very delicate circumstances—as evidence of unguarded expressions might easily have been procured—were happy to escape censure, and did not stand forward at the only time when they could have done so with some probability of success, in support of the constitution, freedom, and religion of their country. The committee, however, did not rest here: with the most unblushing effrontery, although conscious themselves of having to a man complied with the English, they hung out a threat of prosecution for this common and inevitable fault, which damped all who seemed inclined to assert the independence of a Scottish par liament, or the privileges they had obtained from the crown during the late struggle.*

Besides to pinion the country gentlemen more effectually, they tendered a bond to all of whom they were suspicious, which they obliged them to sign, with a sufficient cautioner, each binding themselves —besides disowning the remonstrance—that they should not in any way or manner, directly or indirectly, plot, contrive, speak, or do any thing tending, or what might tend, to the hurt, prejudice, or derogation of his majesty's royal person or any of that royal family—that they should not do any thing, directly or indirectly, tending, or that might tend, to the breach or disturbance of the public peace, nor connive or concur with any person whatsoever who should contrive any such thing; but, to the utmost of their power, stop and let any such plot and doing, and appear personally before the committee, sub-committee, or parliament, upon a lawful citation; and, in case of failure, the parties bound themselves to pay a high fine, besides whatever other punishment might be inflicted.

For a justification of proceedings so unwarrantable, we must look to the sequel; it was not because the parties accused were inimical either to kingly government or to the person or right of Charles, but because the plan was already formed for sweeping from the face of the country, had it been possible, whatever was lovely or of good report—whatever in the institutions of the state or the polity of the Church was calculated to present any obstruction to the tide of obscene licentiousness and faithless despotism that was now fast flowing upon them. Their stretches

* Of the nature of these prosecutions, the reader may form some idea from the following:—"Mr. James Nasmyth, minister of the gospel at Hamilton, was sisted before the committee for words alledged to have been spoken by him many years ago. About the year 1650, when Lambert was in the church, it was alledged he pressed his hearers to employ their power for God, and not in opposition to the gospel, otherwise they might expect to be brought down by the judgment of God as those who went before were!"—*Wodrow*, vol. i. p. 12.

of power against the liberties of the country, do not, however, seem to have occasioned any remonstrance; and the Synod of Lothian was amused with a proclamation for calling a General Assembly, which Mr. William Sharpe had submitted for their amendment; but the last acts of the committee, levying a cess, excited some remark as to the legality of the tax or their power to exact it.

On the 1st of November, a proclamation announced the meeting of parliament; and the same day another, that the king had committed to them the consideration and judging of the conduct of all his subjects during the late troubles, from whom alone he would receive any applications, and promising after his honour and ancient royal prerogative were vindicated, he would grant a free, full pardon and indemnity —a promise which, although conveyed in very specious language, and accompanied by an assurance that there was nothing his royal bosom was more desirous of than that his people should be blessed with abundance of happiness, peace, and plenty, was received with suspicion, and, like almost all the other acts of grace, afforded little relief to the unfortunate, while it secured the persons and plunder of those who had pillaged and oppressed them

BOOK II.

DECEMBER 1660 TO 12TH JULY 1661.

Lord High Commissioner arrives in Edinburgh—Parliament—Its composition—Act of indemnity withheld—Lord Chancellor restored to the Presidentship—Oath of allegiance—Retrogression in reformation work—Divine right of Kings asserted—Solemn League and Covenant repealed—Engagement approved, &c.—Declaration—Resolutioners begin to perceive their error—Middleton amuses the ministers of Edinburgh—Manner of concocting the Act recissory and of getting it passed—Middleton's interview with D. Dickson and part of the Edinburgh presbytery—Distress of the ministers—Dispersion of the Synods—Concluding acts—Trial of Argyle—His behaviour before and at the place of execution—Trial of James Guthrie—His behaviour and execution—Captain Govan—Persecutions of Mr. Traill of Edinburgh—Mr. Moncrief of Scone—Intrepid reply of his wife—Mr. Robert Macwaird of Glasgow—His striking picture of the effects of the Restoration—His accusation—Defence—Banishment—Swinton of Swinton—Sir John Christy and Mr. P. Gillespie's escape—Parliament rises—Samuel Rutherford.

THE Earl of Middleton, Lord High Commissioner, arrived at the ancient Palace of Holyrood on the last day of December 1660. He entered upon his office with great pomp; and, being allowed a princely salary for the support of his establishment, he vied with royalty itself in the profusion of his expenditure. Every preparation had been made for his reception: he was met and conducted to his residence by a large concourse of the nobility and the magistrates of the capital; and the venerable cathedral of St. Giles had been elegantly fitted up with a throne for his Grace and lofts for the parliament.

That parliament which met on the first day of the new year, was one entirely suited for promoting the schemes of the Scottish rulers. The old nobles, who had been active in the cause of the covenant, had almost all died out, their estates had been wasted, and of the new race too many, neglected in their education, were now dependent in their circumstances. When the king arrived, they had flocked to London to put in their claims upon his justice or generosity for their sufferings in the royal cause, and had been received with specious condescension, and sent home with empty pockets and magnificent expectations. But they had learned at court to laugh at sobriety, to ridicule religion, and to consider even common decency a mark of disloyalty, while they looked to a rich harvest of fines and confiscations from the estates of the remonstrators, as a reward for their sacrificing their principles and profession at the shrine of prerogative. The commissioners for counties and burghs were chosen entirely from among those who were considered devoted to the court and averse to the strict Presbyterians. In some cases, when persons of an opposite description had been returned, the ruling party interfered and procured others to be substituted; and to prevent such as were distinguished for their attachment to the cause of religious freedom from offering themselves as candidates, they got them accused of complying with the usurpers, and summoned as criminals.*

From a parliament so constituted, the most servile compliance might have been anticipated; but to ensure their submission, an act of indemnity had been withheld from Scotland; and, while every one dread-

* Were it not that mankind have a strange propensity to reward with injury favours they feel too great to repay, and to heap injustice upon their benefactors in order to conceal their ingratitude, we would be astonished at the conduct of Charles; but having often, in private life, seen that to raise a wretch from penury, was to incur his hatred, if we did not, at the same time, rise in proportion; we confess that the ingratitude of princes to those who have succoured them in distress, ceases to excite those strong feelings of reprobation, which we have often heard men in humbler life, who were themselves guilty of grosser injustice, express against crimes, whose highest aggravation was, that they were committed by persons of rank.

ed his individual safety, the whole assisted in destroying that public liberty which might have afforded a better chance for security than the will of a prince or the favour of a parasite. The regalia, always carried before the commissioner at the opening of a session, were borne—the crown by the Earl of Crawford, the sceptre by Sutherland, and the sword by Mar. The Duke of Hamilton and the Marquis of Montrose rode immediately behind. Mr. Robert Douglas, who had preached the coronation sermon before Charles when he was inaugurated at Scone, delivered upon this occasion a faithful and appropriate discourse from 2 Chron. xix. 6.—"Take heed what you do; for you judge not for man but for the Lord, who is with you in the judgment."

The Earl of Middleton's commission was then presented, and, as had been previously agreed upon, an act was brought forward to restore to the Lord Chancellor the Presidentship of parliament. This act, which struck at the root of the whole reformation in Scotland, deserves particular notice. By several acts of the estates, passed during the troublous times, particularly one of the last, held in 1651, at which the king himself had presided, it was enacted, that, before entering upon business, every member should swear and subscribe the covenant, without which the constitution of parliament would become null and void. To have set aside these statutes openly and at once, was thought too flagrant; but it had also been enacted during the late struggle, that the President of the parliament should be elected by parliament, instead of the Chancellor nominated by the king; and it was therefore proposed to abolish this privilege as trenching upon the royal prerogative. In this act, however, brought forward for that purpose, was inserted an oath of allegiance, which went to annul all preceding oaths, and covertly to revive the abhorred supremacy of the king. It was insidiously worded, in order that those who wished to have an excuse for compliance might take it without appearing undisguisedly to violate their former engagements, yet sufficiently plain to justify a refusal by men who were not altogether prepared to surrender their principles to their interest.

By it the sovereign was acknowledged only supreme governor in the kingdom over all persons and in all causes; and it was declared that no foreign prince, power, or state, nor person, civil nor ecclesiastic, had any jurisdiction, power, or superiority over the same; "and therefore," it was added, "I utterly renounce and forsake all foreign jurisdictions, powers, and authorities, and shall, at my utmost power, defend, assist, and maintain his majesty's jurisdiction aforesaid against all deadly, and never decline his majesty's power and jurisdiction." The consistent and stricter part of the Presbyterians were not imposed upon. They considered, and correctly as it afterwards appeared, that this was a complete acknowledgment of the king's ecclesiastical supremacy, and conferred upon him the power to alter or innovate at his pleasure upon the religion of the country. In parliament, however, almost the whole took the oath without remark, except the Earls of Cassils and Melville of the nobles, and the Laird of Kilburnie of the commissioners, who would not subscribe it unless allowed to limit the king's supremacy to civil matters—an explanation which Middleton was disposed to admit of verbally, but, knowing the extent to which allegiance was to be required, he refused to permit this explanation to be recorded.

Having thus dispensed with the obligation of the covenant as a parliament-oath, and reinstated his majesty in his ecclesiastical power, they proceeded to restore to him a less questionable part of the prerogative—the nomination of the officers of state, privy counsellors, and Lords of Session, the right of convoking and dissolving parliament, of commanding the militia, and of making peace and war. These powers, which are now deemed necessary for the support of the crown in regular ordinary times, had been assumed by the estates of Scotland (1649) on account of their abuse by the English ministers and favourites, at a period when our country, from being the poorest of the two united kingdoms, and the most distant from the immediate presence of the king, was peculiarly liable to be oppressed by those who obtained possession of the royal ear:—and the whole of the succeeding melancholy period evinces but too clearly how well founded was the jealousy entertained of the power intrusted to a monarch who was a non-resident. But what then particularly disgusted the friends of freedom, was, to observe in their re-enactment, the express unqualified avowal of the slavish tenets of the divine rights of kings, and their accountability to God alone, the assertion of which had occasioned all the troubles of the land, had brought Charles I. to the block, and which was eventually to forfeit for the Stuarts the throne of their fathers.

Sudden and astonishing as had been the revolution that had taken place in the public feelings and morals, and outrageously violent as the shoutings of newfangled loyalty had been against the treasons and insults of the remonstrators, still the covenants were esteemed sacred bonds by an imposing number of the worthiest part of the community, whom it might not have been advisable to shock too abruptly. These revered engagements were therefore first attacked obliquely in an act which purported merely to assert a constitutional truth respecting "his majesty's royal prerogative in making of leagues and the convention of the subjects," which, after narrating some enactments forbidding councils, conventions, or assemblies, for determining matters of state, civil or ecclesiastical, without his majesty's command or license, declared that any explanation or glosse that, during these troubles, had been put upon these acts—"as, 'that they are not to be extended against any leagues, councils, conventions, assemblies, or meetings, made, holden, or kept by the subjects for preservation of the king's majesty, the religion, laws, or liberties of the kingdom, or for the public good either of kirk or kingdom,' are false and disloyal."

No opposition having been made to this act, a more decisive followed, annulling the "pretended" convention of estates kept in 1643, which had entered into the Solemn League and Covenant, but which, not having been convoked by the king, although afterwards approved, afforded at least some pretext for disallowing it. Next came an act "concerning the League and Covenant, declaring that there was no obligation on the kingdom by covenant to endeavour, by arms, a reformation of religion in the kingdom of England, or to meddle in any seditious way in any thing concerning the religion and government of the churches of England and Ireland." With this, perhaps, there was little quarrel. The attempts to obtain uniformity in religion, and to procure a hollow profession of the form, where the reality was notoriously wanting, was a political sin, for which the covenanters had suffered severely already, and the repetition of which it might be laudable to prevent; yet, as the Solemn League and Covenant had been formally, fully, and repeatedly sanctioned by all the members of the state in subsequent parliaments, and was by many good men considered irreversible, it might have been more decorous to have allowed it to remain a dead letter, especially as it had been renounced by the English, and could not in such circumstances be acted upon by the Scots. Considerable reluctance was expressed respecting this measure; and, to silence opposition, the commissioner informed the House that he had no orders from his royal master to encroach upon the National Covenant or upon the consciences of the people; but as to leagues with other nations, he conceived they could not now subsist with the laws of the king. One honest man, however, had the courage publicly to avow that he could do nothing against his lawful oath and covenant; and numbers who could not approve of the act, silently withdrew. To make the annulling of the covenant more palatable, the managers sweetened the draught by an act against papists, priests, and jesuits, whose numbers they asserted more abounded of late, and insinuated as if the covenants had been the cause of the increase!

Preparatory to the bloody tragedy with which they were to conclude, an act was passed approving of the engagement, and vilifying in the most bitter terms all who opposed that expedition, ruinous equally to the king and to the country; and another, condemning the transactions respecting the delivering up of Charles I. at Newcastle, and declaring the approval of them by the parliament, 1647, to have been the deed of a few factious, disloyal persons, and not the deed of the nation. All the acts which had been voted were embodied into a declaration, entitled an acknowledgment of his majesty's prerogative, which, together with the oath of allegiance, every person holding a place of public trust was required to subscribe, and all other persons who should be required by his majesty's privy council, or any having authority from them, should be required to take and swear; and whoever should refuse or delay to take them, were not only to be rendered incapable of any office of public trust, but be looked upon as persons disaffected to his majesty's authority and government.

Hitherto, a majority of the Presbyterian ministers —the remonstrators excepted—had remained silent, while those who, after Mr. Douglas, were employed to preach before parliament, shamefully flattered the proceedings of the day, by declaiming against seditious bands and the irregularity of the times, and inculcating the courtly doctrine of gratitude for their gracious deliverance from tyranny and usurpation, and for the miraculous restoration of the king—the duty of unlimited confidence in the best of princes; and some went so far as to recommend Episcopacy as that form of church-government that suited best with monarchy; but when the plans of the managers began to be developed, even the resolutioners were painfully constrained to suspect that they had been duped, and that their brethren who wished at first to make an explicit declaration of their fears, and to supplicate against encroachment, acted the wiser and more reputable part. When too late, they saw the folly of admitting to power men of bad principles, and trusting either to their professions of repentance or the smallness of their number. The ministers of Edinburgh now attempted to stem the torrent; they had frequent interviews with the Earl of Middleton, who, during the progress of the measures, treated them with respect and fair promises. They entreated that, in the oath of allegiance, the supremacy of the king might be restricted to his right as supreme governor in civil affairs, and in ecclesiastical, as defined in the Confession of Faith, ch. 23: that it might be declared by parliament that they did not intend to make void the oath of God: and that an act might be passed ratifying anew the Confession of Faith and Directory of Worship. His Grace politely promised to transmit their desires to the king, and requested that they would draw out an act of ratification, such as they would consider satisfactory, and he would attend to it, which they accordingly did.

But, while he was amusing them in this manner, a measure was in progress—the wildest and most extravagant ever tried in any legislative body—for which, however, the Scottish parliament, by a peculiarity in its constitution, afforded every facility. That peculiarity consisted in having a committee, called the Lords of the Articles, composed of from eight to twelve persons of each estate, who prepared all the bills brought before the House; so that when they were presented the members had little else to do but to vote. This committee, at all times under the influence of the crown, was, in the present instance, completely devoted to the king's pleasure, and ready to approve and propose whatever he desired. Every thing had been so arranged by them, that the parliament was only required to meet in the afternoon of two days in the week,* where

* Before this, it had been the custom for parliament to meet at nine o'clock A. M. and sometimes earlier, while their committees met about seven to prepare the business.

the important acts already noticed, together with others of a civil nature, of scarcely less consequence, had passed precipitately almost without discussion. Even this method, however, seemed too slow for accomplishing the total overthrow of the work of reformation, and an idea was now revived, which had been originally suggested in a meeting at London by Sir George M'Kenzie of Tarbet, for disannulling at one sweep the whole of the parliaments whose proceedings were disagreeable to the present rulers, or presented any obstacle to the establishment of unlimited despotism.

Middleton had brought to Scotland, not only the high monarchical principles, but the shameless manners of the English court, rendered still more disgraceful by the regardless habits of a rough mercenary. Short as were the sessions of parliament, and late in the day as they met, he and his companions occasionally reeled to the House in such a state, that an immediate adjournment became necessary. Their sederunts at the Palace were more protracted; and the most important affairs were settled on these occasions, when all difficulties were got rid of, with a facility far beyond the reach of forenoon-disputants, engaging each other in a dry debate. At some such carousal, a jocular remark of Primrose's is said to have decided the commissioner; and the draught of a bill, rescinding all the parliaments which had met since 1640, as illegal and rebellious, was framed and attempted to be hurried through parliament with the same rapidity as the rest. An unexpected opposition delayed its passage. As "that incomparable king," Charles I., had freely presided at one, and the king himself at two others, some of the best affected to the court did not approve of an act, which they said went to throw a slur upon the memory of the blessed martyr, and was highly disrespectful to his present majesty. What staggered, however, even that assemblage, base and servile as it was, was the danger of destroying all the legal foundations of security for private property. If parliaments, regu iarly constituted in the royal presence, could be thus easily set aside, another parliament following the precedent might make this void, and render the tenures of their rights and possessions as unstable as they would be under the firman of an eastern sultan. To satisfy these, it was expressly provided, that all acts, rights, and securities passed in any of the pretended meetings, or by virtue thereof, in favour of any particular persons for their civil and private interests, should stand good and valid unto them, excepting only such as should be questioned before the act of indemnity; and notwithstanding the efforts of the Earl of Loudon, and a few others, a majority agreed to undo all that had been done in favour of religion and liberty for the preceding twenty years, and to wreath around their necks the yoke that had galled their fathers for other twenty before.

Some indistinct rumours of the rescissory act having reached the ministers of Edinburgh, the presbytery assembled to draw up a supplication, praying that their church-government might be preserved to them amid this general wreck, and that some new civil sanction might be granted in place of the statutes about to be repealed; and three of the most complaisant were deputed to the commissioner, to show it before presenting to parliament. His Grace prevailed upon them to delay doing any thing in the business, and they, who appear to have been very willing to oblige, acceded, and the bill passed, like all the rest, without any representation by the ministers against it. Next day, when they learned it had been voted by a large majority, a deputation of a different stamp, with Mr. David Dickson at their head, waited upon Middleton to remonstrate; but he had attained his object, and they found him in a very different mood. He received their paper in a very discourteous manner, and told them they were mistaken if they thought to terrify him with their papers—he was no coward. Dickson pointedly replied—"He knew well his Grace was no coward, ever since the Bridge of Dee"—a sarcasm the Earl seemed to feel, as he had there distinguished himself, fighting in the cause of the covenant against the king's army. Nor did his chagrin abate when he was reminded of the vows he had made to serve the Lord and his interest, in 1645, when under serious impressions in the prospect of death; but turning round pettishly asked, "What do you talk to me for about a fit of the colic?" and entirely refused to have any thing to do with their supplication.

An evasive deceitful act followed, allowing presbyteries and synods to meet, but promising to make it his majesty's care to settle the government of the church in such a frame as should be most agreeable to the word of God, most suitable to monarchical government, and most complying with the public peace and quiet of the kingdom. It did not tend to allay the fears of the ministers, who wrote an urgent letter to Lauderdale, reminding him of their sufferings for the king, of the steadiness of their loyalty, and their opposition to the heats of some during the times of distraction; and entreating him, by his zeal for his majesty's service, and his love for his mother church, to interpose with his majesty to prevent any prejudice to her established government, and procure the calling of a General Assembly as the king had promised.

Public fasts were now kept in various parishes throughout the country, and the synods met to prepare supplications for some confirmatory act to set the people at rest with regard to their religion. No attention was paid by the secretary to their application, and visiters were sent to the different synods to prevent their taking any disagreeable steps, or dissolve them if they proved refractory. Accordingly, the synod of Dumfries was dissolved by Queensberry and Hartfield, who were both exceedingly drunk at the time, and appear to have dispersed the ministers with very little ceremony, and without any resistance. Fife was equally quietly dismissed by the Earl of Rothes, who entered while they were in the midst of their business; and, ordering them to dismiss in the king's name, they obeyed:* in their respective presbyteries, they afterwards approved of a petition, and declared their adherence to the principles of the church of Scotland. Glasgow and Ayr being the most obnoxious, was discharged by proclamation, after they had drawn up a supplication, which was delayed being presented through the manœuvres of a few among themselves who afterwards became prelatic dignitaries. The synod of Lothian split, and, at the desire of the Earl of Callendar, suspended five of their most pious members, and removed two from their charges before they were themselves forcibly turned off. The northern judi-

* Lamont, in his usual *naïve* manner, thus narrates the transaction:—

"1661, Apryll 2. The Provincial Assembly of Fyfe sat at St. Andrews, where Mr. David Forrest, minister of Kilconquhar, was moderator. After they had sitten a day, and condescended upon a peaper to be sent to his majestie, wishing he might be as good as his word, etc. [This, in reference, he had sent doune to the presbytery of Edinboroughe, Sept. 3, 1660.] As also speaking of another peaper to be intimat in the severall parish churches, to put peopell in mynde of their oath to God in covenant, in caise that episcopacy should againe be established in this land: as also speaking against something done by the present parliament, in cancelling the league and covenant with England, etc. The nixt day, in the afternoon, they were raised by the Earle of Rothes and the Laird of Ardrosse, two members of parliament, (young Balfour Beton being present with them for the tyme,) and desyred them, under the paine of treason, presently to repaire to their several charges, which they accordingly did. In the meane whille, the moderator offered to speake; and Rothes answered, Sir, wither doe ye speake as a private man, or as the mouth of this meeting? If you speake as the mouth of this meeting, you speake high treason and rebellion. After that, Mr. David Forrest followed Rothes to his chamber, and spoke to him; and amonge other things, speaking of the covenant, he said, that few or none of ther meeting bot had ministered the covenant to hundreds, bot for himsef he had tendered it to thousands; and if he sould be silent at this time, and speake nothing of it, bot betray the peopell, he said he wist not what he deserved—hanging were too little for him. Rothes professed to this judicatory that it was sore against his will that he came to that employment. However, many of the ministrie blames Mr. James Sharpe, minister of Craill, for the present chaplaine to his majesties commissioner, Earle of Middleton, for ther scattering; for he wrat over to some of them some dayes before, that a storme was like to breake; and the said Mr. David Forrest said of him that he was the greatest knave that ever was in the kirke of Scotlande."

catures were little disturbed, their majorities generaly "falling in with the times."

The remaining acts of this parliament, respecting ecclesiastical affairs, and which became instruments of cruelty and grounds of persecution, were, the seventeenth, enjoining the 29th of May—the anniversary of the Restoration, also the king's birth-day—to be set apart as a day holy unto the Lord for ever, to be part employed in public prayers, thanksgiving, preaching, and praises to God for so transcendent mercies, and the remaining part spent in lawful diversions suited to so solemn an occasion; and the thirty-sixth, restoring "the unreasonable and unchristian burden of patrons and presentations" upon the church.

Having virtually subverted Presbytery, restored every abolished abuse, and obtained in the preambles of several of their acts repeated expressions of the parliament's detestation and abhorrence of all that was done in the "rebellious and distracted times," it was requisite that those who had been the most strenuous assertors of the civil and religious rights of their country, and who had been the chief instruments of the late Reformation, should be punished for their temerity. Accordingly, the most noble the Marquis of Argyle, who stood first on the list, was, on the 13th of February, brought to trial. He had been sent down from London by sea, along with Swinton of that ilk, in the latter end of 1660, and had encountered that storm in which the records of Scotland were lost;* since when he had lain in the Castle; but the first hurry being over, his case was proceeded in —the commissioner anticipating a reward for his services from the confiscation of his estates.

His activity in the cause of religion, and the great

* These had been seized and sent to London by the English during the civil war, and, upon the Restoration, were ordered to be returned to Scotland; but, as it was supposed the original Covenant which Charles had signed was among them, they were detained on purpose to search for it, in order to destroy it, till late in the season, when the weather became tempestuous, and the vessel that carried them was lost.

power he had long enjoyed, had created him many enemies, and gave rise to many calumnies, which made even his friends dread the investigation. But the most painful endeavours could establish nothing against him, except his compelled submission to the English, after every county in Scotland had acknowledged their superiority. His indictment consisted of fourteen distinct charges narrating almost all the public acts of the nation in which he had had any share, since his first joining the covenanters, till the final protectorate of Richard Cromwell, and attributing to him as treasonable acts, his concurrence with the different parliaments, or his obedience to their orders, and his submission to the usurper's government, and sitting and voting in his parliament, together with having positively advised Cromwell and Ireton, in a conference in 1648, to take away the late king's life, without which they could not be safe, or at least knew and concealed the horrid design. The last charge, which the Marquis strenuously denied, was not insisted on; nor does there appear to have been any foundation for it.

In his reply, he enumerated all the favours he had received from the former and the reigning sovereign, and desired the parliament to consider how unlikely it was that he should have entertained any design to the hurt or dishonour of either. He could say with Paul in another case, the things alleged against him could not be proven; but this he would confess, that, in the way allowed by solemn oaths and covenants, he served his God, his king, and country: he besought those who were capable of understanding, when those things for which he was challenged were acted, to recollect what was the conduct of the whole kingdom at the time, and how both themselves and others were led on in these actions without any rebellious inclination; and entreated those who were then young to be charitable to their predecessors, and to censure sparingly these actions, with all the circumstances of which they were unacquainted; for often the smallest circumstance altered entirely the nature of an action. In all popular and universal insurrections *communis error facit jus: et consuetudo peccandi minuit crimen et pœnam.* As to what he had done before the year 1651, he pled his majesty's indemnity granted in the parliament at Perth; and for what he had done since, under the usurpers, they were but common compliances, wherein all the kingdom did share equally, and for doing which many had express allowance from his majesty, who declared he thought it prudence, and not rebellion, for honest men to preserve themselves from ruin, and thereby reserve themselves till God should show some probable way for his return. Besides, among all those who complied passively, none was less favoured by the usurpers than himself—what he did was but self-defence, and, being the effect of force, could not amount to a crime.

When he had finished, his advocates, Messrs. Sinclair, Cunningham, and M'Kenzie, afterwards Sir George, protested, that, seeing they stood there by order of parliament, whatever should escape them in pleading for the life, honour, and estate of their client, might not thereafter be brought against them as treasonable—a common form and usually sustained; but on this occasion the parliament would not admit the protestation, lest they might allow themselves upon that pretext the liberty of speaking things prejudicial to his majesty's government, and therefore desired them to speak at their peril. His advocates being strangers to his cause, as the ones he wished were afraid to appear, he requested a short delay to prepare his defence fully; but this being referred to the Lords of the Articles, they cruelly denied his reasonable request; upon which he gave in a supplication and submission, throwing himself entirely upon the king's mercy, and entreating the intercession of the parliament on his behalf. This, also, they refused to listen to.

After which, his lordship gave in a bill, desiring to be remitted for trial before the justice court, as the intricacy of his case would require learned judges.

Nor was it to be supposed that every gentleman or burgess could understand points of law; neither were they his peers; and a nobleman should be judged by his peers. His prosecutors, bent upon his ruin, construed this application into a declining the jurisdiction of parliament, and required him to own it, or inform them who had written the petition. The Marquis, perceiving that every possible advantage would be taken against him, was extremely perplexed; but his advisers avowed the paper, and, after a warm debate, the petition was rejected, but the advocates were excused. He then requested to be allowed the benefit of exculpatory proof, and to bring forward witnesses, who could either attest his innocence or give such explanations as would alleviate his guilt; even this, the last privilege of the lowest criminal, he could not obtain, and was commanded immediately to proceed to his defence—likewise an unusual and oppressive mode of procedure, as it had been customary to discuss first the relevancy of the indictment; that is, whether the facts charged actually constituted the crimes alleged, and thus to give the accused a chance of escape from a cumulative treason, or from any legal informality that might occur.

All the Marquis's reasonable requests and objections being thus disposed of, his defences, with the Lord Advocate's replies, duplies, and triplies—papers of enormous length—were fully read before parliament, as tiresome, tedious, and unfair a mode of conducting a trial before a court, consisting of some hundred individuals, as could possibly have been contrived. When ended, a debate ensued, and the Lord Advocate restricted his charge to the acts committed after 1651, a letter having been procured from the king forbidding any person to be prosecuted for any deed antecedent to the indemnity of that year. This letter, which was understood to have been procured by Lauderdale and Lorn—who had staid at London to attend to his father's interest—somewhat disconcerted the managers, who were now persuaded that the secretary had espoused Argyle's cause; and therefore, to counteract this influence, despatched Glencairn and Rothes to court, with a letter from parliament approving of the whole proceedings, accompanied by Mr. James Sharpe, to inform his majesty respecting the state of the Church.

Glencairn actively stirred up the vindictive feelings of the treacherous Monk and the bigoted Hyde, while Rothes reminded Lauderdale of the former treatment he had received from the Marquis, how dangerous a competitor he might yet be if he escaped, and hinted at the imprudence of committing himself too far with a declining faction. Their arguments prevailed; and, from the date of their arrival, repeated expresses were sent down to Scotland, urging forward the trial.

The relevancy having been sustained, proof was led with regard to his compliance with the usurpers; but the evidence was by no means satisfactory, especially to judges almost all of whom had been ten times more deeply implicated than he, and the issue was doubtful; when, after the debate and examination were closed, and parliament was proceeding to consider the whole matter, an express from London knocked violently at the door. Upon being admitted, he presented a packet to the commissioner, which was believed to be a pardon or some warrant in favour of the Marquis, especially as the bearer was a Campbell, but, upon its being opened, it was found to contain a great many letters addressed by Argyle to Monk when commanding in Scotland, which he had perfidiously reserved, to produce, if absolutely necessary, for the conviction of his former friend; and, on being informed by the commissioner's agents of the "scantiness of probation," had transmitted them by post to supply the deficiency. There was now no room for hesitation; the parliament were perfectly satisfied that the rebel English General had received the reluctant submission and forced co-operation of the last royalist nobleman in Scotland who yielded to the fortune of the victorious republicans, and therefore Argyle was guilty of a treason which Monk had obliged him to commit! The proof of his compliance was complete; and next day he was condemned and forfeited. The manner of his execution was put to the vote, "hang or behead," when it was carried that he should be beheaded, and his head placed on the same spike, on the top of the tolbooth, whence Montrose's had been but lately removed.

During the whole of this protracted trial, which lasted from the 13th of February till the 25th of May, his behaviour was meek and composed, although attacked with the most virulent abuse by the reptiles who crouched before him in the hour of his prosperity. When in his own defence he asked, how could I suppose that I was acting criminally, when the learned gentleman, his majesty's advocate, took the same oaths to the Commonwealth with myself? Sir John Fletcher replied to a question he could not answer, by calling him an impudent villain. The Marquis mildly said, he had learned in his affliction to endure reproach. After his case appeared desperate, his friends planned an escape, partly by force, and partly by stratagem, and a number of resolute gentlemen had engaged in it; but, after he had consented, and had even put on a female dress, in which he was to be carried out of the Castle, he changed his mind, threw aside his disguise, and declared he was determined not to disown the cause he had so long appeared for, but was resolved to suffer to the utmost.

When brought to receive sentence, there were but few, and these the most determined time-serving sycophants, in the House, shame or compassion preventing a number who had decided his fate from hearing it announced; yet even they could not help moralizing on the mutability of human glory, though, when he requested a delay of only ten days, that the king might be acquainted with the result of his trial, they refused that short interval, and prevented his last chance of mercy!

He heard his sentence with equanimity. The Earl of Crawford, who pronounced it in absence of the Chancellor, told him he must receive it kneeling, and he immediately knelt, saying, "That I will with all humility." When rising, he remarked, "I had the honour to put the crown upon the king's head, may God bestow on him a crown of glory. Now he hastens me to a better crown than his own."* Then addressing the commissioner and parliament, "you have the indemnity of an earthly king," said he, "among your hands, and have denied me a share in that; but you cannot hinder me from the indemnity of the King of kings; and shortly you must be before his tribunal. I pray he may not mete out such measure to you as you have done to me, when you are called to account for all your actings, and this among the rest."

After sentence he was conducted to the common jail, where his lady was waiting for him. "They have given me," said he as he entered, "till Monday, my dear, to be with you; let us improve it." As she embraced him, she sobbed out—"The Lord will require it! The Lord will require it!" and wept bitterly. Nor could the officer who attended him, nor any who were present, avoid shedding tears at the scene. The Marquis, too, was at first considerably affected, but becoming composed, "Forbear!" said he affectionately to the Marchioness, "forbear! truly I pity them—they know not what they are doing. They may shut me in where they please, they cannot shut out God from me; for my part, I am as content to be here as in the Castle. I was as content in the Castle as in the Tower of London; and as content there as when at liberty; and I hope to be as content on the scaffold as in any of them all." He then added, "he remembered a text that had been cited to him by an honest minister—'When Ziklag was taken and burnt, the people spake of stoning David; but he encouraged himself in the Lord.'"

* Kirkton, p. 103, *et seq.*

The solemn interval he spent in exercises befitting a dying Christian; and though rather of a timid disposition, yet during the short space that now separated him from eternity, and with the immediate prospect of a violent death, his mind was elevated above his natural temper, and he desired those about him to observe "that the Lord had heard his prayers, and removed all fear from him." To some ministers permitted to attend him he said, "that they would shortly envy him who had got before," adding, "mind I tell it you; my skill fails me if you who are ministers will not either suffer much or sin much; for though you go along with these men in part, if you do it not in all things, you are but where you were, and so must suffer; and if you go not at all with them you can but suffer." Mr. Robert Douglas and Mr. George Hutchinson preached in the tolbooth, at his desire, on the Lord's day; and at night his lady, at his particular request, took leave. Mr. David Dickson spent the last night with him that he spent on earth, which passed delightfully in prayer, praise, and spiritual conversation, except a few hours he enjoyed of calm and tranquil repose. On Monday, he rose early, and was much occupied in settling his worldly affairs; but, while signing some conveyances, his spiritual joy was such, that he exclaimed with rapture before the company, "I thought to have concealed the Lord's goodness, but it will not do. I am now ordering my affairs, and God is sealing my charter to a better inheritance, saying, 'Son, be of good cheer; thy sins are forgiven thee.'" He wrote a letter to the king, expressing his satisfaction that nothing had been proved against him but his being forced to submit to the unlawful power of usurping rebels—the epidemic and fault of the time—praying his majesty's princely goodness and favour to his wife and family after his decease, and requesting that his just debts might be allowed to be paid out of his estate. He dined with a number of friends at twelve o'clock; after which he retired a little, and returned from his private devotions in a holy rapture.

A sense of the forgiveness of his sins made the tears of joy run from his eyes; and, turning to Mr. Hutchison, "I think," said he, "His kindness overcomes me, but God is good to me; he lets not out too much of it here, for he knows I could not bear it;" and thinking the time was expired, added, "Get me my cloak—let us go;" but being told that the clock had been put back, he answered they were far in the wrong, and kneeled down and prayed. As he ended, notice was sent that the bailies waited him, upon which he called for a glass of wine, and asked a blessing. Then he declared his readiness—"Now let us go and God go with us." When leaving the room, he said to those who remained, "I could die like a Roman, but choose rather to die as a Christian. Come away, gentlemen; he that goes first goes cleanliest." Calling Mr. Guthrie as he went down, he embraced him and took farewell. Mr. Guthrie's parting benediction was—"My lord, God hath been with you, he is with you, and He will be with you; and such is my respect for your lordship, that, if I were not under the sentence of death myself, I could cheerfully die for your lordship."

The Marquis was accompanied to the place of execution by several noblemen and gentlemen in mourning. He walked steadily down the street, and, with the greatest serenity, mounted the scaffold, which was filled with his friends, of whom he had given in a list, and whose names were contained in a warrant subscribed by the commissioner. After Mr. Hutchison had prayed, his lordship addressed the spectators. He did not attempt any explanation of his conduct. "I came not here," were his humble expressions, "to justify myself but the Lord, who is holy in all his ways and righteous in all his works, holy and blessed is his name. Neither came I to condemn others. I know many will expect that I should speak against the hardness of the sentence pronounced against me, but I will say nothing of it. I bless the Lord, I pardon all men, as I desire to be pardoned of the Lord myself: let the will of the Lord be done." He then, as in the presence of God, disclaimed having entered upon the work of reformation from any motive of self-interest or personal dissatisfaction with the government. He had ever been cordial in his desires to bring the king home, and in his endeavours for him when he was at home; nor had he ever corresponded with his enemies during the time he was in the country. "I confess," he continued, "many look on my condition as a suffering condition; but I bless God, He who hath gone before, hath trode the wine-press of the Father's wrath, by whose sufferings I hope my sufferings shall not be eternal. I shall not speak much to those things for which I am condemned, lest I seem to condemn others. I wish the Lord to pardon them. I say no more."

Then changing the subject, he continued—"There are some, and those not openly profane, who, if their private interest go well, they care not whether religion or the church of God sink or swim. But, whatever they think, God hath laid engagements on Scotland. We are tied by covenants to religion and reformation, and it passeth the power of all magistrates under heaven to absolve a man from the oath of God. It is the duty of every Christian to be loyal; but God must have his as well as Cæsar. Religion must not be secondary. They are the best subjects who are the best Christians. These times are like to prove very sinning times or very suffering times; and let Christians make their choice; and truly he that would choose the better part would choose to suffer. Others that will choose to sin will not escape suffering. Yet I cannot say of mine own condition, but that the Lord in his providence hath mind of mercy to me even in this world; for if I had been more favourably dealt with, I fear I might have been overcome with temptations, as many others are, and many more I fear will be; yea, blessed be his name, I am kept from present evil and evil to come! I have no more to say but tc beg the Lord, since I go away, he would bless them who stay behind."*

Having again spent some time in devotion, he distributed some last tokens of remembrance to the friends who were with him. To the Earl of Caithness, his son-in-law, he gave his watch, saying, with a smile, it was fit for men to pay their debts; and having promised him that watch, he now performed it. After his doublet was off, and immediately before he laid his head upon the block, he addressed those near him—" Gentlemen, I desire you and all that hear me, again to take notice and remember, that, now when I am entering into eternity and to appear before my Judge, and as I desire salvation and expect eternal happiness from him, I am free from any accession, by knowledge, contriving, counsel, or any other ways, to his late majesty's death; and I pray the Lord to preserve our present king his majesty, and to pour his best blessings upon his person and government; and the Lord give him good and faithful counsellors." Mr. Hutchison, his attendant minister, on bidding him finally adieu, used a Scottish phrase, peculiarly emphatic—" My lord, now hold your grip sicker." The appropriate force of the expression was felt by the sufferer. " You know, Mr. Hutchison, what I said to you in the chamber, I am not afraid to be surprised with fear;" and the Laird of Skelmorlie, who took him by the hand at this awful moment, felt that no tremour in his veins belied the assertion. He then knelt, offered up his last prayer, and upon dropping his hands, the appointed signal, the axe of the maiden fell, and his spirit fled to his God and Saviour. His body was carried to Dunoon, and buried in Kilmun church.

Argyle has ever, by the unanimous verdict of his Presbyterian countrymen, been considered a martyr, not for the form, but for the reality of their religion.

* Sir George M'Kenzie, an unquestionable evidence, says—" At his death he showed much stayedness, as appeared by all his gestures, but especially by his speaking to the people, without any commotion, and with his ordinary gestures."—*History*, p. 47.

The form, perhaps, he might have consented to modify—the essence he never durst think of forsaking. There was a consistency in his adherence to his principles that claims our admiration, especially as he sealed his testimony by his blood. He may have given, as many of the excellent men of his day did, an undue importance to points of inferior moment, but the fundamental truths of the gospel were his hope, as, in so far as we can trust the testimony of his friends, its precepts had been the rule of his life. It is refreshing to know that his persecutors did not share his spoil. Through the intercession of Lauderdale, Lorn procured from the king all his father's estates and titles, except that of Marquis.

Mr. James Guthrie, minister of Stirling, remarkable for his piety, zeal, and consistency in the cause of reformation-principles, followed his friend to trial and judgment.* He was peculiarly obnoxious to Middleton, having pronounced sentence of excommunication upon him, and was considered the chief of the remonstrators, who had uniformly resisted communion with the malignants; but he was no less distinguished for his intrepid opposition to the government of Cromwell, whom he had boldly stigmatized as an usurper, at the time when all those who now made such flaming professions of loyalty had crouched before him. Revered and popular among the lower ranks, he was not less respected among the worthy of the higher; for, although constrained by terror to condemn, no political victim was ever sacrificed with more reluctance by the subordinate ranks of the priesthood of mammon, than was James Guthrie; and even the Moloch at whose shrine he was

* "He was the son of the Laird of Guthrie, and so a gentleman. When he was regent in St. Andrew's, he was very episcopal, and was with difficulty persuaded to take the covenant. There goes a story, that, when he first yielded to join the covenanters in Mr. Samuel Rutherford's chamber, as he came out at his door, he mett the executioner in the way, which troubled him; and the next visit he made thither, he mett him in the same manner again, which made him apprehend he might be a sufferer for the covenant, as indeed he was."—*Kirkton's Hist.* p. 109.

immolated, expressed his regret, and bore testimony to his worth—"Had I known," said the callous-hearted Charles, when he heard of Mr. Gillespie being suffered to live, "that they would have spared Gillespie, I would have saved Guthrie!"—a noble testimony, but happily too late to deprive that holy man of the honour his Lord had provided for him with them who were slain for the word of God, and for the testimony which they held. He was arraigned before a court, of which the director and the president were his personal enemies, and of which a majority had already prejudged his case. His pursuers were men who had yielded to the blast that he had braved, who had deserted their prince in the hour of his extremity, had flattered the very powers that he had withstood, yet now came forward with a flagrant effrontery to charge him with favouring an usurpation to which they had done homage, but which he had suffered for withstanding.

On the 20th of February, he received his indictment, the general charges of which were—his accession to the remonstrance—his writing and publishing that abominable pamphlet, "The Causes of God's Wrath"*—his contriving and writing, and subscribing "The humble Supplication of 23d August last;" but, chiefly, his declining, in the year 1650, his majesty's power in matters purely ecclesiastical, which branch of the royal prerogative the present managers

* "The Causes of God's Wrath," printed after the fatal defeat at Worcester, which ruined the hopes of the Presbyterians and their covenanted King, contained a faithful and pungent enumeration of the sins of all ranks, public and personal, in which the misconduct of the royal family and of the nobles—their defections from duty and the oaths of the covenant in public, and the immorality and ungodliness of their conduct in private—were treated with great plainness and particularity, accompanied with strong exhortations to repentance as the only way to avert the judgments of an offended God. Nor were the sins of the ministry or the people slightly passed over; it was an earnest, deep call upon the nation to consider their ways at a time of great public suffering, when the land had been scourged by the presence of two armies, of which their own had not been the least oppressive, and when a threatened famine and an actual scarcity were afflicting them. Its truth was its treason—it had the honour of being burnt.

were determined to assert, as they traced, and justly, the chief, if not the whole, of the misery the nation had endured under the king's father and grandfather, to the opposition made by the ministry to this anti-scriptural jurisdiction, or, in the language of Sir George M'Kenzie, "because this principle had not only vexed King James, but was the occasion of much rebellion." The indictment, framed upon certain obsolete or repealed acts in favour of popery, prelacy, or the kingly power, passed before the last full establishment of Presbytery, charged him with convoking the lieges without warrant or authority to the disturbance of the state and church. After it had been read, he addressed the Lord Chancellor—

"He was glad," he said, for he pled his own cause, "that the law of God was named first as being indeed the only supreme law, to which all other laws ought to be subordinate; and there being an act of the first parliament of James VI., by which all clauses of laws or acts of parliament repugnant to the word of God were repealed, he hoped their lordships would give most respect to this, that he might be judged by the law of God especially, and by other laws in subordination thereto. As to the acts of parliament upon which he was arraigned, he asserted the legal maxim, that where any difference between acts occurs, the last is that only which is to be considered obligatory; and he further affirmed, what almost all his judges had previously, repeatedly, and upon oath allowed, that it must also be granted that laws and acts of parliament were to be understood and expounded by those solemn public vows and covenants contracted with God by his majesty and subjects, which were not only declared by the laws of the land to have the strength of acts of parliament, but, both by the law of God and common law and light of all the nations in the world, are more binding and indispensable than any municipal law and statute whatever."

The general charge of abetting Cromwell, he defied all the world to prove if he had justice allowed him; nor was it attempted. His approval of the remonstrance he did not deny, but this he only did in a legal manner, as a member of a legal assembly. His participation in the authorship of "The Causes of God's Wrath," he avowed and defended. But in this he said he acted merely and singly from a constraining power of conscience to be found faithful as a minister of the gospel, in the discovering of sin and guiltiness, that it being acknowledged and repented of, wrath might be taken away from the house of the king and from these kingdoms. "Your lordship knows," continued he, "what charge is laid upon ministers of the gospel, to give faithful warning to all sorts of persons, and how they expose their own souls to the hazard of eternal damnation, and the guilt of the blood of those with whom they have to do, if they do not this. And you do also know, that the prophets and apostles of our Lord Jesus Christ himself did faithfully warn all men, though it was their lot, because of the same, to be reckoned traitors and seditious persons. My lord, I wish it seriously to be pondered, that nothing is asserted in these 'Causes' as matter of sin and duty, but what hath been the common received doctrine of the Church of Scotland, the truth of which is confirmed from the word of God; and as to matters of fact, as far as regards the royal family, they are no other than are mentioned in the solemn public causes of humiliation condescended upon and kept by the whole Church jointly, and his majesty and family, with the commission of the General Assembly and committee of estates, before his coronation at Perth."

He also avowed the "Supplication" at Edinburgh, which he vindicated as containing nothing more than a humble petition concerning those things to which his majesty and all his subjects were engaged by the solemn irreversible oath of the covenant, with a serious representation of the dangers threatening religion, and the duties of that sacred obligation, and did only put his majesty in remembrance of holding fast the oaths of the covenant. The meeting was presbyterial, and therefore legal; and was, besides, a quiet, orderly convocation, without tumult, and requiring no particular warrant.

Respecting his declining the king's authority in things sacred, he unhesitatingly acknowledged that he did decline the civil magistrate as a competent judge of ministers' doctrine in the first instance.* His authority in all things civil, he said he did with all his heart allow; but such declinations were agreeable to the word of God, which clearly holds forth that Christ hath a visible kingdom, which he exercises in or over his visible members by his spiritual officers, which is wholly distinct from the civil power and government of the world—to the Confession of Faith and doctrine of the Church of Scotland, which acknowledge no head over the Church of Christ but himself, nor any judgment or power in or over his Church, but that which he hath committed to the spiritual office-bearers thereof under him, and had been the ordinary practice of that kirk since the time of the reformation from Popery; and were also agreeable to, and founded on, the National Covenant and Solemn League and Covenant, by which the king's majesty himself, and all the subjects of that kingdom, were bound to maintain the doctrine, worship, discipline, and government of that Church, with solemn vows and public oaths of God. "Upon these grounds, therefore," said he, "it is that I gave in and do assert that declination for vindicating the cause, dignity, and royal prerogative of Jesus Christ, who is King of kings and Lord of lords, but with all due respect to his majesty, his greatness, and authority." Then, after discussing the several acts of parliament that had been quoted, he thus concluded an able and argumentative speech:—

"That I did never purpose or intend to speak or act any thing disloyal, seditious, or treasonable against

* The error of these good men was, in allowing the civil magistrate the right of judging of a minister's doctrine in any case whatever, so long as he kept within the proper bounds of his pastoral duty, and inculcated only religious tenets, and did not meddle with seditious or treasonable matters.

his majesty's person, authority, or government, God is my witness; and that what I have written, spoken, or acted, in any of those things wherewith I am charged, hath been merely and singly from a principle of conscience; that, according to the weak measure of light given me of God, I might do my duty in my station and calling as a minister of the gospel. But because the plea of conscience alone, although it may extenuate, cannot wholly excuse, I do assert that I have founded my speeches, writings, and actings, in these matters, on the word of God, and on the doctrine, Confession of Faith, and laws of this Church and kingdom—upon the National Covenant of Scotland, and the Solemn League and Covenant between these three kingdoms. If these foundations fall, I must fall with them; but if these sustain and stand in judgment, as I hope they will, I cannot acknowledge myself, neither I hope will his majesty's commissioner and the honourable court of parliament judge me, guilty either of sedition or treason."

This trial lasted from the 20th of February till the 15th of April; and the most strenuous efforts were made to induce Mr. Guthrie to submit and plead for mercy. He was even offered a bishopric; but he deemed the object for which he contended too important to be yielded up for any consideration of temporal aggrandizement. When the protracted proceedings were drawing to a close, on the 11th of April, after his defences, which were very elaborate, had been read, he finished his pleading by a pointed and solemn appeal, which was heard with the most profound attention, and induced a number to withdraw, declaring, in the language of Scripture, "They would have nothing to do with the blood of that righteous man."

Addressing the Chancellor, "My lord," said the intrepid minister in conclusion, "I shall, in the last place, humbly beg—having brought such pregnant and clear evidence from the word of God, so much divine reason and human law, and so much of the common practice of the kirk and kingdom in my own defence; and being already cast out of my ministry, driven from my dwelling, and deprived of my maintenance, myself and my family thrown upon the charity of others; and having now suffered eight months' imprisonment—that your lordships would put no further burden upon me. But, in the words of the prophet, 'Behold! I am in your hands, to do to me what seemeth good to you.' I know for certain that the Lord hath commanded me to speak all these things, and that if you put me to death you shall bring innocent blood upon yourself and upon the inhabitants of this city. My lord! my conscience I cannot submit; but this old crazy body and mortal flesh I do submit to do with whatever you will, whether by death, by banishment, or imprisonment, or any thing else, only I beseech you ponder well what profit there is in my blood; it is not extinguishing me or many others that will extinguish the covenant and the work of reformation since 1638. No! my bondage, banishment, or blood, will contribute more for their extension than my life or liberty could, were I to live many years. I wish to my Lord Commisioner, his Grace, and to all your lordships, the spirit of judgment, wisdom, and understanding, and the fear of the Lord, that you may judge righteous judgment, in which God may have glory, the king honour and happiness, and yourselves peace in the great day of accounts." But all was of no avail; his death was determined on as an example to the ministers, and he was found guilty, upon his own confession, of the charges brought against him. Sentence was delayed till the 28th of May, when the doom of a traitor was pronounced by the Earl of Crawford, in absence of the Chancellor. As he arose from his knees—for he had been ordered to kneel—"My lords," said he, "may never this sentence more affect you than it does me; and let never my blood be required of the king's family!" He had assisted in managing his defence with an eloquence, acuteness, and legal knowledge, that drew forth the admiration of the professional gentlemen who were his advocates.

When his case was decided, and he was removed to wait till his sentence was written out, while he remained amid the soldiers, and officers, and servants of the court, he afterwards declared he never felt more of the sensible presence of God, of the sweet intimations of peace, and the real manifestations of divine love and favour, than when surrounded with all their bustle and confusion. From that time till he went to the scaffold, he remained in a serene, tranquil frame of mind. On the day of his execution, June 1, several of his friends dined with him, when not only his cheerfulness, but even his pleasantry, did not forsake him. After dinner, he jocularly called for a little cheese, of which he was very fond, but had been forbid by his physicians to eat on account of a gravelish complaint, saying, "I hope I am now beyond reach of the gravel."

He delivered his last speech from the ladder with the same composed earnestness with which he was wont to deliver his sermons. "He thanked God that he suffered willingly, having had it in his power to have made his escape, or by compliance to have obtained favour, but he durst not redeem his life with the loss of his integrity." "I bless God," he proceeded, "that I die not as a fool, not that I have any thing wherein to glory in myself. But I do believe that Jesus Christ came into the world to save sinners, whereof I am chief; through faith in his righteousness and blood, I have obtained mercy, and through him and him alone have I the blessed hope of a blessed conquest over sin and Satan, death and hell, and that I shall attain unto the resurrection of the just, and be made partaker of eternal life. I know in whom I have believed, and that he is able to keep that which I have committed to him unto that day. I have preached salvation through his name; and as I have preached, so do I believe, and do recommend the riches of his free grace and faith

6*

in his name unto you all, as the only way whereby ye can be saved."

"And," continued he, "as I bless the Lord I die not as a fool, so also that I die not for evil-doing. God is my record, that in these things for which sentence of death is passed against me, I have a good conscience. My heart is conscious of no disloyalty. The matters for which I am condemned, are matters belonging to my calling and function as a minister of the gospel; such as discovering and reproving of sin, the pressing and holding fast of the oath of God in the covenant, and preserving and carrying on the work of reformation according thereto, and denying to acknowledge the civil magistrate as the proper, competent, immediate judge in causes ecclesiastical." He then warned his hearers that the wrath of God was hanging over the land for that deluge of profanity that was overflowing it; for their perjury and breach of covenant; ("Be astonished, O ye heavens, at this! shall he break the covenant and prosper? shall the throne of iniquity have fellowship with God, which frameth mischief by a law?") for their ingratitude; for their dreadful idolatry and sacrificing to the creature—a corruptible man, in whom many had placed almost all their salvation and all their desire; for a generation of carnal, time-serving ministers, men who minded earthly things, enemies to the cross of Christ, who pushed with the side and shoulder, who strengthen the hands of evil-doers, and make themselves transgressors by studying to build again what they did formerly warrantably destroy.

Next, he earnestly exhorted the profane, the lukewarm, and the indifferent, to repentance, and the godly to confidence and zeal, expressing his belief that God would neither desert his people nor cause in Scotland. "There is yet," exclaimed he, "a holy seed, a precious remnant, whom God will preserve, and bring forth; but how long or dark our night may be, I do not know; the Lord shorten it for the sake of his chosen. In the mean while, be patient, steadfast, and immovable, always abounding in the work of the Lord. Beware of snares, decline not the cross, and account the reproach of Christ greater riches than all the treasure of the world. Let my death grieve none of you. I forgive all men the guilt of it, and I desire you to do so also. Pray for them that persecute you; bless them that curse you; bless, I say, and curse not!" After bearing testimony to the faith of the gospel, the doctrine and discipline of the Church of Scotland, the protestation, and against the course of backsliding then afoot in the land, he ended in this strain of triumphant exultation, well becoming a martyr for the truth—"Jesus Christ is my light and my life, my righteousness, my strength, and my salvation, and all my desire. Him! O him! do I with the strength of all my soul commend unto you; blessed are they that are not offended in him. Bless him, O my soul! from henceforth even for ever. Rejoice, rejoice all ye that love him; be patient and rejoice in tribulation. Blessed are you, and blessed shall you be for ever and ever. Everlasting righteousness and eternal salvation is yours; all is yours; and ye are Christ's, and Christ is God's!" His last words were—" Remember me, O Lord, with the favour thou bearest to thy people. O visit me with thy salvation, that I may see the good of thy chosen; that I may rejoice in the gladness of thy nation; that I may glory with thine inheritance. Now let thy servant depart in peace, since my eyes have seen thy salvation!"

An obscure individual, named William, sometimes Captain, Govan, was executed along with Mr. Guthrie. He met death with the same joyful confidence, resting on the same sure foundation. For what specific charges he suffered, is uncertain. In his speech which he left, he says it was for laying down his arms at Hamilton, as all the company did. Sir George M'Kenzie alleges it was for joining in the English army in 1651. "But so inconsiderable a person," he adds, "had not died if he had not been suspected to have been upon the scaffold when King Charles the First was murdered, though he purged himself of this when he died; and his guilt was, that he brought to Scotland the first news of it, and seemed to be well satisfied with it." His chief crime, however, appears to have been that he was a pious, consistent, and zealous Presbyterian. Mr. Guthrie was turned off first; and his behaviour must have tended greatly to strengthen his fellow-sufferer, who, in his last speech, after exhorting the licentious and the lukewarm to repent, remarked—"As for myself, it pleased the Lord, in the fourteenth year of my age, to manifest his love to me; and now it is about twenty-four years since, all which time I professed the truth which I suffer for and bear testimony to at this day, and am not afraid of the cross upon that account. It is sweet! it is sweet! otherwise how durst I look on the corpse of him who hangs there with courage, and smile upon that gibbet as the gate of heaven?" When he had ended, he took a ring from off his finger, and gave to a friend, desiring him to take it to his wife and tell her—he died in humble confidence, and found the cross of Christ sweet. Christ, he added, had done all for him; and it was by him alone he was justified. Being desired to look up to that Christ, he replied—"He looketh down and smileth upon me;" and mounting the ladder—"Dear friends," said he to those around him, "pledge this cup of suffering before you sin, as I have now done; for sin and suffering have been presented to me, and I have chosen the suffering part." When the rope was put about his neck, he observed—"Middleton and I went out to the field together upon the same errand; now I am promoted to a cord and he to be Lord High Commissioner; yet for a thousand worlds would I not change situations with him! Praise and glory be to Christ for ever!"

Besides those who suffered unto death at this time, many others were prosecuted and punished, by removal from their office, imprisonment or exile.

Among these, the most conspicuous were, Mr. Robert Traill, minister of the Greyfriars' church, Edinburgh. He had been in the Castle while it held out against Cromwell, had encouraged the governor and garrison to be faithful to their trust, and had received a severe wound during the siege; yet he was now charged with disloyalty and a participation in all the obnoxious transactions for which Mr. Guthrie laid down his life. His indictment had been drawn up, as all the libels of that time were, with great acrimony and peculiar virulence of expression, to exaggerate the crime of disloyalty, which formed the prominent feature of the accusation. In replying, Mr. Traill averred he durst appeal to the Lord Advocate's own conscience, whether he believed him to be such an one as he had represented him, and complained of bitter and injurious words, but abstained from any angry retort. "I have not," was his meek answer, "so learned Christ; yea, I have learned of him not to render evil for evil, nor railing for railing, but contrariwise blessing; and therefore I do from my heart pray for the honourable drawer up of the libel, as I would do for myself, that the Lord would bless him with his best blessings, and would give him to find mercy in the day of the Lord Jesus!" When the remonstrance was presented, he was confined in the garrison; but, with respect to the other charges, his replies were similar to Mr. Guthrie's, although not perhaps quite so strongly expressed assertions of the legality, propriety, and the imperative necessity of ministers being faithful in the discharge of their duty. He had been seven months confined before being brought to trial; and to that he alludes in the following solemn conclusion of his defence:—

"Now, my lord, I must in all humility beg leave to entreat your lordship that you would seriously consider what you do with poor ministers, who have been so long kept, not only from their liberty of preaching the gospel, but of hearing it—that so many congregations are laid desolate for so long a time, and many poor souls have put up their regrets on their deathbed for their being deprived of a word of comfort from their ministers in the hour of their greatest need! The Lord give you wisdom in all things, and pour out upon you the spirit of your high and weighty employment, of understanding and the fear of the Lord, that your government may be blessed for this land and kirk—that you may live long and happily—that your memory may be sweet and fragrant when you are gone—that you may leave your name for a blessing to the Lord's people—and that your houses and families may stand long and flourish to the years of many generations—above all, that you may have solid peace and heart-joy in the hour of the breaking of your heart-strings, when pale death shall sit on your eyelids—when man must go to his long home and the mourners go about the streets: for what man is he that liveth and shall not see death? or who can deliver himself from the power of the grave? Even those to whom he saith, ye are gods, must die as men; for it is appointed to all men once to die, and after death the judgment, and after judgment an endless eternity! Let me therefore exhort your lordship, in the words of a great king, a great warrior, and a holy prophet—Be wise, be taught, ye rulers of the earth; serve the Lord with fear, and rejoice before him with trembling. Kiss the Son, lest he be angry, and ye perish from the way, when his wrath is kindled but for a little. Then blessed with all those, and those only, be who put their trust in him. Now the Lord give you, in this your day, to consider the things that belong to your eternal peace, and to remember your latter end, that it may be well with you world without end!"

An address such as this, from a prisoner at the bar to his judges, who had his life and death in their hands, could not fail to have been productive of a powerful effect upon the minds of such as were not altogether hardened against every impression, and presents the sufferer for truth and a good conscience upon a commanding elevation, unattainable in any other cause, fearless of personal safety, and anxious only that, while he be found faithful in the service of his master, his persecutors may enjoy the same privilege. How forcibly does it recall the Apostle's address to Agrippa—"I would to God, that not only thou, but also all that hear me this day, were both almost and altogether such as I am, except these bonds." Mr. Traill was remitted to prison, where he lay for some time, and was afterwards banished to Holland. While uncertain of his fate, he thus wrote to another minister from his prison—"Your imprisoned and confined brethren are kindly dealt with by our kind Lord, for we have large allowance from him could we take it. We know it fares the better with us. You and such as you, mind us at the throne. We are waiting from day to day not knowing what man will do with us. We are expecting banishment at the best; but our sentence must proceed from the Lord, and whatsoever it be, it shall be good as from him, and whithersoever he send us, he shall be with us; for the earth is the Lord's and the fulness thereof."

A remarkable trait in all these proceedings is, that the men now persecuted for alleged disloyalty were the men who, when the throne was prostrate, and when these their persecutors had in general deserted the cause as desperate, rallied round the standard of royalty, refused to bow to the invaders, and had suffered for their attachment to the legitimate prince! and it seemed as if the measure of ingratitude meted out to them, was to be in proportion to the steadfastness with which they had adhered to the fortunes of that family in their lowest depression.

Mr. Alexander Moncrief, minister of the gospel at Sconie, in Fife, had particularly distinguished himself by his loyalty during the usurpation and domination of the English—and had subjected himself to imprisonment by boldly praying for the king; and so far had he been from joining with the sectaries, that he presented a petition to Monk against their toleration; but he had approved of the remonstrance, and had assisted in drawing up "The Causes of God's Wrath;" and he was therefore a proper object for persecution. Highly esteemed in the country where he lived, the greatest interest was made to procure his life; and two ladies of the first rank presented a handsome service of plate to the Lord Advocate's wife—a practice it seems not uncommon in these times!—to procure his interference; but the plate was returned, and they were told that nothing could be done to save him. The Earl of Atholl, likewise, and several members of parliament, were anxious to protect him, but were informed that he could expect no mercy, unless he would consent to change his principles. When this was told to his wife, her reply showed her to have been a woman of a similar spirit. "Ye know that I am happy in a good husband, to whom I have ever borne a great affection, and have had many children; but I know him to be so steadfast to his principles, where conscience is concerned, that nobody need speak to him upon that head; and, for my part, before I would contribute any thing that would break his peace with his Master, I would rather choose to receive his head at the cross!" Yet the numerous applications in his favour from persons of influence—without his knowledge—procured a mitigation of his punishment; and, after a tedious confinement, he was only rendered incapable of all civil or ecclesiastical employment, deprived of his living, and forbid to enter his parish.

Mr. Robert Macwaird, minister, Glasgow, who had likewise maintained his loyalty to his king in the face of his enemies, was included in the noble band of sufferers; but the accusation against him differed somewhat from the others. When he perceived the general and awful course of defection from the very profession of religion, and the design to overturn the whole covenanted work of reformation, he commenced a series of sermons, in his week-day exercise, from that striking text, Amos iii. 2. "You only have I known of all the families of the earth; therefore I will punish you for all your iniquities." In these, he first addressed himself to his hearers, and pressed upon their consciences their personal sins—for these worthies, who stood in the front of the battle while contending earnestly for the national religion, never failed to inculcate the inutility and danger of a public profession without personal holiness—from personal, he ascended to general and national sins; and, adverting to the open profligacy and backsliding which pervaded a nation once so high in profession, and so favoured in privilege, he pathetically asked, "Alas! may not God expostulate with us, and say, ye are backslidden with a perpetual backsliding, and what iniquity have you found in him? We are backslidden in zeal and love. The glory of a begun reformation in manners is eclipsed, and an inundation of profanity come in. Many who once loved to walk abroad in the garment of godliness, now persecute it. The faithful servants of Christ are become enemies, because they tell the truth. The upright seekers of God are the marks of the great men's malice." And, interjecting the most remarkable prayer—"May it never be said of faithful ministers and Christians in Scotland, 'We have a law, and by this law they must die'"—he continued, "Backsliding is got up to the very head and corrupts the fountains; and wickedness goeth forth already from some of the prophets through the whole land! Are these the pastors and rulers that bound themselves so solemnly and acknowledged their former breaches? How hath the faithful city turned an harlot?"

These expressions, and many others of a like import, excited the enmity of those whom they convicted, and to whom the exhortations to repent and to return were addressed in vain; and some of the apostate tribe transmitted to the managers information against the preacher, as having been guilty of treason. The following passage was that upon which the charge chiefly rested. After entreating his audience to mourn, consider, repent, and return—to wrestle, pray, and pour out their souls before the Lord, he encouraged them, by remarking, that "God would look upon these duties as their DISSENT from what was done prejudicial to his work and interest, and mark them among the mourners in Zion." Then came the treason! "As for my own part, as a poor member of the church of Scotland, and an unworthy minister in it, I do this day call upon you who are the people of God to witness, that I humbly offer my *dissent* to all acts which are or shall be passed against the covenants or work of reformation in Scotland. And, secondly, protest, that I am desirous to be free of the guilt thereof, and pray that God may put it upon record in heaven." For this discourse he was arrested; and, on the Thursday following Mr. Guthrie's execution, was brought before the parliament.

Expecting nothing else than to follow that great man to heaven from the scaffold, he was equally courageous and unhesitating in his behaviour; and, when called upon to reply, June 6th, thus honestly avowed his sentiments:—"My lord, I cannot, I dare not, dissemble, that, having spoken nothing but what I hope will be the truth of God when brought to the touchstone, and such a truth as, without being guilty of lese-majesty against God, I could not conceal while I spoke to the text, I conceive myself obliged to own and adhere to it. So far from committing treason in this, I am persuaded that it was the highest part of loyalty towards my prince, the greatest note of respect I could put upon my superiors, the most real and unquestionable evidence of a true and tender affection to my countrymen and the congregation over whom the Holy Ghost made me, though most unworthy, an overseer, to give seasonable warning of the heavy judgment which the sin of Scotland's backsliding will bring on, that so we may be instructed at length to search and try our ways and turn to the Lord, lest his soul be separated from us; for wo unto us if our glory depart! No man will or ought to doubt whether it be a minister's duty to preach this doctrine in season and out of season, which yet is never unseasonable, and to avow that the backslider in heart shall be filled with his own ways; and if any man draw back, his soul shall have no pleasure in him. And if so, what evil have I done, or whose enemy am I become for telling the truth?

"But in order to remove any thing that may seem to give offence in my practice, I humbly desire it may be considered that a ministerial protestation against, or a dissent from, any act or acts which a minister knows and is convinced to be contrary to the word of God, is not a legal impugnation of that or these acts, much less of the authority enacting them, which it doth rather presuppose than deny; it is just a solemn and serious attested declaration, witness, or testimony, against the evil and iniquity of these things, which, by the word of God, is a warrantable practice, as is clear from Samuel, where the prophet was directed by the Lord himself to obey the voice of the people, howbeit yet protest solemnly unto them, and show them the manner of the king that shall reign over them; also Jeremiah xi. 7. There is no act of parliament declaring that it shall be treason for a minister to protest, in the Scripture sense, against such acts as are contrary to the covenant and the work of reformation; nay more, there were acts by which the covenants and vows made to God for reformation in this church, according to his will revealed in his word, received civil confirmation; and I, as his unworthy servant, was authorized to protest that these rights be not invaded—that these vows be not broken!

"Nor may I conceal, that, when I reflect upon and remember what I have said and sworn to God in the day when, with an uplifted hand to the Most High, I bound my soul with the bond of the covenant, and engaged solemnly, as I should answer to the great God, the searcher of hearts, in that day when the secrets of all hearts shall be disclosed, never to break these bonds, nor cast away these cords from me, nor to suffer myself, either directly or indirectly, by terror or persuasion, to be withdrawn from owning them—when I recollect that, had they been even things indifferent, I durst not have shaken them off when I had sworn to God, and consider that, instead of this, they were duties of indispensable obligation antecedently to all oaths, and remain unalterably binding independently of them—and when I considered my duty as a minister, to give warning, to declare, testify, and bear witness against the sin of violating these covenants, in order to avoid the wrath that shall follow, and that under no less a threatening than banishment from the presence of the Lord and the glory of his power—I had no choice.

"Now I humbly beseech I may not be looked upon as a disloyal person, either as to my principles or practice; and so clear am I that there was neither iniquity in my heart, nor wickedness in my hands, against his majesty, that I only wish the informer's conduct, be he who he may, in the place where I live, were compared with mine, and the issue of my trial depended on this—whether he or I had shown most loyalty during the prevalence and usurpation of the enemy; but I suspect he has rather a little more prudence than to agree to such a test. But as for me, my lord, while I wait the coming forth of my sentence from his presence, whose eyes behold the things that are equal, I declare, that however I cannot submit my conscience to men, yet I humbly, as becometh, submit my person."

This case appears to have been ably managed; and the parliament delayed proceeding to any immediate decision. In the interval, he presented a supplication withdrawing the words "protest and dissent," as too legal and forensic, substituting the words "declaring and bearing witness." The reasons which he assigned for so doing are satisfactory, and show that the witnesses of this period did not stand with obstinacy upon any irrational punctilio, or foolishly rush upon suffering for the sake of unmeaning distinctions or of favourite phrases. "I am brought," are his expressions, "to offer this alteration, not so much, if my heart deceive me not, for the fear of prejudice to my person—though being but a weak man, I am easily reached by such discomposing passions—as from an earnest desire to remove out of the way any, the least, or remotest, occasion of stumbling, that there may be the more ready and easy access, without prejudice of words, to ponder and give judgment of the matter; and that, likewise, if the Lord shall think fit to call me forth to suffer hard things on this account, it may not be said that it was for wilful and peremptory stickling to such expressions; whereas, I might, by using others, without prejudice to the matter, and no less significant, have escaped the danger; and lest I should seem to insinuate that a minister of the gospel could not have sufficiently exonered his conscience without such formal and legal terms." But it was necessary to get rid of men whose abilities were dreaded by their apostate brethren, and whose consistent piety would have been a standing reproach to the new prelates. He was therefore, before parliament rose, sentenced to banishment, though, by an uncommon stretch of moderation, he was allowed to remain six months in Scotland—one of them in Glasgow to arrange his affairs—and empowered to receive his next year's stipend.

What rendered these rigorous proceedings towards the ablest, the most pious, and most conscientious loyalists, more flagrantly unjust, was, the lenity shown to others who had been deeply implicated in active compliances with the usurpers, not only after their power became irresistible, but even while Charles was in the country and at the head of an army. The Laird of Swinton had been suspected, in the year 1650, of corresponding with Cromwell, and being summoned to answer before the parliament at Perth, was forfeited for failing to appear, on which he joined the English, and was appointed a judge; but having now turned a quaker, he was pardoned, and went to the north, where he succeeded in making a few proselytes. Sir John Chiesly, also, who had acted cordially with the English, and been forfeited by the same parliament, was passed over; but his safety was attributed to the influence of money; for rapacity and venality characterized almost every member of government, and every court of justice, from the Restoration to the Revolution.

The escape of Mr. Patrick Gillespie was more surprising, as he was personally disagreeable to the king, who had repeatedly refused to listen to any solicitations on his behalf. Gillespie was a minister in Glasgow, and afterwards principal of the College. He had been the most conspicuous of the remonstrators—had approved of "The Causes of God's Wrath," and had been appointed principal by the English commissioners, or sequestrators as they were called*

* At the time when the English ruled, the church of Scotland was divided and subdivided into a variety of sections. The remonstrators themselves divided; some of them, among whom were, Messrs. P. Gillespie, Samuel Rutherford, James Durham, William Guthrie of Fenwick, Robert Traill, and other eminently pious men, complied with the ruling powers on the Christian principle of obedience to the powers that be, and the absolute necessity of the case; but they were still more obnoxious to the resolutioners, because they so far agreed with the sectaries, in only considering as members of the church persons who gave proof of practical godliness, and opposed the principle of promiscuous communion and general membership. Against this schism, Principal Baillie was very violent. "This formed schism," says he, in a letter to Mr. W. Spang, "is very bitter to us, but remediless, except on intolerable conditions, which our wise orthodox divines will advise us to accept:—We must embrace, without contradiction, and let grow, the principles of the remonstrants, which all reformed divines, and all states in the world, abhor. We must permit a few heady men to waste our church with our consent or connivance. We must let them frame our people to the sectarian model—a few more forward ones among themselves, by privy meetings, to be the godly party; and the congregation, the rest, to be the rascally malignant multitude; so that the body of our people are to be cast out of all churches; and the few who are countenanced, are fitted, as sundry of them already have done, to embrace the errors of the time for their destruction." *Letters*, vol. ii. p. 375. The other section of the remonstrants refused to acknowledge in any manner the power of the usurper, lamented the toleration of sectaries, and maintained, with the resolutioners, the legitimate principles of a national church—that all who attended were to be considered members of that church, unless excommunicated for openly immoral conduct or disobedience to the order and discipline of the church. At the head of this section were Mr. James Guthrie, Warriston, and many others, who bore

—had been a great favourite with Cromwell—had preached before him—prayed for him as chief magistrate—and had received from him several valuable gifts—all which were now brought forward as charges against him. But he had many friends in the House, and was induced to profess civil guilt and throw himself upon the king's mercy. His concessions, it is alleged, were strained beyond what he intended, and represented as of great importance at the time, as he had been eminent among his brethren; and it was supposed his example would have a mighty influence in inducing the more scrupulous to give way. They were, however, grievous to the Presbyterians and not satisfactory to his majesty; but they procured a mitigation of his punishment, which was commuted to deprivation of his office, and confinement to Ormiston and six miles round.

On the 12th of July, the parliament rose; and, on the last day of that month, their public acts were proclaimed, with the usual formalities, from the cross of Edinburgh—a ceremony that employed the heralds and other functionaries from ten o'clock in the forenoon till six at night.

About the same time, Samuel Rutherford was relieved by death.

testimony by their blood to the sincerity of their profession. It is worthy of remark, that the first class were chiefly the older, the second the younger, race of the Presbyterians.

BOOK III.

AUGUST, A. D. 1661—1662.

Lord High Commissioner sets out for court—His reception—Deliberations of the Council—Episcopacy resolved upon as the National Religion of Scotland—Glencairn, Rothes, and Sharpe appointed to carry the tidings to Edinburgh—King's letter--Privy Council announce the overthrow of Presbytery—Forbid the election of Presbyterian Magistrates in Burghs—Prosecute Tweeddale—Ministers summoned to London to be episcopally ordained—Their characters—Their consecration—Grief of the Presbyterians—Re-introduction of Episcopacy—Restrictions on the press—Witch-craft—Synods discharged and Bishops ordered to be honoured by royal patent—Their consecration—Parliament restores their rank—Asserts the King's supremacy—The Covenants declared unlawful—Acts of fines—Defeated—Lord Lorn—Blair and other ministers deprived—King's birth-day—Middleton's visit to the West and South—Case of Mr. Wylie—Brown of Wamphrey—Livingston, &c.—Middleton removed and Lauderdale appointed.

Leaving the government in the hands of the privy council,* Middleton, after parliament adjourned, set out for court, where he was received by the Earl of Clarendon, Lord Chancellor, the Duke of Ormond, and all the cavalier party, with the greatest congratulations for having quenched the fanatic zeal of Scotland, and carried his majesty's prerogative beyond what any preceding monarch when present, had ever claimed.

At a council held upon his arrival, Charles, who utterly detested Presbytery, expressed himself highly

* The chief members of which were—The Earl of Glencairn, chancellor; Crawford, treasurer; Rothes, president; Lauderdale, secretary. Members—Dukes of Lennox and Hamilton; Marquis of Montrose; Earls of Errol, Marischal, Mar, Atholl, Morton, Cassils, Linlithgow, Perth, Dunfermline, Wigton, Callender, Dundee, &c. &c.—*Wodrow*, p. 87.

gratified at the report of what he had done; but his counsellors were divided. Lauderdale and some others, who knew perfectly that the established religion was deeply rooted in the affections of Scottishmen, where unwilling to hazard a change; and even some who wished an Episcopacy were yet averse to its being too rashly introduced.* Middleton, however, who had been previously tutored, immediately addressed the king—"May it please your sacred majesty: You may perceive by the account I have now given of your affairs in Scotland, that there is no present government as yet established in that church. Presbytery is, after a long usurpation, now at last rescinded—the covenant, whereby men thought they were obliged to it, is now declared to have been unlawful—and the acts of parliament, whereby it was fenced, are now removed; so that it is arbitrary to your majesty to choose what government you will fix there; for to your majesty this is by the last act of supremacy declared to belong. But if your majesty do not interpose, then Episcopacy, which was unjustly invaded at once with your royal power, will return to its former vigour."

Glencairn followed, and affirmed that the insolence of the Presbyterian ministers had so disgusted all loyal subjects, that six for one longed for the Episcopalian government, which had ever inculcated obedience and supported the royal interest; whereas, Calvinism and Presbytery had never been introduced

* When the lords went first up to welcome the king, the question was debated what form of Government should be established in the Scottish Church. "Middleton and Clencairn were resolute for bishops, pronouncing they would both compose the church and manadge it to the king's mind; Lauderdale opposed it stiffely, affirming the king should thereby lose the affectiones of the people of Scotland, and that the bishops should be so far from enlargeing the king's power, that they would prove a burdine too heavy for him to bear; and therein he proved als true a prophet, as he was a faithful friend to the king. Within some few days, Glencairn came to visit Lauderdale, and told him he was only for a sober sort of bishops, such as they were in the primitive times, not lordly prelats. Lauderdale answered him with ane oath, that since they hade chosen bishops, they should have them higher than any that ever were in Scotland, and that he should find."—*Kirkton*, p. 134.

into any country without blood and rebellion, and instanced, with the most preposterous absurdity, the struggles for freedom at the Reformation—in France, during the civil war—in Holland, when they revolted from Spain—and now twice in Scotland; once by the Regent Murray, when Queen Mary was banished, and lastly in 1637. Rothes added although he had not seen the rise of the innovations, yet he had witnessed the ruin of the engagement and the treatment of the king by that persuasion. Lauderdale contended that the proposition was of too great importance to be slightly determined. and required much thought and much information; for, upon their resolution, depended the quiet of the Scots—a people very unmanageable in matters of religion—and advised that either a General Assembly should be called, the provincial Synods consulted, which, as composed of ministers and laymen, would acquaint his majesty with the inclinations of his subjects—or, he might call the ablest divines on both sides, and learn their sentiments, if either of the other proposals were approved of. Middleton replied that all these methods would only tend to continue Presbytery; for it was probable the power of the ministers which had been so irresistible of late, would preponderate in all. They would easily procure ruling elders of their own cast to be chosen, and both would be unwilling to resign the power they possessed; at all events, the leading men whom the inferior clergy must follow, durst not quarrel the resolutions of their rabbies, who would adhere to the oaths they had taken, and stoutly defend their own supremacy; besides to call General Assemblies or Synods, were to restore them, and thus to infringe the act rescissory.

The Earl of Crawford, whose treasurer's rod was a desirable object for Middleton, had declined mingling in the debate, which the Chancellor of England observing, requested his majesty that he might be desired to give his opinion, in order that he might either disclaim Presbytery or displease the king, and thus put his principles or his place in jeopardy; for it appeared to be a settled rule among the courtiers of Charles, that whatever Scottishmen were allowed to interfere in the public affairs of their native country, should sacrifice either their conscience or their interest.

Crawford perceived the Chancellor's aim, and vehemently urged that provincial synods might be consulted, assuring his majesty, the king, that six for one in Scotland were in favour of Presbytery. "The offences of the reformers," he warmly contended, "were not to be charged upon the Reformation: the best innovations were ever attended with much irregularity, and therefore it was better to continue that government which had now past all these hazards—at first unavoidable—than risk another, which, at its outset, must be unhappy in the same inconveniences. Nor did the act rescissory cut off Presbytery, for it was secured by acts of General Assemblies, which had been countenanced by his majesty's father's commissioners, and were yet unrepealed."

The Duke of Hamilton supported him, and affirmed that the reason why the act rescissory had so easily passed, was, because his majesty had promised to continue Presbytery in his letter addressed to the ministers of Edinburgh. Clarendon closed the debate, by observing that Crawford had owned all that ever was done in Scotland in their rebellion; "and God preserve me," said he, "from living in a country where religion is independent of the state, and clergy may subsist by their own acts; for there all churchmen may be kings." The king then told them that he perceived a majority were for Episcopacy, and therefore he resolved to settle it without any further delay.

Immediately after, Glencairn and Rothes were despatched to Edinburgh, accompanied by Mr. Sharpe, to convey his majesty's determination to the council. Were it not that, in humble life, we see men equally base and shameless where their own self-interest is concerned, we might wonder at the unblushing effrontery of the royal communication; yet the pitiful evasion and vile duplicity in which it was couched, render the king's letter at once an object of detestation and contempt. That the reader may compare it with his former to the ministers of Edinburgh, I give it at full length:—

"Charles R. Right trusty and well-beloved cousins and councillors, We greet you well. Whereas, in the month of August, 1660, We did, by our letters to the Presbytery of Edinburgh, declare our purpose to maintain the government of the church of Scotland as settled by law; and our parliament having since that time not only rescinded all the acts since the troubles began, but also declared all these pretended parliaments null and void, and left to us the settling and securing of church government: Therefore, in compliance with that act rescissory, according to our late proclamation, dated at Whitehall the 10th of June, and in contemplation of the inconveniences from the church government, as it hath been exercised these twenty-three years past—of the unsuitableness thereof to our monarchical state—of the sadly experienced confusions which have been caused during the late troubles, by the violence done to our royal prerogative, and to the government, civil and ecclesiastical, settled by unquestionable authority, We, from respect to the glory of God and the good and interest of the Protestant religion; from our pious care and princely zeal for the order, unity, peace, and stability of that church, and its better harmony with the government of the churches of England and Ireland, have, after mature deliberation, declared to those of our council here, our firm resolution to interpose our royal authority for restoring of that church to its right government by bishops, as it was before the late troubles, during the reigns of our royal father and grandfather, of blessed memory, and as it now stands settled by law. Of this our royal pleasure concerning church government you are to take notice, and to make intimation thereof in such a way and manner as you shall judge most expedient and effectual. And we require you, and every one

of you, and do expect, according to the trust and confidence we have in your affections and duty to our service, that you will be careful to use your best endeavours for curing the distempers contracted during those late evil times—for uniting our good subjects among themselves, and bringing them all to a cheerful acquiescing and obedience to our sovereign authority, which we will employ, by the help of God, for the maintaining and defending the true reformed religion, increase of piety, and the settlement and security of that church in her rights and liberties, according to law and ancient custom. And, in order thereto, our will is, that you forthwith take such course with the rents belonging to the several bishopricks and deaneries, that they may be restored and made useful to the church, and that according to justice and the standing law. And, moreover, you are to inhibit the assembling of ministers in their several synodical meetings through the kingdoms until our further pleasure, and to keep a watchful eye over all who, upon any pretext whatever, shall, by discoursing, preaching, reviling, or any irregular or unlawful way, endeavour to alienate the affections of our people, or dispose them to an ill opinion of us and our government, to the disturbance of the peace of the kingdom. So, expecting your cheerful obedience and a speedy account of your proceedings herein, We bid you heartily farewell. Given at our court, at Whitehall, August 14, 1661, and of our reign the thirteenth year, by his majesty's command.'
(Signed) "LAUDERDALE."

The privy council received with all due humility this intimation of the royal pleasure; and, on the 6th of September, an act was drawn up and published, announcing to the people of Scotland the overthrow of their beloved Presbytery, under whose shade they had reposed with so much tranquillity during the few last years of the much abused and unreasonably hated protectorate, and the re-establishment of that system against which their fathers had ever contended. A proclamation overturning the freedom of elections, accompanied the act for overturning the constitution of the Church—so naturally and nearly are civil and ecclesiastical tyranny connected. The royal burghs were commanded, under the highest penalties, to elect none for their magistrates who were fanatically—an epithet which it now became fashionable to apply to the conscientious Presbyterians—inclined; and such and so sudden had been the change wrought by the transfer of power, that this illegal dictation was universally obeyed. Nor did their conduct towards one of their own number evince a greater regard for their own privileges or the rights of parliament, than their ready servility had done for the religion and liberty of their country. Tweeddale and Kincardine had pressed the council to request the king that he would consult provincial synods, who would declare the sense of the country; and, at all events, relieve his majesty from obloquy whatever might be the ultimate decision. This proposition, however, would have shown too much deference to men whom it was intended to bring to unconditional subjection, and was refused accordingly; but Charles was informed of Tweeddale's hesitation, and an order was procured for his imprisonment, not indeed ostensibly for his opinion delivered in council, but for what was or ought to have been still more sacred, for his judgment and voice in parliament, because he had spoken in vindication of Mr. James Guthrie, and had not voted him guilty of death! It was to no purpose that he pled the freedom allowed in parliament, where he was a counsellor upon oath and expressly indemnified by law for what was spoken there; and the danger which every member would thus incur who voted any person accused of treason innocent, if a majority should happen to find him guilty. He was sent prisoner to the Castle, and was only, upon his submission and petition, permitted to confine himself to Yester and three miles round, finding caution to the amount of one hundred thousand merks to answer when called for! Eight months after, when it was thought his discipline had taught him obedience, he was, through the mediation of the council, relieved; and, when his relation Lauderdale came into power, he joined his government.

Although his majesty could establish Episcopacy by proclamation, the peculiar holiness which was supposed necessarily to belong to the office of a bishop, it was beyond his power to confer. This essential attribute of a prelate, which had passed, as was believed, untainted from the apostles, through all the corruption, vileness, and abomination of the church of Rome, had, by hands crimsoned in the blood of the saints, and defiled with all the pollutions of their brethren, been communicated to the dignitaries of the English hierarchy, upon whom it still rested in all its imaginary purity and vigour. But the feeble portion of the sacred virus that had reached Scotland upon a former occasion, when James VI. procured the inoculation of his hierarchate, was now confined to one aged and almost superannuated subject, Mr. Thomas Sydeserf, formerly bishop of Galloway; and he had been excommunicated by a General Assembly. It was therefore resolved that a select number of the Scottish ministers should be consecrated by priests who had never been polluted by any unhallowed contact with Presbyterians; and Messrs. Sharpe, Fairfoul, and Hamilton were summoned to London* to receive the holy unction.

James Sharpe, designed for the primacy, was already the object of detestation to every one who had the smallest regard for the Presbyterian profession, or for consistency of principle. Andrew Fairfoul, promoted to the archbishopric of Glasgow, possessed considerable learning, better skilled, however, in physic than in theology—a pleasant, facetious companion, but never esteemed a serious divine. He had taken the covenant and was first minister in Leith, then in Dunse. Mr. James Hamilton, brother to Lord Belhaven, created bishop of Galloway, was also a covenanter, and minister of Cambusnethan. His abilities were not above mediocrity, and his cunning was more remarkable than his piety. They were, however, joined at London by Mr. Robert Leighton, a man of a very different description, whose meek and gentle spirit, unfitted for the stormy region of political polemics, delighted more in communion with God than in contending with his fellows, and who, counting himself a stranger and a pilgrim upon earth, was only anxious to diffuse the gospel of the kingdom, and shed around him the charities of life. He was educated during the reign of pseudo-episcopacy, and never was a thorough Presbyterian. His character and views may be estimated from a circumstance which occurred during that period of his life when he was minister of Newbattle. Some of his zealous co-presbyters urging on him the duty of "preaching to the times," (by no means an unnecessary one, however, in its proper place,) he mildly replied—"When so many of my brethren are preaching to the times, they may spare one poor minister to preach for eternity." He had retired to London to enjoy the privacy he loved, and was unwillingly dragged forward to assist in carrying Episcopacy to Scotland.*

A commission, under the great seal of England, was directed to the bishops of London and Worcester, and some other suffragans of the diocese of Canterbury, to officiate upon this important occasion; but an unexpected difficulty occurred by Dr. Sheldon proposing to set aside the Presbyterian ordination altogether and commence *de novo.* Sharpe quoted the case of Bishop Spottiswood, whose Presbyterian ordination had been sustained when he was consecrated, and for a while resisted the proposal; but the other was peremptory, and would not hear of the validity of any other than prelatic imposition of hands; and Sharpe, who had now gone too far to recede for a trifle, submitted to enter his new pro-

* There is just one point in Leighton's character that appears unaccountable, that is, after he had solemnly sworn the covenants, and enforced them upon others, how he could ever turn an Episcopalian

fession by the lowest step, that he might attain the wretched object of his ambition—to him a woful eminence. In the month of December, they were with great pomp, and before a splendid assemblage of nobility at Westminster, passed and raised through the various degrees of the craft, from preaching-deacons to mitred bishops, in one day, which was concluded by a magnificent entertainment given by the new-made prelates to their English brethren and a select party of Scottish and English nobles.

Convinced at length of their error, the honest Presbyterians, of all parties, lamented that their intestine divisions should have been allowed to divert them from attempting the security of their religion, and that they should have indulged in bitterness of spirit against each other about matters of comparatively lesser moment, while the common enemy was making such rapid, though covert, advances against their establishment. Uncertain how long they might enjoy that liberty, they now throughout Scotland directed the attention of their hearers to the principles of their church, and the points in dispute between them and the Episcopalians*—they held congregational fasts in every corner of the land to la-

* The points in dispute between the Presbyterians and Episcopalians were of much more vital importance than modern Presbyterians seem to be aware of. They comprehended doctrinal points—the form of church government, the ceremonies, the festivals, and the forcible intrusion of the whole system upon the nation, in virtue of the king's spiritual supremacy. The very essence of Christianity was at stake. The grand fundamental doctrine which Luther asserted at the Reformation, was justification by faith, in opposition to justification by works; and a more clear statement of this essential article of Christian belief will nowhere be found than in his exposition of the Epistle to the Galatians—to this all was subsidiary. He found that attacking the rites, ceremonies, and fooleries of Rome was wasting shot against pitiful outworks, the fall of which was of no importance, while the main rampart and the citidel frowned defiance. It was the same with all the reformers; and it was now a revival of the old question. The Episcopalians were in general Arminians, and the Presbyterians contended for "the faith" once delivered to the fathers; and this faith was the doctrinal creed embodied in the covenants. This should always be kept in view. The other points were not of little moment; but this was the foundation.

ment over the misimprovement of their privileges and deprecate the impending wrath of God—and they continued their parochial duties among a mourning people, who, with a general sadness, anticipated the lamentable change. Their synods had been forbid; but they met with little interruption in their presbyterial duties till the bishops were installed, when they were informed that their power of ordination had ceased. This intimation was first made by the council to the presbytery of Peebles, when, in the month of December, they were proceeding to induct Mr. John Hay to the kirk of Manner; and from thenceforth all presentations to benefices were ordered to be directed to the archbishops or bishops within whose diocese the vacant church might lie.

The re-introduction of Episcopacy into Scotland was accompanied by a restoration of all the most severe restrictions upon the liberty of the press and a revival of the absurd and flagitious proceedings against poor, old, and friendless creatures, ignorantly or maliciously accused of witchcraft. The council, upon an information that George Swinton and James Glen, booksellers in Edinburgh, had printed and sold the speeches of the Marquis of Argyle and Mr. James Guthrie, with other seditious and scandalous publications, such as the "Covenanter's Plea," ordered the Lord Advocate and Lord Provost of Edinburgh, to seize upon such books and papers, and prohibit them and the rest of the printers from printing any other books or pamphlets without a warrant from the king, parliament, or council; and, "for preventing false intelligence," they granted liberty to a creature of their own, Robert Mein, keeper of the letter-office, Edinburgh, to print the Diurnal, then the only newspaper in the kingdom. Commissions for the trial of witches were at the same time issued to gentlemen in almost every shire, and great numbers of unfortunate creatures, chiefly poor decrepit old women, were tortured and murdered upon the most contradictory, ridiculous, and incredible absurdities, which were alleged against them; or upon the incoherent ravings which, after being kept for nights without sleep, and tormented without intermission, in the height of a delirium, they uttered as their confessions. And yet such convictions stand upon record as being in consequence of "clear probation" or voluntary confessions! But it is deserving of especial notice, that these trials took place chiefly in the north and east—the districts least infected with "fanaticism."*

This eventful year was closed by a letter from the king, December 28, ordering the council to discharge by proclamation all ecclesiastical meetings in synods, presbyteries, and sessions, until authorized by the archbishops or bishops upon their entering upon the government of their respective sees; and requiring that all due deference and respect should be given by the lieges to these dignitaries, or, to use the words of the king, "that they have all countenance, assistance, and encouragement from the nobility, gentry, and burghs, in the discharge of their office and service to Us in the church; and that severe and exemplary notice be taken of all and every one who shall presume to reflect or express any disrespect to their persons, or the authority with which they are intrusted"—an ominous and unholy introduction to a Christian ministry, which sufficiently marked the nature of the proposed establishment; bore witness

* The Dunbar witches were famous in East, as the Borrowstounness witches were in West, Lothian. It is, however, among the melancholy and unaccountable problems in the history of the human mind, that persons of excellent understanding were implicated in these and similar transactions. In England, even Judge Hale condemned two. Had the witches, or wizards, been tried for operating upon the fears and the superstitions of their country folk, as the Africans in the West Indies and on their own coasts operate on the fears and superstitions of each other by the *obi*, *bitter water*, and other really noxious practices, their persecution might have been proper, and their punishment just; but, dancing reels with Satan, and flying through the air upon broomsticks, were accusations so truly ridiculous, that, how they came to be ever gravely listened to, is passing strange. Dr. Hutchinson says, "the word *witch*, in old English, according to Dr. More, signifies *a wise woman;* in the vulgar Latin, it is *venefica a poisoner*."—*Hist. Essay on Witchcraft*, p. 183.

to the known dislike of the people towards such a priesthood, and the strong probability that pastors created by royal patent, and sanctified by prelatic palmistry, would be received with any thing but respect or affection by the flock over whom they were to have the oversight.

The new year, 1662, was ushered in by a proclamation, January 9, from the privy council, announcing, in terms of the king's letter, the final extinction of Presbytery. Formerly, such a decree would have encountered at any rate a formidable show of opposition from the denounced ecclesiastical judicatories; nor would they have separated without at least bearing testimony against this unwarrantable invasion of their legal right. But the blind confidence that the Presbyterians had so unaccountably reposed in the king, produced a species of fatuity; nor would they believe till they experienced the truth of the prognostications of the more discerning, who saw from the first the ill-dissembled hatred Charles bore to Presbyterianism as well as to piety. They were like men amazed at the greatness of the calamity; and although some few of them attempted to draw up petitions to the council, no united effort was made to vindicate the oppressed church.

An obsequious crowd of nobility, clergy, and gentry, awaited the arrival of the new bishops, and obeyed to the letter the orders of the king. From Cockburnspath to the capital, their numbers increased; and, as the procession rolled on, it assumed more the splendour of some earthly potentate marching to take possession of a newly-acquired conquest, than that of spiritual guides entering upon the humble duties of a gospel ministry. They were greeted on their approach to Edinburgh with martial music, and received at the gates by the magistrates in their robes,* and spent several successive days in sump-

* Leighton alone declined all public show. When he understood the manner in which it was proposed to receive them, he left the cavalcade at Morpeth, and came privately to Edinburgh. After-

tuous entertainments. The primate, vieing with the chief nobility in the elegance of his equipage as well as the magnificence of his banquets, displayed upon the occasion a handsome London-built chariot, and was attended by lackeys in purple liveries. Shortly afterwards, in great pomp, he took possession of his see;* then, returning to Edinburgh on the 7th of

wards, he told Dr. Burnet, "he believed they were weary of him, for he was very weary of them."

* Lamont gives the following account of Sharpe's visit on this occasion:—"As for Mr. Sharpe, he came to Fiffe, Apryl 15th, and dyned that day at Abetsaa, Sr. Andrew Ramsays, formerly provest of Edenboroughe, his house, and that night came to Lesly, being attended by divers both of the nobilitie and gentrie. The nixt day being Weddensday, the 16th Apr., he went to St. Androws from Lesly, attended from the Earle of Rothes his house, with about sixty horse; bot by the way divers persons and corporations (being wretten for in particular by the said Earle of Rothes a day or two before) mett him, some at ane place and some at ane other, viz. some from Fawkland, Achtermowghtie, Cuper, Craill, and about one hundred and twenty horsemen from St. Androws and elsewhere; so that once they were estimat to be about seven or eight hundred horse. The nobilitie ther were, Earle of Rothes, Earle of Kelley, Earle of Leven, and the Lord Newarke; of gentrie, Ardrosse, Lundy, Rires, Dury, Skaddowory, Doctor Martin of Strandry, and divers others. All the way the said Archbishope rode thus, viz. betwixt two nobelmen, namely, Rothes on his right, and Kelley on his left hand. No ministers were present ther safe Mr. William Barclay, formerly deposed out of Fawkland, and Mr. William Comry, minister of St. Leonards Colledge, that came foorth with the Bishope his sone out of St. Androws to meit his father. (He dwells in the Abbay in Mr. George Weyms house, that formerly belonged to B. Spotswoode, Archb. of St. Androws.) That night ther supped with the said Bishope, the Earles of Rothes, Kelley, Newarke; Ardrosse, Lundy, Strandry, and divers others; and divers of this dined with him the nixt day. As for Rothes and Ardrosse, they lodged with him all night. On the Sabbath after, he preached in the towne church in the forenoone, and a velvet cushion in the pulpitt before him. His text, 1 Cor. ii. 2, 'For I determined to knowe nothing amonge you, save Jesus Christ, and him crucified.' His sermon did not run mutch on the words, bot in a discourse of vindicating himselfe and of pressing of episcopacie and the utilitie of it; shewing, since it was wanting, that ther hath beine nothing bot trowbels and disturbancies both in church and state. Apryl 30, 1662, he tooke journey for Edenboroughe, being accompanied with about fifty horse, most of them of the citie of St. Androws; and, in his way, he gave the ladys at Lundy a visit at Lundy: he cam with only five or six horse, and himselfe staid a short whille, toke a drink (bot did not dine), and was gone againe" *Diary*, p. 183–4.

May, consecrated other six bishops in the Abbey of Holyroodhouse.

This ceremony, which had been deferred till the arrival of the Commissioner, was conducted in the grandest and most imposing style. His Grace, and all the nobles and gentlemen who had come to town to attend parliament, together with the magistrates of the city, were present; and none were admitted but by tickets. The two archbishops who officiated were in their full canonicals—black satin gowns, white surplices, lawn sleeves, copes, and all the long desecrated garments, known to the Presbyterians of that day by the contemptuous epithets of their forefathers—"Rags of Rome." The others wore black satin gowns. The passage leading from the pews, where the bishops elect sat, to the altar, and the space before the altar, were covered with rich carpets. Mr. James Gordon, one of the northern ministers, preached the consecration sermon from 1 Cor. iv. 1: "Let a man so account of us as of the ministers of Christ, and stewards of the mysteries of God;" in which, pointing out the errors of the former, he exhorted the new prelates to beware of encroaching on the nobles, nor exceed the bounds of their sacred function. They were then led from their places by the archbishop of Glasgow, and by him presented to the primate who presided, and set them apart according to the ritual of the Church of England, and to whom they vowed clerical obedience during all the days of their lives. The bishops this day consecrated were—*Dunkeld*, George Halyburton, late minister of Perth; *Ross*, George Patterson, minister of Aberdeen; *Moray*, Murdoch Mackenzie, minister of Elgin; *Brechin*, David Strachan, minister of Fettercairn; *Argyle*, David Fletcher, minister of Melrose; *The Isles*, Robert Wallace, minister of Barnwell, Ayrshire;* none of whom were men either of distin-

* George Wiseheart, chaplain to Montrose, and author of the elegant Latin romance which goes under the name of his memoirs was consecrated bishop of Edinburgh at St. Andrews, on the 3d of

guished talents or exemplary piety, all had appeared zealots in the cause of the covenant. Common report attributed to them a private dissoluteness of character which might be exaggerated; but for their apostasy from a cause which they had urged with more than ordinary heat, no apology was ever attempted. Conviction could not be alleged, and as self-interest appeared the only ostensible reason, they sunk in the estimation of the people in proportion to the respect in which they had been previously held; while they returned the contempt with which they were deservedly treated, by hatred and persecution—a consequent usual with renegades, who ever remorselessly pursue to degradation and death the steadfast members of the religion they have betrayed, whose unshaken integrity is a standing reproof of their temporizing baseness.

Next day, May 9, the parliament met; and their first act was to restore the bishops to the exercise of their episcopal function, precedence in the church, power of ordination, inflicting of censures, and all other acts of church discipline; and this their office they were to exercise only with "the advice and assistance of such of the clergy as they should find to be of known loyalty and prudence." Without entering into any of the puzzling questions respecting the divine right of any form of church government, they at once founded their Prelacy upon a principle most repugnant to Presbytery—the spiritual supremacy of the king—"Forasmuch as the ordering and disposal of the external government and policy of the church doth properly belong unto his majesty as an inherent right of the crown, by virtue of his royal prerogative and supremacy in causes ecclesiastical." In the preamble were narrated as the causes of its re-establishment, the disorders and exorbitancies that had been in the church, the encroachments upon the prerogative and rights of the

June, and Mr. David Mitchell, minister of Edinburgh, bishop of Aberdeen. Sydeserf had Orkney.

crown, the usurpations upon the authority of parlia ments, and the prejudice inflicted on the liberty of the subject ever since the invasion made upon the bishops and episcopal order—a form of church government pronounced most agreeable to the word of God, most convenient and effectual for the preservation of truth, regularity, and unity, most suitable to monarchy, and the peace and quiet of the state: "THEREFORE his majesty and his estates did redintegrate the state of bishops to their ancient places and undoubted privileges in parliament and all their other accustomed dignities." Nor was it among the least strange enactments of this extraordinary act, that whatever his majesty, with the archbishops and bishops, should determine respecting the external order of the church, was "previously" declared valid and effectual.

Immediately upon this act being passed, a deputation of six members, two noblemen, two barons, and two burgesses, was sent to the prelates, who were waiting in the primate's lodgings to invite them to take their seats. They were accordingly conducted in state to the House—the two archbishops first, walking between two noblemen, the Earls of Kellie and Wemyss, and the bishops following, attended by the barons, gentlemen, and the magistrates in their robes. When they entered, a congratulatory speech was made them from the throne, the act restoring them was read, and the parliament adjourned on purpose that the spiritual lords might have the pleasure of dining with his Grace, the Commissioner who, to do them the greater honour, walked on foot with them in procession to the Palace. They were preceded by six macers with their maces, next three gentlemen-ushers, then the purse-bearer uncovered. The Commissioner and Chancellor followed, with two noblemen on their right and the two archbishops on their left. A select party of noblemen and members of parliament, with the bishops, made up the goodly company, who, "at four of the clock, sat down to ane sumptuous entertainment, and remained at table till eight."

The bishops, as now thrust upon the Scottish church, differed widely from those intruded by James VI. They pled no scriptural authority, but an act of parliament, as the source of their power, and acknowledged, in its fullest sense, a temporal prince as the supreme head of the church. The old bishops were only a set of constant moderators in the synods and presbyteries, possessing merely a sort of negative voice, and were nominally at least responsible to the General Assembly; but the whole form of Presbytery was now swept away, and the prelates were amenable to no church courts; nor could any assembly of ministers meet, but under their sanction, or by their permission.

Having subverted the religion of the country, the next and most natural step was to eradicate, if possible, the principles of civil liberty. The sycophantish estates, therefore, proceeded to declare rebellious and treasonable those positions for which their fathers had contended unto blood, and which their children asserted at the point of the sword:—That it is lawful in subjects, upon pretence of reformation, or any other pretence whatsoever, to enter into leagues or covenants, or to take up arms against the king: or that it is lawful for subjects, pretending his majesty's authority, to take up arms against his person or those commissionated by him, or to suspend him from the exercise of his royal government, or to put limitations on their due obedience and allegiance. As, notwithstanding the acts of the former session, the Presbyterians did not conceive themselves loosened from what they considered the oaths of God—ratified by the highest ecclesiastical and civil authorities of the land—the National Covenant, and the Solemn League and Covenant, these were now declared unlawful oaths; the subjects were relieved from their obligations; the acts of Assembly respecting them, which had received the sanction both of the parliament and of the king, but had hitherto escaped notice, were annulled; and all ratifications, by whatsoever authority, cassed and made void. At the same time, it was enacted, that if any person should, by writing, printing, praying, preaching, or remonstrating, express any thing calculated to create or cherish dislike in the people towards the king's supremacy in causes ecclesiastic, or of the government of the church by archbishops and bishops, as now settled, they were to be declared incapable of enjoying any place or employment, civil, ecclesiastical, or military, and liable to such further pains as the law directs; that is, liable to the pains of that detestable statute against leasing-making, of whose extent a notable specimen was speedily given in the case of Argyle. This was followed by an act obliging all persons in public trust to subscribe a declaration in which the whole of the transactions, since the commencement of the troubles, were affirmed to have been illegal and seditious, and the covenants unlawful oaths, unwarrantably imposed against the fundamental laws and liberties of the kingdom, and not obligatory either on themselves or others.

By another retrospective act, repeating the restoration of patronage, it was ordained that all the ministers who had entered to parishes since the year 1649, had no right to their stipends; and their charges were pronounced vacant, until they should procure presentations anew from the lawful patrons and collocation from the bishop of the diocese, which he was enjoined to give to the present incumbents, upon application, before the 20th of September following; failing which, the presentation was to fall to the bishop *jure devoluto;* and, to conclude the series of enactments intended to establish Episcopacy upon a firm and immovable foundation, amid the ruins of Presbytery, all professors and teachers in universities and colleges were required to take the oath of allegiance on pain of deprivation—all ministers were ordered to attend the diocesan synods, and pay all clerical obedience to their superiors under the like penalty—and all meetings in private houses, for religious exercises, which might tend to alienate this people from their lawful pastors, were strictly forbidden. Nor were any persons to be permitted to preach in public or private, to teach any school, or act as tutor in the family of any person of quality, without the license of the ordinary of the diocese.

Ecclesiastical matters being thus arranged, and the session apparently drawing to a termination, Lauderdale so strongly pressed a bill of indemnity, that Middleton could no longer get it avoided; but he introduced, as an accompaniment, the act of fines, which in numerous instances rendered it nugatory.

Last year a complaint had been made to parliament of the losses sustained by the Earl of Queensberry from the forces under Colonels Strachan and Kerr in 1650, estimated at two thousand pounds sterling, when a committee, consisting of the Earl of Eglinton, Lord Cochrane, the Sheriff-depute of Nithsdale, and some others, was appointed to meet at Cumnock, to inquire who had served in that army, and to proportion the same upon such of the guilty as were able to pay, which was accordingly done; and a number of gentlemen who were opposed to the measures of the present government, were assessed to make good the damage alleged to have been suffered by his lordship. This easy but arbitrary method of rewarding his supporters, and punishing or silencing his opponents, having excited no murmurs among the pusillanimous legislators, the plan was now followed out by the Commissioner, and a secret committee appointed to inquire who had been the most eminent compliers under the usurpers, in order that their estates might be taxed to raise a sum sufficient to compensate the king's friends for what they had suffered as malignants during the time of the late troubles. Their report included nearly nine hundred noblemen, gentlemen, and tenants; and the money to be produced from their fines amounted to about eighty-five thousand pounds sterling—an enormous sum at that time, to be arbitrarily and vexatiously levied by political adversaries without any check, there being neither accusation nor trial, nor any crime alleged, of which those who now assumed the name of the king's friends, had, in general, been far more guilty than they.

The act of fines, iniquitous and unjust in principle, was rendered still more so by the manner in which the list was made up. It included the names of many who were dead, absent from the country, or infants at the breast at the time! They were represented as favouring the usurpers. Others were inserted from private revenge; and several were named who were living upon the parish. But the chief weight of the imposition was intended to fall upon such as had been distinguished for eminent piety and a consistent Christian walk in their different stations, who were deemed singular in a time of general profession, when religion was the fashion, but who were destined to show the power of the gospel in a day of general apostasy, when religion was persecuted and a profession ridiculed.

Lauderdale, who saw that the produce of these fines was intended to strengthen the Commissioner's party, strenuously, though ineffectually, endeavoured to thwart the measure; and Middleton, justly supposing that such conduct would cool the king's affection for his secretary, despatched Tarbet to London to complete his ruin. The ostensible purpose of his mission was to submit the act of indemnity to the king, and to obtain his sanction to a clause for excepting twelve persons, to be named by the parliament, from the benefit of the act, as incapable of holding any place of public trust. Lauderdale knew that he was aimed at, and exerted his every art and influence to prevent the exception as unjust, but the Duke of York and the English Chancellor, who were jealous of his influence, supported the clause; and the king gave his consent to the proposed exception.

An incident which he could not have foreseen—so capricious is the fate of royal favourites—prevented his fall, and gave him the ascendancy his enemies were seeking to destroy. Middleton, who wished to procure for himself Argyle's estates, when disappointed by their gift to his son, harassed the young Earl by every means in his power, and procured that they should be burdened with an immense debt, which so irritated his lordship, that he expressed himself very freely in a confidential letter to Lord Duffus, saying, "he hoped that he would procure the friendship of Clarendon," and, in reference to the proceedings in parliament, used these words—"then the king will see their tricks." This letter being intercepted at the post-office, a capital charge of lying between the king and parliament was founded upon it, and a letter written to the king, requesting that Argyle might be sent down prisoner to stand trial. At Lauderdale's earnest entreaty, he was sent down not a prisoner, and with express instructions that no sentence should be executed till his majesty saw and approved it. Lorn, when brought to trial, convinced that any defence before such a tribunal would be vain, made none, but threw himself on the royal mercy, declaring the innocence of his intentions, and noticing gently the provocation he had received. He was pronounced guilty of death by parliament, but the king shortly after remitted his punishment.

During these discussions, Tarbet had been gradually undermining Lauderdale's influence, and, by his insinuating manners, had so far gained on Charles, that the fall of the favourite seemed no very distant or doubtful event, when the indiscretion of Middleton or his friends blighted all their flattering prospects. Afraid openly to attack the present ministers, an act was brought into parliament for incapacitating twelve persons by ballot, and lists were so formed that Lauderdale and Crawford were included in the number; and so anxious was Middleton to insure their dismissal, that, as soon as the act passed, he ratified it without ever communicating it to the king. Lauderdale, who had been apprised of the whole proceedings by the vigilant gratitude of Argyle before the official intelligence reached court, seized the opportunity of representing the affront offered to his majesty in such glaring colours, that, when the act arrived, he refused it his sanction, with a sarcastic remark, that the proceedings of his Scottish ministers were like those of madmen, or of men that were perpetually drunk.

Knowing the aversion of the Presbyterian ministers to the proposed changes, the privy council, before the bishops returned from court, endeavoured to overawe them and prevent opposition. They began with Mr. Robert Blair, an eminent and aged minister, that it was necessary to remove from his charge at St. Andrews to make room for Sharpe, to whom he was particularly obnoxious on account of his having the preceding year, by order of the presbytery, faithfully reproved him for his deceitful dealings at court, and his proudly grasping after the archbishopric. Although at an advanced age and in delicate health, the venerable saint was summoned before the council at Edinburgh, and examined as to his steadfastness in the principles he had professed through a long and honourable life: when it was found that he held fast his integrity, he was first sequestered from his parish, and confined successively to Musselburgh, Kirkaldy, and Couston; and then, in his last sickness, forced to send in his presentation to the council, to prevent his being dragged to Edinburgh while labouring under a mortal disease.

Upon the bishops' arrival, it was deemed necessary to make an example of some of the most steadfast and distinguished Presbyterians in the west, as that part of the country had ever been remarkable for attachment to their profession. The Chancellor was, in consequence, directed to require the attendance of such ministers as he thought fit; and by the suggestion of the prelates, wrote to Messrs. John Carstair, Glasgow; James Nasmyth, Hamilton; Matthew Mowat, and James Rowat, Kilmarnock; Alexander Blair, Galston; James Veitch, Mauchline; William Adair and William Fullerton, at St. Quivox, as if he had merely wished the assistance of their advice. Upon their arrival, however, in Edinburgh, they were charged with holding disloyal principles, and particularly with some expressions they had used in their sermons. From the charge of disloyalty, they easily vindicated themselves, and desired that the particular passages in the offensive sermons might be pointed out; but these the Chancellor was unable to produce, and they were dismissed from their first interview, with a hint that the easiest way to get rid of further trouble, would be to comply with the king's pleasure and acknowledge his bishops. When they would not consent to this, they were detained in town till the parliament met. No valid charges, however, being found against them, they were carried before the Lords of the Articles, and commanded as a test of their loyalty, to subscribe the oath of allegiance.

As they were the first Presbyterian ministers to whom this oath had been tendered, they required a few days to consider—for they deemed it an object of high importance that they should be fully satisfied in their own minds as to their line of duty—lest, on the one hand, they should wound their consciences by the sin of denying the supreme kingship of Christ in his Church, or incur the charge of disloyalty by refusing obedience to him whom they considered their rightful sovereign. They therefore set apart some time for solemn prayer to ask of the Lord light and direction. Then, after serious deliberation, they gave in their explication of the oath—which contained a brief but distinct statement of the principles upon which they and all the succeeding consistent Presbyterians refused to subscribe—what continued afterwards always to be pressed upon them under the false and insidious name of the oath of allegiance, while in fact and verity it was an explicit oath of supremacy. "They heartily and cheerfully acknowledged his majesty as the only lawful supreme governor under God within the kingdom, and that his sovereignty reached all persons and all causes, as well ecclesiastic as civil, having them both for its object; albeit it be in its own nature only civil, and extrinsic as to causes ecclesiastical; and, therefore, they utterly renounced all foreign jurisdictions, powers, and authorities, and promised with their utmost power to defend, assist, and maintain his majesty's jurisdiction aforesaid." For this explanation six of the ministers—Messrs. Adair and Fullarton having through favour been passed over—were committed close prisoners to the public jail, where they were confined for several weeks; and the paper being laid before parliament, it was put to the vote—"whether process them criminally, or banish them?"—when it was carried to banish them. Upon a representation to the commissioner by Mr. Robert Dougal, that the sentiments of the explication were sound and orthodox, and such as would be approved by the whole reformed churches abroad, the sentence of banishment was changed into deprivation. But their churches were declared vacant, and they were ordained to remove their families and leave the possession of their manses and glebes at Martinmas next, their stipends for the current year were seized, and themselves forbid to reside within the presbyteries where their churches lie, or within the cities of Glasgow or Edinburgh.

Conscientious ministers were not only entrapped by these tyrannical yet pitiful devices, but likewise harassed by the rigorous enforcement of the act for celebrating the king's birth-day as an "holyday." A proclamation was issued ordering its observance by the ministers, under pain of deprivation; and numbers were deprived of their year's stipend for non-observance.* But such had been the retrograde progress from the sobriety of their former profession, that within little more than one short year, the return of this holyday had become throughout the land the signal of universal riot and drunken uproar, particularly in these towns that had the misfortune to be burghs. On this occasion, Linlithgow signalized

* The same day had already been set apart as a day of thanksgiving for nis restoration!

itself, not only by its outrageous loyalty, but by its shameless and profane contempt for the bonds their fathers had held so sacred, and they themselves had solemnly sworn to observe. After the farce of church-going which occupied the forenoon, bonfires were kindled in every corner of the streets in the afternoon. The magistrates, accompanied by the Earl of Linlithgow, assembled in the open area before the council-house, around a table covered with comfits, the beautiful gothic fountain all the while spouting from its many mouths French and Spanish wines, when the curate opened the evening service by singing a psalm and repeating what was either a long blessing or a short prayer. The company then tasted the confections and scattered the rest among the crowd. An irreverent pageant closed this part of the performance.

At the cross, an arch was erected upon four pillars, on the one side of which stood the statue of an old hag, having the covenant in her hand, with this superscription—"A glorious Reformation;" on the other, the figure of a Whig, with "the remonstrance in his hand, inscribed 'no association with malignants;' while the devil, in the form of an angel of light, surmounted the keystone, having a label issuing from his mouth—'Stand to the cause.'" On the pillar, beneath the covenat, were painted rocks, (distaffs,) reels, and repenting-stools. The other, under the remonstrance, was adorned with brechams, (horse collars,) cogs, (wooden dishes,) and spoons. Within the arch, on the right, was drawn "a committee of estates," with this legend—"Act for delivering up the King." Opposite was placed "a commission of the kirk," and, in prominent characters, "Act of the West Kirk." In the middle of the arch hung a tablet with this litany—

From covenanters, with uplifted hands;
From remonstrators, with associate bands;
From such committees as governed this nation;
From kirk commissions and their protestation;
Good Lord, deliver us.

Upon the back of the arch, Rebellion was depicted under the guise of Religion, in a devout attitude, with eyes turned up to heaven, holding Rutherford's "Lex Rex" in her right hand, and in her left, "The Causes of God's Wrath." Around her were scattered acts of parliament, of committees of estates, General Assemblies, and commissions of the kirk, with all their protestations and declarations for the last twenty years; and above was written "Rebellion is as the sin of witchcraft." At drinking the king's health, a lighted torch set the fabric in a blaze; and a number of concealed fireworks exploding, the whole was instantly reduced to ashes, whence arose two angels, bearing a tablet with the following lines:—

Great Britain's monarch on this day was born,
And to his kingdom happily restored—
The queen's arrived—the mitre now is worn—
Let us rejoice this day is from the Lord.
Fly hence, all traitors, who did mar our peace—
Fly hence, schismatics, who our church did rent—
Fly covenanting, remonstrating race—
Let us rejoice that God this day hath sent.

The magistrates, with the Earl, then withdrew to the Palace, where a large bonfire was lighted in its noble court; and the king, queen, with other loyal toasts, were drunk; after which the festivities of the semi-sacred carnival were concluded by the magistrates and a number of the inhabitants walking in procession through the town and "saluting every person of account."

Parliament rose on the 9th of September, and the privy council entered upon the full exercise of their tyrannical powers, which had been acknowledged and vowed to by the obsequious legislature, who thus paved the way for their own lower degradation By an act of the 10th, the diocesan meetings which had been deferred on account of the lords, archbishops, and bishops being engaged in attending their parliamentary duty, were appointed to be held within all dioceses of the south upon the second Tuesday of October,. excepting that of Galloway, which, together with Aberdeen and some in the Highlands,

Islands, and the north, were to keep the third Tuesday of the same month, at which all parsons, vicars, (uncouth titles in Presbyterian ears,) and ministers were required to be present, under pain of being considered contemners of his majesty's authority. Every step taken to thrust Episcopacy forcibly upon an unwilling people, was accompanied by some new act of injustice and oppression to their respected ministers. It was requisite that those of the capital should set an example of obedience; and therefore, unless they also would apostatize and violate their oaths and their consciences by acknowledging the present Episcopacy, and concurring in their discipline, before the 1st of October, they were to be deprived of their office and banished the city—an arbitrary punishment, for which the oppressors had not even the authority of their own iniquitous parliament.

The western brethren being the most refractory, Middleton determined to proceed thither with a quorum of the council to enforce in person the obnoxious decrees. Accordingly, about the latter end of September, accompanied by Earls Morton, Linlithgow, Callender, and Lord Newburgh, with the king's lifeguard,* the clerk of the council, and a great retinue of attendants, he set out upon his progress, preceded by macers and military music. Burghs and nobles regaled the party as they passed, evincing their affection for the hierarchy by prodigal hospitality, while their guests, conformably to the manners of the English court, displayed their loyalty by pushing it to the most disgusting and loathsome excess. In districts remarkable for the strict soberness of their manners, scenes of revelry and profane riot

* The king's guard was chiefly composed of those who had, during the civil wars, been attached to the royal party, and who had expected mountains of gold at the Restoration; but, as the whole revenues of the kingdom could not have satisfied their claims and their cupidity, and "the merry monarch" and his higher satellites could spare nothing from their own licentious expenses, they, who had been unaccustomed to honest industry, had no other resource left but to enter the army.

were exhibited by the Commissioner and his Episcopalian propaganda that astonished the decent, while it afflicted the pious portion of the inhabitants. Their streets were disturbed by midnight inebriety; and men who had conscientious scruples about drinking healths at all, heard with sensations approaching to horror, that in some of these debauches the devil himself had had his health drunk! Ecclesiastical matters do not seem to have much disturbed the thoughtless "joyeosity" of this outrageous crew till they came to Glasgow, when Fairfoul entered a grievous complaint to Middleton, that, notwithstanding the acts of parliament and the time that had elapsed, not one of the younger ministers who had entered the church since 1649, had acknowledged him as archbishop—that he had incurred all the hatred attached to his office without obtaining any of the power; and, unless his Grace could devise some method for securing obedience, a bishop would be merely a cipher in the state. Middleton, a rough mercenary, requested the bishop's directions. The archbishop, like a true son of a temporal priesthood, knew of no better remedy than force. He proposed that all the ministers who had entered since the year 1649, and who would not submit to receive collation and admission from the bishop before the 1st of November, should be peremptorily banished from their houses, parishes, and the bounds of their presbyteries; and he assured the Commissioner that, if this were rigorously enforced, he did not believe there were ten in the whole of his diocese who would choose to lose their stipends.

A council was summoned, upon his Grace's representation, to meet in the front hall of Glasgow College; but when the worthies assembled, the whole, except one or perhaps two, were in a high state of excitation, or, as Wodrow phrases it, flustered with drink.* Sir James Lockhart of Lee, the only sober

* "There was never a man among them," says Kirkton, "but he was drunk at the time, except only Lee."—*Hist. Church of Scot.* p. 149.

member present, attempted to reason the matter. He affirmed that, so far from accomplishing its object, such an act would have a diametrically opposite effect—that the young ministers would suffer more than the loss of their stipends before they would acknowledge the bishops, and the inevitable consequences would be desolation in the country and discontent among the people. But reasoning was altogether out of the question. An act according to the archbishop's wish was agreed to without dispute, although it was not quite so easily drawn up—"whether," adds the honest historian, "for want of a fresh man to dictate or write, I know not." It was, however, sufficiently severe; not only did the non-conforming ministers forfeit their current year's stipend and incur the penalty of banishment, but their parishioners who should repair to their sermons were subjected to the same punishment as the frequenters of private conventicles. Besides this desolating act, the council passed two of a more private nature, incapacitating individuals—Mr. Donald Cargill, minister of the barony parish, Glasgow, (with whom we shall frequently meet in the course of the Annals,) and Mr. Thomas Wylie, minister of Kirkcudbright. This latter was a distinguished member of a distinguished presbytery, which had not one conformist in their bounds, and was among the very few that presented petitions against their illegal discontinuance nor desisted from fulfilling their ministerial functions till compelled by force.

He early foresaw the approaching blackness that was about to overspread the land, and, anticipating for himself and his people a share in the general calamity, he was earnestly desirous to dispense the sacrament of the Lord's Supper before the cloud came on. A general seriousness seems also to have pervaded the country side; for, on the Sabbath appointed for its administration, June 8, the number of communicants who offered was so great, that they could not all join in one day, and he intimated that on the Sabbath following, he would again dispense the ordinance, when those who had not participated might come forward. On Monday, after sermon, he received a letter informing him that the presbytery had been summoned to Edinburgh for holding their meetings after the council had prohibited them. But he determined to proceed in his work, leaving the consequences to Providence, and he was favoured to conclude the solemnity without further interruption. On the Monday, however, certain news arriving that a party was to be in the town that night to apprehend him, he withdrew, and next day they searched his house narrowly for him; but the bird for this time had escaped the snare of the fowler. He continued under hiding, till, through the exertions of his wife and the friendship of Lord Kenmure, he was allowed to return to his parish on the 10th of September. Now, without any new accusation, he was included in the same sentence with Donald Cargill, and ordered to be banished beyond the Tay.

England, on the 24th of August preceding, had exhibited the sublime and heart-stirring spectacle of upwards of two thousand of the ablest, most upright, and most devout ministers in the land, surrendering without hesitation their livings, rather than violate their consciences by conforming to the restored national church. Yet, with this instance before his eyes, of obedience to God in preference to subjection to men, the Commissioner could not understand how persons with large families would voluntarily throw themselves upon the world, and leave their homes without any certain dwelling-place, rather than submit to a change which the prelates and he had found so easy; but they feared to sin; and now that a century has rolled by, and they and their oppressors rest in the grave together, who would not say that they did not act the wisest part, who preferred a good conscience, and trusted to the faithfulness of Him who has promised never to leave, never, never, to forsake his servants, rather than to place their confi dence in princes, and their trust in the sons of men? Of what value are the mitres now, for which the prelates in Scotland destroyed their usefulness, and which sat so uneasily for a few troubled years upon their heads? At the time, the case was dreadfully trying. When a man's temporal interest comes in competition with his profession, then will appear the strength of his religious principle. Nearly four hundred ministers of the church of Scotland stood this severest of all tests. Turned from their houses in the midst of winter, and deprived of their stipends, they went out not knowing whither they went. Never did Scotland witness such a Sabbath as that on which they took leave of their parishioners; and the mourning and lamentation that filled the south and west, was only equalled by the hatred and detestation excited against those who were the authors of so much sorrow, who, for their own ambitious and worldly schemes, ruptured ties so sacred and so dear as those that had subsisted between the Presbyterian ministers and their affectionate congregations.

It was questioned at the time, and even since, whether Presbyterian ministers did not act improperly in all at once throwing up their charges? That they acted scripturally, is plain. They continued to exercise their calling as long as they could. When illegally forbid, they continued to preach, acting upon the apostolic precept of obeying God rather than man; but when a tyrannical power, under the form of parliamentary or council enactments, was ready to use force in ejecting them, then, as ministers of the gospel, they had no other resource left than to shake off the dust of their feet and go to another city—they bore testimony against their persecutors and retired. Following the advice of James v. 10, they took the prophets, who had spoken in the name of the Lord, for an example of suffering and of patience.

That they acted, even in political view, in the very best manner that their circumstances admitted, is I think, demonstrable. They showed to the people that it was not the fleece but the flock that had been the object of their care, and imprinted upon their minds a sense of the worth of the truth for which they were contending, beyond what they could have done in any other manner; and that truth was one written as with a sunbeam throughout the whole New Testament—that Christ is the king and the head of his church, and that whatever form of church government does not acknowledge this, is essentially antichristian. It is not less evident, that the prelatists, as well as the papists, gave that dignity and power to another; and the solemn and universal testimony which so many godly men lifted up at once against acknowledging such unholy usurpation, has not lost its effect even unto this day—an effect it never could have had, had the ministers resisted and allowed themselves to have been thrust out one by one.

From Glasgow, Middleton and his Episcopalian reformadoes pursued their route, confirming their churches in the south, through Galloway as far as Wigton; and, upon the last day of October, returned to Holyroodhouse.

On his arrival, the Commissioner was assailed by what was to him unexpected intelligence, that the whole south and west were thrown into confusion; and, enraged to find that both the archbishop and himself had so entirely miscalculated, he expressed his astonishment at the unaccountable conduct of the "madmen" with a volley of oaths and execrations the now fashionable dialect of the court—and, on the first meeting of council, caused letters to be sent off express to his lordship and the primate, requesting their presence and advice. Meanwhile, they proceeded in the usual course of endeavouring to intimidate the humbler refractory by their rigour to the more eminent. Mr. Hugh M'Kail, chaplain to Sir James Stewart of Kirkfield, a youth of high promise, was forced into voluntary exile because he had defended in a sermon what he considered the scriptural mode of church government. Mr. John Brown of Wamphrey, well known by his historical, controversial, and practical writings, not less respected for his piety than for his learning, having reproved some ministers for attending the Archbishop of Glasgow's diocesan

Synod, styling them perjured, was banished to Holland—at that time the asylum of the persecuted; there he remained for many years, and, by his seasonable publications, strengthened the hands of the sufferers in his native land, and proved a thorn in the side of their tyrannical government.

Mr. John Livingston, more honoured of God as the means of converting sinners to Christ than almost any minister of the Church of Scotland since the Reformation, then minister at Ancrum, because he would not promise to observe the 29th of May as an holyday, nor take the oath of allegiance without any explanation, was subjected to a like punishment, as were Messrs. Robert Traill of Edinburgh, Neave of Newmills, and Gardner of Saddle. Mr. Livingston, in the true spirit of a Christian patriot, after sentence was pronounced, thus replied—" Well! although it be not permitted me to breathe my native air, yet into whatsoever part of the world I may go, I shall not cease to pray for a blessing to these lands, to his majesty, the government, and the inferior magistrates thereof; but especially for the land of my nativity!" In the same excellent spirit, having been denied the privilege of paying a farewell visit to his wife, children, and people, he addressed a pastoral letter to the flock of Jesus Christ in Ancrum. Their sins and his own, he told them, had drawn down this severe stroke; and, while it was their part to search out and mourn for them, "it is not needful," he adds, "to look much to instruments. I have from my heart forgiven them all, and would wish you to do the like, and pray for them that it be not laid to their charge. For my part, I bless his name, I have great peace in the matter of my sufferings. I need not repeat, you know my testimony of the things in controversy:—Jesus Christ is a king, and only hath power to appoint the officers and government of his house. It is a fearful thing to violate the oath of God, and fall into the hands of the living God. It could not well be expected," he proceeds to remark, and the remark is applicable in all similar cases when religion has been in repute among a people—"there having been so fair and so general a profession throughout the land, but that the Lord would put men to it; and it is like it shall come to every man's door, that, when every one according to their inclination, may have acted their part—and He seems to stand by—He may come at last and act his part, and vindicate his glory and truth. I have often showed you that it is the greatest difficulty under heaven to believe that there is a God and a life after this; and have often told you that, for my part, I could never make it a chief part of my work to insist upon the particular debates of the time, as being assured that if a man drink in the knowledge and the main foundations of the Christian religion, and have the work of God's Spirit in his heart to make him walk with God, and make conscience of his ways, such an one shall not readily mistake Christ's quarrel, to join either with a profane atheist party or a fanatic party. There may be diversity of judgment, and sometimes sharp debates among them that are going to heaven; but, certainly, a spirit guides the seed of the woman, and another spirit the seed of the serpent."

Several of lesser note were treated with not much less harshness, been ordered to confinement in distant places of the country, without the means of subsistence, and debarred from preaching in the rugged and barren districts to which they were banished.

Such, however, was the outcry the wide desolation of the church had occasioned, that the council were convinced they had acted with unwise precipitation, and endeavoured in some measure to retrace their steps. The author of the mischief, Fairfoul, though repeatedly called upon, does not appear to have assisted their deliberations, which were protracted, till the month of December, when a proclamation was issued, extending the time allowed ministers for procuring presentations and collocation to the 1st of February, but ordering those who neglected to do so to remove from their parishes and presbyteries; and such of them as belonged to the dioceses of St. Andrews and Edinburgh, to go into banishment beyond the Tay. The older ministers, who had not been touched by the Glasgow act, and had hitherto remained exercising their parochial duties among their people, because they had not attended the diocesan meetings, were confined to their parishes. The people who left the hirelings intruded upon them, travelling sometimes twenty miles to hear the gospel, were now ordered to attend their parish churches, under a penalty of twenty shillings for every day's absence; and because in those places where the ministers, in view of separation from their flocks, had celebrated the sacrament of the Lord's Supper to multitudes assembled from the surrounding districts—and much of the divine presence had appeared among them—these were stigmatized as unlicentiate confluences of the people; and the discourses delivered under such circumstances, with more than ordinary fervour, and accompanied with more than ordinary power, abused as the extravagant sermons of some ministers of unquiet and factious spirits—special engines to debauch people from their duty, and lead them to disobedience, schism and rebellion; therefore every incumbent was prohibited from employing more than one or two of his neighbours at a communion without a license from the bishop, or admitting the people of any other parish to participate of the sacrament with out a certificate from his curate.

This was the last of Middleton's acts in Scotland. His rival, Lauderdale, had so well employed the access he had to the king to undermine his influence, that he was called to court to answer charges of having encroached upon the royal prerogative by the balloting act, and defrauded the royal treasury by appropriating the fines. While the affair was under discussion, Lauderdale procured an order to delay levying the fines due the first term and dismiss the collector. Middleton, who saw that this was a deadly blow at his interest in Scotland, countermand ed the royal letter upon alleged verbal authority which Charles either never gave, or found it con venient to disown; and this completed his ruin. His rashness and inconsideration were too palpable to be denied; but, by the interest of his friends, Clarendon and the Bishop of London, his fall was softened, and he was sent into a kind of honourable banishment as governor of Tangiers. There he continued to indulge his habits of intemperance, and, falling down a stair in a fit of intoxication, broke his right arm so severely, that the bone protruded through the flesh, and, penetrating his side, a mortification ensued, which terminated his life.

Middleton, who never appears to have had any serious religion, was the friend of Lord Clarendon—a statesman bigoted to Episcopacy, rather on account of its political than its spiritual advantages—and employed by him for rearing in Scotland, upon the ruins of Presbytery, which he detested, an establishment more in accordance with those high notions of the prerogative which, notwithstanding the melancholy example of the first Charles, were adopted and cherished by the court of his son. Well calculated for carrying through the most despotic measures by force, he must be acquitted of the mean duplicity of Charles's letter to the ministers of Edinburgh, the obloquy of which rests upon the crafty politics of Sharpe. When first shown it, he considered it as opposed to Episcopacy, and expressed his regret; but when told that, upon rescinding all the laws in favour of Presbytery, then Episcopacy remained the church government settled by law, he observed, "that might be done; but for his part he was not fond of making his majesty's first appearance in Scotland to be in the character of a cheat." Once, however, fairly embarked, he never hesitated, and concurred with the bishops in their every project, however treacherous or oppressive. He first overturned the Presbyterian church government, which had been settled under as solemn sanctions, and as strong legal guarantees, as can ever possibly be devised to secure any religious establishment, and then sent to the scaffold, from motives of avarice and revenge, the noblest ornaments of that religion, whose only crime was adhering to a profession he himself had, with uplifted hand, sworn to support.

In council, he unwarrantably extended the tyrannical acts of his servile parliament, and wantonly laid waste hundreds of peaceable and flourishing congregations. With a cunning worthy the priesthood of Rome, he invited numbers of unsuspecting ministers from distant parts of the country to Edinburgh, as if to consult them on the affairs of the church, then ensnared them by insidious questions, and punished their unsuspecting simplicity with deprivation, imprisonment, and exile. Without any shadow of law, and without the form of a trial, he turned ministers from their congregations—prohibited them from preaching, praying, or expounding the Scriptures, and sent them to the most distant corners of the land, or forced them to seek an asylum in foreign countries—then intruded on the desolated parishes worthless and incapable hirelings—and concluded his career by commanding the people to attend upon their ministrations under a severe and oppressive penalty. His own expatriation to the barren coast of Africa was looked upon by the sufferers as a righteous retribution, and his melancholy end as an evident mark of divine displeasure; nor could the coincidence between his own rash imprecation and the manner of his death fail to strike the most careless. Like many other political hypocrites, with a zeal as furious as false, he had sworn and subscribed the covenants when it was the fashion of the time to do so; and, on retiring from the place where he had taken these vows upon him, he said to some of those who were with him, "that that was the pleasantest day he had ever seen; and if ever he should do any thing against that blessed work, he had been engaging in," holding up his right arm, "he wished that it might be his death!" The enormous fines he imposed, he never was empowered to exact; and, in return for impoverishing his country, he died an exile and a beggar.

Lauderdale having succeeded in removing his formidable antagonist, from thenceforth for a number of years almost solely directed Scottish affairs. The Presbyterians, who believed that he was secretly attached to their cause, anticipated better days under his protection; but ambition was his master-passion, and to it he was prepared to sacrifice all his early attachments and principles. While religion appeared the only road to power in the state, he had been foremost in the ranks of the covenanters; and, by the warmth of his professions, and the consistency of his conduct, had gained the confidence of those who were sincerely devoted to the cause; but when the path of preferment on Charles's restoration struck off in an opposite direction, he deserted to the prelates, and evinced the sincerity of his change by at once forsaking his sobriety of manners, and apostatizing from his form of religion; and, as he understood well the principles he betrayed, and at one time certainly had strong convictions of their truth, his opposition was proportionably inveterate, and he became outrageously furious at whatever tended to remind him of his former "fanaticism."

BOOK IV.

DECEMBER, A. D 1662—1664.

State of the West and South—Bishops—Curates—Their reception—Tumult at Irongray—Commission sent to Kirkcudbright and Dumfries—Field-preaching—Rothes and Lauderdale arrive in Scotland—Parliament—Warriston's arrest and execution—Principal Wood of St. Andrews and other ministers silenced and scattered—Troops ordered to enforce the Acts of Parliament—Their outrages—Sir James Turner—High Commission Court—Its atrocities—Privy Council—Its exactions—Prohibits private prayer-meetings or contributing money for the relief of the sufferers—William Guthrie of Fenwick laid aside—Donaldson of Dalgetty's case—Death of Glencairn—Political changes.

WHILE these struggles were going forward at court, the affairs of Scotland were in a state of the most woful confusion. Almost the whole parishes in the west and south had been deprived of their ministers; and as their own churches remained vacant, the people in crowds flocked to those where the few old Presbyterian ministers were yet allowed to officiate. These assemblies having been denounced by the council's proclamation, attracted the attention of the soldiers; and numerous parties patrolled the country to disturb the meetings and levy the fines to which offenders were liable.

When the vacant charges came to be filled, (1663,) new sources of disturbance arose. No preparation had been made for such an exigence as had now arisen. The regular candidates for the ministry were too few; and of these but a small proportion were willing to pursue their studies under the direction of the bishops, or accept of Episcopal ordination. The north was therefore ransacked, and a great number of ignorant, uneducated young men, not more deficient in talents and acquirements than in decent common moral conduct,* were hastily brought forward to supply the places of the ejected ministers, who in general were both pious, learned, and of respectable abilities; many of them eminently so, and all laborious in the discharge of their duties, exemplary in their lives, and dear to their people. These presentees, who were contemptuously styled by the people "bishops' curates," when intruded upon them without any regard to their wishes or choice, were received in many places with the most determined opposition; in some, they were compelled to retire; and, in others, obliged to enter by the windows, the doors being built up; and thus literally to display the scriptural characteristic of spiritual thieves and robbers. The Presbyterian ministers had uniformly classed prelacy and popery together; and, at the settlement of the new clergy, the prelates justified the charge by employing the military to enforce their ecclesiastical appointments, and ordaining their parsons at the point of the sword. The patrons, in most cases, had allowed their rights to devolve upon the bishops; and thus the whole undivided obloquy rested on their consecrated heads, which was not lessened when some of the careless or profane heritors, to ingratiate themselves with the rulers, feasted the clergy at their settlements, and, aping the loyalty of their superiors, conducted their entertainments with an equally jovial disregard of decency and temperance.

But there was also an opposition of a more solemn and impressive nature offered by the serious part of the people in different parishes, who received the

* Bishop Burnet, himself an Episcopalian, thus characterizes them:—"They were the worst preachers I ever heard. They were ignorant to a reproach; and many of them were openly vicious. They were a disgrace to their order and the sacred function, and were indeed the dregs and refuse of the northern parts. Those of them who were above contempt or scandal, were men of such violent tempers, that they were as much hated as the others were despised."

intruders when they came among them with tears, and entreated them earnestly to be gone, nor ruin the poor congregations and their own souls. Neither of these methods, however, had any effect; the thoughtless wretches entered upon that awful charge —the care of souls—as if they had been taking forcible possession of an heritable estate to which they had a legal right.*

As the south had been favoured with remarkably faithful pastors, the strongest resistance appeared there. Irongray was the first settlement where open "tumultuating" took place. The curate not being able to obtain peaceable admission, returned with a party of soldiers to force an entrance, when a band of women, led on by a Margaret Smith, attacked the guard with stones, and triumphantly beat them off the field. Margaret, the fair heroine, was brought to Edinburgh, and sentenced to slavery in Barbadoes; but she "told her tale so innocently," that the managers, not yet steeled to compassion, permitted her to return home. The parish was not, however, allowed to escape with impunity. Upon hearing of this disturbance, and a similar one at Kirkcudbright, the privy council, as if the country had been in an actual state of rebellion, appointed the Earls of Linlithgow, Galloway, and Annandale, with Lord Drumlanrig and Sir John Wauchope of Niddry, to proceed on a commission of inquiry to that district, attended by a hundred horse and two hundred foot of the king's guard, with power to suppress all meetings or insurrections of the people, if any should happen.

At Kirkcudbright, the commission held several diets, and examined a number of witnesses. Of about thirty-two women whom they apprehended,

* The following appears to have been the clerical mode of infeftment:—At the admission of Mr. John Ramsay to the parish of Sconie, in Fife, "Mr. Jossia Meldrum, minister of Kingorne, after sermon ended, he tooke his promise to be faithfull in his charge of that flock: and ther was delivered to him the bibell, the keys of the church doore, and the bell-tou."—*Lamont's Diary*, p. 192.

five were sent to Edinburgh; and Bessie Laurie, with thirteen others, was bound over to keep the peace. Lord Kirkcudbright—who had declared if the minister came there he should come over his body, and that he would lose his fortune before he should be preacher there; but at the same time admitted, that, if the minister had come in by his presentation, he could have raised as many men as would have prevented a tumult—was transmitted under a guard to Edinburgh. James Carson of Fenwick, the late provost, although not in power, and John Ewart, who had refused to accept the office, because they had declined interfering upon the occasion, were also sent prisoners to the capital, where they were kept in confinement several months;* besides, in addition, being severely fined. The five women were sentenced to stand at the cross of Kirkcudbright two hours on two market days, with labels on their foreheads denoting their crimes, and thereafter to find bail to keep the peace. New magistrates were appointed for the burgh, who, on accepting the nomination, signed a bond in their own name and that of the haill inhabitants of the place, binding and obliging them, and ilk one of them, during their public trust, and all the inhabitants, to behave themselves loyally, and in all things conform to his majesty's laws, made and to be made, both in civil and ecclesiastical affairs! and besides, to protect the Lord Bishop of Galloway, the minister of the burgh, and any other ministers that were or should be established by authority.

* The following singular order was issued by the council on this occasion; and it deserves to be noted, that it was issued the very first meeting after the archbishops had taken their seats as members:—"June 23d. The lords of council being informed that ministers and other persons visit the prisoners for the riot at Kirkcudbright, now in the tolbooth of Edinburgh, and not only exhort but pray for the said persons to persist in their wicked practices, affirming that they are suffering for righteousness' sake, and assure them that God will give them an outgate—recommend it to the keeper to notice who visits them, and what their discourse and carriage is when with them."—*Wodrow*, vol. i. p. 188.

At Dumfries, the commission also examined witnesses, but the mighty insurrection dwindled into a "great convocation and tumult of women;" yet the whole party, horse and foot, were quartered upon the parish, and a bonus levied for remunerating the clerks. The whole heritors were likewise compelled to sign a bond of passive obedience to laws known and unknown, in terms similar to that of the magistrates of Kirkcudbright.*

Instead of reconciling the people, or terrifying them back to the churches, these severities exasperated them; nor was it to be expected that they would willingly attend the ministrations of men, whose preaching they despised, and who were thus ushered in. Outrageous expressions of dislike were not, however, approved of by the godly and judicious Presbyterians; they mourned in private over the desolation of the church, and sought, by attending the family exercises of the younger ministers who were "outted,"† but sojourned among them, to receive that instruction, and enjoy that social worship, of which they were so tyrannically deprived! Sometimes the numbers who assembled to enjoy this privilege were so great, that a house could not contain them, and the minister was constrained to officiate without doors; till at length they increased so much that they were under the necessity of betaking themselves to the open fields; and, like him whose servants they were, beneath the wide canopy of heaven, preached the gospel of the kingdom to multitudes upon the mountain's side. Mr. John Welsh and Mr. Gabriel Semple began the practice of field-preaching, which quickly increased, and, to the great alarm of the bishops, had pervaded almost every

* The council ordered to be advanced for this expedition, the sum of five hundred pounds to the soldiers as part of their pay, one hundred and twenty pounds to the Earl of Linlithgow, and fifty pounds to the Laird of Niddry for their expenses; so that probably these petty squabbles would cost the two parishes not much under one thousand pounds sterling, equivalent to nearly five in later times.

† "Outted," turned out of their churches.

quarter of the country, when the political arrangements being completed, Rothes arrived as commissioner to open the parliament.

Lauderdale accompanied the Earl to Scotland, professedly to inquire into the origin of that conspiracy against his majesty's royal prerogative—the balloting act;—in reality to secure his own ascendancy in Scotland, and, by pushing to the utmost the advantage he had gained over the Middleton faction, to prevent any attempt being made against him from that quarter for the future. The Chancellor made some feeble show of opposition, but the universal spirit of submission to the will of the crown which pervaded the higher classes, and their selfish eagerness to obtain a share in the spoils of their unhappy country, not only blighted every appearance of patriotism, but precluded every plan of association among the aristocracy themselves for maintaining their own rank and station independent of the minions of the court. The Presbyterians who rejoiced in Middleton's fall, soon found that they had gained very little by the change. At the first diet of council, (June 15, 1663,) the two archbishops were admitted, with Mr. Charles Maitland, Lord Hatton, Lauderdale's brother; but Crawford having refused the declaration, was deprived of the treasurership, and Rothes, the commissioner, that same day was appointed to succeed him in the office.

On the 18th, parliament met, and, by an alteration in the method of appointing the Lords of the Articles —allowing the spiritual lords first to name eight temporal lords, then the temporal lords to choose eight spiritual; and these sixteen, or such of them as were present, to elect the representatives of the barons and burghs—they virtually gave up the privilege of nominating this important committee, to the servants of the crown, and surrendered the last check they had upon the prerogative. The tyranny of the council was next legalized, and a practice introduced which continued till the Revolution:—the most oppressive acts of the former sessions, together with the acts of council, enlarging and explaining their vindictive clauses, were approved of by a retrospective declaratory enactment; and every mode of persecution which had been adopted upon trial since last session, was incorporated into the statute law of the kingdom. Thus an act against separation and disobedience of ecclesiastical authority—introduced early in the session—besides recapitulating all the penalties to which the non-conforming ministers had been previously subjected, ordained those who still dared to preach in contempt of law, or did not attend the diocesan meetings, to be punished as seditious persons, and despisers of the royal authority. Absence from church on Sunday—a finable offence—was now denounced as sedition; and whoever wilfully should withdraw from the ministrations of the parish priest, however incapable he might be, were, if noblemen, gentlemen, or heritors, to lose the fourth part of their yearly income—if yeomen, tenants, or farmers, such proportion of their movables, after payment of their rents, as the council should think fit, not exceeding a fourth part—but if a burgess, his freedom, along with the fourth of his movables, and, in addition, the council was authorized to inflict such corporeal punishment as they should see proper. The declaration was ordered by another act to be taken by all who exercised any public trust; and persons chosen to be counsellors or magistrates of burghs, if they declined to subscribe, were declared for ever incapable of holding any office, or exercising any occupation, trade, or merchandise. To complete the organization of the hierarchy, an act was passed for the establishment and constitution of a National Synod, bearing the same resemblance to the estates of Scotland that the Houses of Convocation did to the English parliament: both emanated from his majesty's supremacy, and consisted of the bishops and their satellites, only the Scottish assembly was to meet in one place, and was even more servilely abject than their elder Episcopalian sister, and could not be constituted without the presence of the king or his commissioner. The balloting act was, after long investigation, rescinded with every mark of detestation, the parliament declaring they had never consented to any such thing! and, that it might not appear in judgment against them, was ordered to be erased from their minutes. Sensible that the measures now pursued in Scotland must necessarily lead to insurrection, and that a military force would be requisite to carry them into effect, Lauderdale procured from this servile crew the offer of an army of twenty thousand foot and two thousand horse, to be raised for his majesty's service when required, under the ridiculous pretence of preserving Christendom against the Turks!! This number never was demanded; and it was alleged that the secretary had carried the measure to ingratiate himself with the king, and to show him what assistance he might derive from Scotland in any attempt to destroy the liberties of England. From the beginning, the Scots had been harassed by the king's guard, but from this date the troopers were more unsparingly employed to enforce clerical obedience, while the act hung *in terrorem* over the heads of the dissatisfied Presbyterians, and afterwards became the foundation of the militia.

Middleton's first session set in blood; Rothes' closed under as deep a stain. Sir Archibald Johnston, Lord Warriston, had been forfeited and condemned by parliament when Argyle and Guthrie were arraigned, but escaping to the Continent, had remained concealed in Holland and Germany, chiefly at Hamburgh, till most unadvisedly, in the latter end of 1662, he ventured to France. Notice of this having been carried to London, the king, who bore him a personal hatred for his free admonitions when in Scotland,*

* "The real cause of his (Warriston's) death, was not his activity in public business, but our king's personal hatred, because when the king was in Scotland he thought it his duty to admonish him because of his very wicked, debauched life, not only in whoredom and adultery, but he violently forced a young gentle-woman of quality. This the king could never forgive, and told the Earle of Bristol so much when he was speaking for Warriston."—*Kirkton's Hist. of the Church of Scot.* p. 173.

Arrest of Lord Warriston.

sent over secretly a confidential spy, known by the name of "Crooked Murray," to trace him out and bring him to Britain. By watching Lady Warriston, Murray soon discovered her lord's retreat at Rouen in Normandy, and had him seized while engaged in the act of secret prayer. He then applied to the magistrates, and, showing them the king's commission, desired that they would allow him to carry his victim a prisoner to England. The magistrates, uncertain how to act, committed Warriston to close custody, and sent to the French king for instructions. When the question was debated in council, the greater part were for respecting the rights of hospitality, and not giving up his lordship till some better reasons were shown than had yet been given; but Louis, who was extremely desirous to oblige Charles, and sympathized cordially in his antipathies against the Protestant religion and liberty, ordered him to be delivered to the messenger, who carried him to London and lodged him in the Tower in the month of January, 1663. While the parliament was sitting in June, he was sent to Scotland with a letter from the king, ordering him "to be proceeded against according to law and justice," and landed at Leith on the 8th, whence, next day, he was brought bareheaded to the tolbooth of Edinburgh. Neither his wife, children, nor any other friend, were permitted to see him, except in presence of the keeper or guard, and that only for an hour, or at furthest two at a time, betwixt eight o'clock in the morning and eight at night. Here he was detained till July 8th, when, no more trial being deemed necessary, he was brought before parliament to receive judgment. His appearance on this occasion was humiliating to the pride of human genius, debilitated through excessive bloodletting and the deleterious drugs that had been administered to him by his physicians,* the faculties of

* "Through excessive blood-letting and other detestable means used by his wicked physician, Doctor Bates, who they say was hired either to poison or distract him, and partly through melancholy, he had in a manner wholly lost his memory." *Kirkton's Hist.* p. 170.

his soul partook of the imbecility of his body, and, on the spot where his eloquence had in former days commanded breathless attention, he could scarcely now utter one coherent sentence. The prelates basely derided his mental aberrations, but many of the other members compassionated the intellectual ruin of one who had shone among the foremost in the brightest days of Scotland's parliamentary annals. When the question was put, whether the time of his execution should be then fixed or delayed, a majority seemed inclined to spare his life, which Lauderdale observing, rose, and, contrary to all usage or propriety, in a furious speech, insisted upon the sentence being carried into immediate effect; the submissive legislators acquiesced, and he was doomed to be hanged at the cross of Edinburgh on the 22d of the same month, and his head fixed upon the Nether Bow Port, beside Mr. Guthrie's.

Mr. James Kirkton, author of the "History of the Church of Scotland," who visited him, says—"I spake with him in prison, and though he was sometimes under great heaviness, yet he told me he could never doubt his own salvation, he had so often seen God's face in the house of prayer." As he approached his end, he grew more composed; and, on the night previous to his execution, having been favoured with a few hours' profound and refreshing sleep, he awoke in the full possession of his vigorous powers, his memory returned, and he experienced in an extraordinary degree the strong consolations of the gospel, expressing his assurance of being clothed with a white robe, and having a new song of praise put into his lips, even salvation to our God, which sitteth upon the throne, and to the Lamb!

Before noon, he dined with great cheerfulness,

Mr. C. K. Sharpe, the editor, thinks his mental imbecility was occasioned in some measure by fear, and quotes a passage from one of Lord Middleton's letters to Primrose. "He pretends to have lost his memory," &c. "He is the most timorous person ever I did see in my life," &c. *Note.* But it was not to be expected that Middleton would allude in the most distant manner to any thing that could be supposed to countenance in the least the then general belief.

hoping to sup in heaven, and drink of the blood of the vine fresh and new in his Father's kingdom. After spending some time in secret prayer, he left the prison about two o'clock, attended by his friends in mourning, full of holy confidence and courage, but perfectly composed and serene. As he proceeded to the cross, where a high gibbet was erected, he repeatedly requested the prayers of the people; and there being some disturbance on the street when he ascended the scaffold, he said with great composure—"I entreat you, quiet yourselves a little, till this dying man deliver his last words among you," and requested them not to be offended that he used a paper to refresh his memory, being so much wasted by long sickness and the malice of physicians. He then read audibly, first from the one side and then from the other, a short speech that he had hurriedly written—what he had composed at length and intended for his testimony having been taken from him. It commenced with a general confession of his sins and shortcomings in prosecuting the best pieces of work and service to the Lord and to his generation, and that through temptation he had been carried to so great a length, in compliance with the late usurpers, after having so seriously and frequently made professions of aversion to their way; "for all which," he added, "as I seek God's mercy in Christ Jesus, so I desire that the Lord's people may, from my example, be the more stirred up to watch and pray that they enter not into temptation."

He then bare record to the glory of God's free grace and of his reconciled mercy through Christ Jesus—left "an honest testimony to the whole covenanted work of reformation"—and expressed his lively expectation of God's gracious and wonderful renewing and reviving all his former great interests in these nations, particularly Scotland—yea, dear Scotland! He recommended his poor afflicted wife and children to the choicest blessings of God and the prayers and favours of his servants—prayed for repentance and forgiveness to his enemies—for the king, and blessings upon him and his posterity, that they might be surrounded with good and faithful counsellors, and follow holy and wise counsels to the glory of God and the welfare of the people. He concluded by committing himself, soul and body, his relations, friends, the sympathizing and suffering witnesses of the Lord, to his choice mercies and service in earth and heaven, in time and through eternity:—"All which suits, with all others which he hath at any time by his Spirit moved and assisted me to make, and put up according to his will, I leave before the throne, and upon the Father's merciful bowels, the Son's mediating merits, and the Holy Spirit's compassionating groans, for now and for ever!"

After he had finished reading, he prayed with the greatest fervour and humility, thus beginning his supplication—"Abba! Abba! Father, Father, accept this thy poor sinful servant, coming unto thee through the merits of Jesus Christ." Then he took leave of his friends, and again, at the foot of the ladder, prayed in a perfect rapture, being now near the end of that sweet work he had been so much employed about, and felt so much sweetness in through life. No ministers were allowed to be with him, but his God abundantly supplied his every want. On account of his weakness, he required help to ascend the ladder. Having reached the top, he cried with a loud voice—"I beseech you all who are the people of God not to scorn at suffering for the interest of Christ, or stumble at any thing of this kind falling out in these days. Be encouraged to suffer for him, for I assure you, in the name of the Lord, he will bear your charges!" This he repeated again while the rope was putting about his neck, forcibly adding—"The Lord hath graciously comforted me." Then asking the executioner if he was ready to do his office, and being answered that he was, he gave the signal, and was turned off, crying—"Pray! pray! praise! praise!" His death was almost without a struggle.

Sir Archibald Johnston, Lord Warriston, was an early, zealous, and distinguished Covenanter, and bore a conspicuous part in all the remarkable transactions of the times, from 1638 till the Restoration. The only blemish which his enemies could affix to his character was, what he himself lamented, his accepting office under the usurpers, after having previously so violently opposed this in others, when yet every prospect of restoring the Stuart family seemed hopeless, and when numbers of his countrymen and of his judges themselves had submitted to a tolerant commonwealth, that did not burden the conscience with unnecessary oaths, or require any compliances which might not, in the circumstances of the case, have been considered venial, if not justifiable. His talents for business were of the first order. His eloquence was ready, and his judgment clear. He was prompt and intrepid in action, and adhered steadily to his Presbyterian principles, notwithstanding his officiating under a liberal government of a different persuasion—conduct we now allow to be not incompatible with integrity. His piety was ardent, and, amid a life of incessant activity, he managed to spare a larger portion of time for private devotion than many of more sequestered habits. He habitually lived near to God, and died in the full assurance of hope.

Parliament having sat upwards of three months, rose on the 9th of October. Even during its sitting, the council never intermitted their oppressive acts; and, so far was this branch of the legislature from interfering to check their immoderate abuse of power, that they had shown themselves upon every occasion the willing instruments of their oppression, ready when called upon to legitimate without a murmur their foulest usurpations. On the other hand, the executive acted as the humble tools of the prelates, ready to support their most arrogant assumptions or gratify their cowardly and cruel revenge. St. Andrews, the primate's seat, first required to be thoroughly cleansed; and all who would not countenance the archbishop in his treachery, were of necessity removed as unwelcome remembrancers of his former profession. Mr. James Wood, principal of the Old College, pious, learned, and assiduous in his duty, who had been an intimate friend and companion of Sharpe's, and one of the many excellent men who had been his dupes, was, on the 23d of July, summoned before the council and required to show by what authority he came to be principal. Without being suffered to offer any remarks, when he acknowledged "that he was called by the Faculty of the College at the recommendation of the usurpers," the place was declared vacant, and he was commanded to confine himself within the city of Edinburgh till further orders.

Yet such was the estimation in which he was held, that his enemy, though by falsehood, endeavoured to shelter his apostasy under the shadow of his name. Not long after this, when Mr. Wood was on his deathbed, March 1664, and greatly weakened by disease, Sharpe called once or twice upon him; and he having said, as a dying man in the immediate view of eternity, that he was taken up about greater business than forms of church government, and that he was far more concerned about his personal interest in Christ than about any external ordinance, Sharpe took occasion to spread a report that he had said Presbyterian government was a matter of no consequence, and no man should trouble himself about it, which coming to the sufferer's ears, he emitted a declaration before witnesses of his unshaken attachment to Presbytery as an ordinance of God, and so precious that a true Christian is obliged to lay down his life for the profession thereof, if the Lord should see meet to put him to his trial.

Along with Mr. Wood, a great number of ministers from every quarter of the country, were removed from their charges, some confined to Edinburgh, others banished beyond the river Ness—all forbid to preach the gospel under the threatening of severer penalties. Heavy were the complaints of the clergy, the ministers refused to attend their Synods, and the people persisted in neglecting their sermons. The council, therefore, appointed "the Lords Archbishops of St. Andrews and Glasgow, the Marquis of Montrose, the Lord Secretary and Register, to wait on the Lord Commissioner, his Grace, to think on a general course what shall be done, as well anent those ministers that were admitted before 1649, and carry themselves disobediently to the laws of the kingdom, as those who were admitted since." While the committee were deliberating, the evil increased; and, on the 30th of the same month, six of the west country ministers were before the council to answer the heavy charge of "convocating great multitudes of his majesty's subjects for hearing their factious and seditious sermons, to the great scandal of religion and prejudice of the government of the church." To shorten their labours, however, and probably upon a report of the archbishops and their assistants, a most harassing and contradictory act was passed, commanding all "outted" ministers, under pain of sedition, *i. e.* being processed criminally, to remove themselves and their families twenty miles from the bounds of their own parishes, six miles from every cathedral, and three miles from every royal burgh, thus depriving them of any means of support they might have derived from their own industry or that of their families, in the only places of trade or traffic, and scattering them among strangers, far from the bounty or assistance of their friends. But as one "outted" minister only could reside in one parish, the act, besides, involved an alternative of death or apostasy; for the whole of Scotland could not have accommodated the sufferers, and no relaxation could be obtained but from the privy council or the bishop of the diocese. The older ministers, who still continued to preach, but withdrew from the Synods, were now to be treated as contemners of his majesty's authority.

To enforce their acts, the privy council ordered the Earl of Linlithgow to send as many troops to Kirkcudbright as, with those already there, would make up the number of eightscore footmen with their officers in that district. Sir Robert Fleming was directed to march two squads of his majesty's lifeguards to the west, and to station one in Paisley and the other in Kilmarnock. The object of these military missionaries was to episcopalize the refractory south and west, by collecting the fines and compelling subjection to the bishops and their curates. Sir James Turner, who had signalized himself by his zeal in fighting for the covenant, was singled out to superintend the pious service in the south, which he performed so much to the satisfaction of his employers, that, on the 24th of November, a letter of thanks was recommended to be written him "for his care and pains taken in seeing the laws anent church government receive due obedience." The excesses which were committed under sanction of these orders and commendations, were never attempted to be justified, though the parties afterwards mutually endeavoured to shift the blame from themselves When it was deemed necessary to make the General the scape-goat, it was asserted that he had exceeded his instructions; but he averred, and with greater probability of truth, that he had not even acted up to their tenor.* The exactions were enormous; and, as the fines for non-attendance were generally appropriated by the soldiers, they were summarily levied, and not unfrequently to far more than the legal amount. The process against nonconformists, in places where there were Episcopalian incumbents, was short. The curates were the accusers—the officers of the army, or sometimes even private sentinels, the judges—no proof was required—and no excuse was received, except money. If a tenant or householder were unwilling or unable to pay, a party was quartered upon him, till ten times the value of the fine was taken, and he was ruined, or, as they termed it, "eaten up;"† then, after every

* "Sometimes not exceeding a sixth part, seldom a halfe."—*Turner's Memoirs*, p. 114.

† To understand the meaning of this phrase, it is necessary to

thing else was gone, the household furniture and clothes of the poor defaulters were distrained and sold for a trifle.

The soldiery employed in this execrable work, were the lowest and most abandoned characters, who readily copied the example of their officers—measured their loyalty by their licentiousness, and considered that they served the king in proportion as they annoyed the Whigs. Religion was the object of their ridicule. In the pious hamlets where they quartered, family worship was interrupted by mockery or violence; and "The Cotter's Saturday Night," not only treated with derision, but punished as a violation of the laws of the land! Upon the Sabbath, the day peculiarly devoted by the Covenanters to holy rest, and the quiet performance of their sacred duties—for the Covenanters made conscience of the moral obligation of the Sabbath—a scene of dismay and distress hitherto unknown was commonly exhibited; and the day to which they had in other times looked forward as the glory of the week, was now dreaded as the signal of their renewed torments. Multitudes were brutally driven to church, or dragged as felons to prison; and hesitation or remonstrance provoked only additional insult or blows. Lists of the parishioners were no longer kept for assisting the minister in his labours of love, but were handed over to the troopers, with directions for them to visit the families, and to catechise them upon their principles of loyalty and their practice of obedience to their parsons. After sermon, the roll was called by the curate, when all absent without leave were delivered up as deserters to the mercy of the military. At churches where the old Presbyterian ministers were yet allowed to remain—for a few still continued to preach at their peril, or through the interest of some influential person—the outrage and

recollect the situation of the rural tenantry in Scotland about this time. They lived almost entirely upon the produce of the lands they rented, and kept usually a small stock of oatmeal, cheese, and salted provisions, as public markets were almost wholly unknown.

confusion were indescribable. As they were generally crowded, the forsaken bishops and their underlings were enraged, and the soldiers were instigated to additional violence. Their custom was to allow a congregation peaceably to assemble, while they sat carousing in some alehouse nigh at hand, till public worship was nearly over; then they sallied forth inflamed with liquor, and, taking possession of the church-doors or churchyard-gates, obliged the people, whom they only suffered to pass out one at a time, to answer upon oath whether they belonged to the parish; if they did not, although their own parish had no minister of any kind, they were instantly fined at the pleasure of the soldiers; and if they had no money, or not so much as would satisfy them, their Bibles were seized, and they were stripped of their coats if men, or their plaids if women; so that a party returning from such an expedition, appeared like a parcel of villanous camp-followers, after an engagement, returning from a battle-field, laden with the spoils of the wounded and slain.

To such an extent had these plunderings been carried, that even the privy council found it necessary to interfere. Towards the end of the year, they issued an explanation of their former acts, and restricted the exactions of the soldiery, "allenarly to the penalty of twenty shillings Scots, from every person who staid from their parish churches on the Sabbath-days.*

[1664.] Even this symptom, small as it was, of moderation, was not at all agreeable to the prelates. Like all upstarts, suddenly raised beyond their expectations, their arrogance became insupportable, and could brook no opposition. Glencairn, in particular, who had been so instrumental in their rise, began to

* Three of the prelates died in course of the past year. Bishop Mitchell of Aberdeen, who was succeeded by Burnet; Sydeserf, who was succeeded in the bishopric of Orkney by Mr. Andrew Honeyman, formerly minister of St. Andrews; and Archbishop Fairfoul of Glasgow, who was succeeded in the arch-episcopate by Bishop Bur net of Aberdeen; Dr. Scougall being appointed to that see.

feel the truth of what he had been repeatedly told—"that the bishops would never rest content with being second in the state, and that moderate Episcopacy was all a jest." He had said to Rothes that "it was the noblemen's interest to repress the growing power of bishops, otherwise they would be treated by them now as they had been before 1638." This remark being carried to Sharpe, he treated the Chancellor with great *hauteur*, and publicly threatened to destroy his interest at court—an affront that Glencairn could never forget, and which is said to have preyed upon his spirits to his dying day.

Fearing a relaxation of "the wholesome severities," the primate hastened to London with heavy complaints against many of the noblemen, for their backwardness in executing the laws made in favour of the church; and, through the influence of the English bishops and high churchmen, prevailed upon the king to re-establish in Scotland the most detested of all the arbitrary courts that had been abolished—the High Commission Court.

His majesty, by virtue of his royal prerogative in all causes and over all persons, as well ecclesiastic as civil, granted the most exorbitant powers to that antitype of the Inquisition. It consisted of thirty-five lay members,* and of all the prelates, except Leighton, who had the honour to be excluded from the nomination; and any five constituted a quorum, pro-

* The following were the lay members:—The Chancellor, Treasurer, Duke of Hamilton, Marquis of Montrose, Earls of Argyle, Atholl, Eglinton, Linlithgow, Home, Galloway, Annandale, Tweeddale, Leven, Moray; Lords Drumlanrig, Pitsligo, Fraser, Cochrane, Halkerton, Bellenden, the President of the Session, the Register, the Advocate, Justice-Clerk; Charles Maitland, the Laird of Philorth, Sir Andrew Ramsay, Sir William Thomson; the Provosts of St. Andrews, Aberdeen, Glasgow, Ayr, and Dumfries, Sir James Turner, and the Dean of Guild of Edinburgh. From among these, the primate, who managed the whole, could easily pick out a quorum to suit his purposes; and thus he got rid of all the members of the privy council who had either the spirit or the policy to resist his unbounded presumption—a presumption heightened by his being now ordered to take precedence of the Chancellor, the nobility, and all the officers of state.

vided always an archbishop or bishop was of the number. Under pretext of seeing all the acts of parliament and council in favour of Episcopacy put in vigorous execution, they were authorized to suspend or depose, fine, and imprison all ministers who dared to exercise any of their sacred functions without the license of a bishop—who should preach in private houses or elsewhere—who should keep meetings for fasts or for the administration of the sacrament of the Lord's Supper not approven by authority: to summon, call before them, and punish all who should speak, preach, write, or print to the scandal, reproach, or detriment of the government of the church or kingdom as now established—and all who should express any dissatisfaction at his majesty's authority. The commanders of the forces and militia, the magistrates of every description, were required to apprehend and incarcerate delinquents upon their warrants, and the privy council to direct letters of horning for payment of the fines—one half of which was appropriated to defray the expenses of the court, and the other to be employed for such pious uses as his majesty should appoint. And by a final comprehensive clause, the High Commission, or their quorum, were authorized to do and execute whatever they should find necessary and convenient for his majesty's service—for preventing and suppressing of schism and separation—for planting of vacant churches—and for procuring of reverence, submission, and obedience to the ecclesiastical government established by law.

By this instrument the whole kingdom was laid at the feet of the prelates; for no quorum of the Commission could be complete without a bishop, while five bishops could form a quorum without a layman. The practice was agreeable to the constitution of the court, and such as may always be expected where churchmen are intrusted with civil authority. True ministers of Christ would never in their ministerial capacity accept it, and worldlings who have assumed that sacred office to serve purposes of ambition, have ever been the greatest curse of Christendom. The records have been mislaid or lost, but the cases that remain, amply justify the epithets bestowed upon this nefarious tribunal by all who have mentioned it.

James Hamilton of Aikenhead, near Glasgow, was among the first brought before them, accused of not hearing Mr. David Hay, curate of the parish—Cathcart—in which his estate was situate. His defence was, the unclerical and ungentleman-like conduct of the clergyman. In collecting his stipend, which he did rigorously, Mr. Hay had borne particularly hard upon some of Mr. Hamilton's tenants, and, in consequence, a quarrel had ensued, in which the curate had descended to very intemperate and abusive language, and in return had been not less roughly answered. Mr. Blair, the "outted" minister, happening accidentally to be upon the spot, interfered, and rescued Hay from the hands of his furious parishioners. When the affray was over, Mr. Blair spoke seriously to the curate, and represented how opposite it was to his own interest for him to turn informer against his people. Hay, in return, thanked him for his kindness and advice, and gave him his solemn promise that he would follow it; yet within a very short time, he went to Glasgow and "delated" (*i. e.* denounced) them to the archbishop, who immedialy despatched Sir James Turner, then in the west, with a party of soldiers, to seize the delinquents. When Mr. Hamilton came to be informed of the circumstances of the affair, he considered the low prevaricating conduct of Hay as so base, that he would never again enter the church door, and he kept his promise; for this he was fined a fourth part of his yearly rent. When he had paid the fine, the court was so fully sensible of the misconduct of Hay, that the Archbishop of Glasgow came forward and promised that he would be removed, but insisted that Mr. Hamilton should come under an obligation to hear and acknowledge the minister he meant to place in his room, and, upon refusing to do any such thing till he knew who that person should be, he was mulcted another fourth of his income, and remitted to the archbishop to give him satisfaction as to his loyal and peaceable behaviour. The prelate, however, not being satisfied, he was again summoned before the court, upon some vexatious charges of keeping up the church utensils and session-books from the curate. Offering to swear he knew nothing at all about them, he was accused of not assisting the curate in the session when called upon, and suffering some of his family to absent themselves from church! Whether he might have been able to acquit himself of these heinous crimes is uncertain, for Rothes cut the business short, by telling him he had seen him in some courts before, but never for any thing loyal, and therefore tendered him the oath of allegiance. He had no objections, he replied, to take the oath of allegiance, were it not mixed up with the oath of supremacy. Sharpe, interrupting him, said "that was the common cant, but it would not do." Then he requested to be allowed to explain, but was politely answered by the president—"he deserved to be hanged!" and, upon refusing to become bound for all his tenants' good behaviour, he was fined three hundred pounds sterling, and sent to confinement in Inverness, to remain during pleasure!

John Porterfield of Douchal, an excellent person, singled out for more than common oppression, was summoned also for not hearing. He alleged the unfounded calumnies the curate had spread against him as the reason why he could not wait upon his ministry. The reason was allowed to be cogent, and, at his own desire, he was permitted to prove it. His first witness bore him out in all that he advanced, and his vindication would have been complete; but he was too much respected and esteemed in the neighbourhood, and his acquittal might have encouraged others. His proof was therefore stopped, and he was required to take the oath of allegiance. As had been expected, he stuck at the supremacy, and offered an explanation. The natural consequence followed—the curate was sent home to enjoy his incumbency, and Porterfield, for daring to offer a defence, was sentenced to pay a fine of five hundred pounds sterling, his estate sequestrated till it should be paid, and himself confined to the town of Elgin, where he continued for four years.

Mr. Alexander Smith, who had been turned out of his parish of Cowend, Dumfries-shire, by the Glasgow act, had since then resided at Leith; but having been guilty of preaching or expounding the Scriptures privately in his own house, was called before the court to be examined. In answering some of the queries Sharpe had put to him, he omitted the primate's titles, and only styled him, Sir, which Rothes observing, meanly truckling to the priest, asked him, "if he knew to whom he was speaking?" "Yes, my lords, I do," answered the prisoner firmly; "I speak to Mr. James Sharpe, once a fellow-minister with myself." For this high misdemeanour, the worthy man was immediately laid in irons and cast into the filthiest corner of the prison—the thieves' hole. He was afterwards banished to one of the desolate Shetland Isles.

At the settlement of Ancrum parish, where a James Scott, who had been presbyterially excommunicated, was appointed to fill the place of Mr. Livingston, a country woman by the name of Turnbull, with more zeal than prudence, attempted, as he was going to be inducted to dissuade him from undertaking the pastoral charge of so unwilling a people; and when he would not stop to listen to her reasoning seized him by the cloak. Impatient at this detention, he turned in wrath upon the female remonstrant, and beat her unmercifully; which unmanly conduct provoking some youths present, they threw a few stones, but none of them touched Scott or any other person. This pitiful affair was instantly magnified into a seditious tumult, and the ringleaders were apprehended by the Sheriff and thrown into jail—a punishment certainly more than adequate to the offence, but it was no sufficient atonement for the indignity done to the clergy, and the business was brought before the

High Commission; there these ministers of mercy sentenced the woman to be whipped through Jedburgh—her two brothers, married men with families, they banished to Virginia—and four boys, who confessed that they had each thrown a stone, were first scourged through the city of Edinburgh, then burnt in the face with a hot iron, and, finally, sold as slaves, and sent to the island of Barbadoes, which severe punishment they endured with a patient constancy that excited much admiration.

Bad as were the other courts in Scotland at this time, there was at least a probability that even a Presbyterian might by accident escape if accused, but before the High Commission no such thing was known. If proof was wanting, the declaration and the oath of allegiance were always at hand; and as the conscientious adherents of that persuasion were well known when brought before them, their trial was as short as their fate was certain. The exorbitant assumptions of the prelates were for some time supported by Rothes, but at length so disgusted the nobility, and brought such odium upon the court, that few of them would countenance its proceedings. While the uniform and flagrant injustice of their sentences rendered men desperate, who, rather than answer their summons, suffered themselves to be outlawed, or withdrew into voluntary exile in Ireland; till, in little more than a year and a half, the detested Crail court, as it was commonly called,* sank first into contempt and then into disuse.

Presbyterians in the north of Ireland being at this time also subject to persecution from the bishops, the ministers pursued in one country sought occasionally refuge in the other. John Cruickshanks and Michael Bruce who had fled to Scotland this year, and were preaching with much success to the conventicles in the west, were in consequence denounced as rebels, (June 23,) and power given to

* It was so called, because Sharpe, who was the author of the court, and took precedence of all its members, had been minister of Crail.

the officers and the commanders of the forces to seize them.

While the High Commission was in its vigour, the privy council was thrown into the background; yet in its temporary shade it was not unmarked by streaks of persecution, equally vivid with any of the lineaments of its co-tyrannous judicatories. The declaration was forced by them upon all who held places of public trust; and their exertions were stimulated by a letter from the king, commanding that "upon no terms was any explication or declaration to be admitted upon the subscription of any;" yet some few of the royal burghs refused, and several of the shires hesitated; but a peremptory proclamation produced a very general compliance—for the conscientious demitted their offices, and the privy council supplied their places with successors who were less scrupulous. Nor did any of the burghs evince the smallest inclination to assert their rights or privileges, or persist in any election that was disagreeable to the managers.

His majesty likewise called their attention early this year to the fines imposed by Middleton's act, which the Presbyterians were beginning to think had been forgotten, and for which leniency Lauderdale had received much unmerited credit. After several communications and delays, it was finally intimated, in the month of November, by proclamation, that the iniquitous imposition would be exigible—the first moiety at Candlemas, and the other at Whitsunday 1665.

Prohibited from preaching, several of the "outted" ministers who resided in Edinburgh, with others of those who feared the Lord, and that thought upon his name, were in the habit of meeting together in those days of sad calamity for social prayer in private houses. This, also, was a nuisance that required to be removed; and information having been given by the prelates or their underlings, the council issued a warrant to the magistrates of the city, "to cause search to be made anent the keeping of any such meetings, and that they acquaint the Lord Chancellor with what they discover, and the persons' names, that order may be taken about the same." This was followed by a mandate for all such ministers as had hitherto been allowed to remain by sufferance in Edinburgh, or any burgh, instantly to remove to the distances required by their former act, under the severest penalties of law. But the most nefarious of their acts, and one opposed to every good or amiable feeling of the human heart, was that of April 29, forbidding any contribution to be made, or money collected, for the relief of those who had been ejected from their livings, banished from their friends, and prohibited from settling in places where themselves or their families might have earned an honest subsistence. The proclamation bears strong marks that its authors were ashamed of so gross a violation of the dictates of common humanity. It is worded in such an ambiguous manner as to be capable of the most severe application, yet so as to be explained away when requisite. For jesuitical falsehood, and heartless tyranny, the production is matchless:—"The lords of his majesty's privy council being informed that, without any public warrant or authority, some disaffected persons to the present establishment, presume and take upon them to require contributions from such persons as they please, and do collect sums of money, which are, or may be, employed for carrying on of their private designs, prejudicial to the peace of the kingdom and his majesty's authority; and considering that such courses and underhand dealing may strengthen seditious persons in their practices and designs, to disturb the peace, if they be not timeously prevented. Therefore, in his majesty's name, they do prohibit and discharge all persons whatsomever, to seek or demand any contributions or supply, or to receive any sums of money. As likewise discharge all persons to grant or deliver any contributions to any persons whosoever shall require the same, unless it be upon occasions as have been publicly allowed and known, and heretofore practised; and that they have a special warrant and allowance of the lords of the privy council, or lords of the clergy within whose dioceses these collections are to be made: with certification, that if they contravene, they shall be proceeded against as persons disaffected to the present government, and movers of sedition."*

Shortly before the Restoration, and within the few years that had elapsed since it had pleased God to remove a great number of his most eminent servants, who had sustained the heat and burden of the day, during the troublous times of civil dissension, others had been honoured to suffer death, imprisonment, or exile for the word of God, and for the testimony of Jesus Christ; and of those who remained, the prelates were extremely anxious to get rid. Among them, William Guthrie of Fenwick was too conspicuous to escape. He had, through the interposition of the Earl of Eglinton and the Chancellor, been allowed to continue so long, but the crowds who were attracted to his church from the neighbouring and even distant parishes, and the blessing of God which in a remarkable manner followed his preaching, provoked the jealousy of the prelates, particularly Archbishop Burnet, who, when requested by Glencairn to overlook him, displayed his inveteracy by replying—"That shall not be done; it cannot be; he is a ringleader and keeper up of schism in my diocese;" and Glencairn was not long dead before he was suspended by his Grace. Such, however,

* Too much liberality in Christians towards their brethren, or even pastors, suffering in the cause of Christ, is a fault of very rare occurrence. There they often withhold more than is meet, and find in their experience that it tendeth to penury; for the Lord has many ways of taking from his people the money they think they can employ better than by lending to him; and perhaps many of the excellent persons who in this reign suffered the spoiling of their goods, might have to regret that they had not more freely contributed to supply the wants of their more needy fellow-christians. But no man knoweth either love or hatred from outward dispensations; and it is impossible for others to say, whether as a rebuke or a trial, the persecutors were permitted to plunder the devoted south and west.

was the respect in which Mr. Guthrie was held, that it was with difficulty he could find a curate to pronounce his sentence, and not till he had procured him a guard of soldiers and bribed him with the sum of five pounds. But Mr. Guthrie strictly forbade any opposition, and rather called them to fasting and prayer. Early on the Sabbath on which his church was declared vacant, he preached, as usual, two sermons from the latter part of that text, Hosea xiii. 9, "O Israel, thou hast destroyed thyself; but in me is thine help"—only had the whole service over before nine o'clock.

Shortly after, the curate with a party of soldiers arrived, and, leaving the privates outside, entered the manse with the officers. Rudely accosting Mr. Guthrie, he told him that the bishop and committee, after much lenity shown to him for a long time, were constrained to pass the sentence of suspension against him for not keeping presbyteries and synods with his brethren, and for his unpeaceableness in the church, of which sentence he was appointed to make public intimation unto him, and for which he had a commission under the Archbishop of Glasgow's hand. Mr. Guthrie answered—"I judge it not convenient to say much in answer to what you have spoken; only whereas you allege there hath been much lenity shown toward me—be it known unto you, that I take the Lord for a party in that, and thank him for it; yea, I look upon it as a door which God opened to me for preaching this gospel, which neither you nor any man else was able to shut, till it was given you of God. And as to that sentence passed against me, I declare before these gentlemen—the officers of the party—that I lay no weight upon it, as it comes from you or those who sent you: though I do respect the civil authority who, by their law, laid the ground for this sentence; and were it not for the reverence I owe to the civil magistrate, I would not surcease my preaching for all that sentence. And as to the crimes I am charged with, I did keep presbyteries and synods with my brethren;

but I do not judge those who now sit in these to be my brethren, but men who have made defection from the truth and cause of God: nor do I judge those to be free or lawful courts of Christ that are now sitting.

"And as to my unpeaceableness, I know I am bidden follow peace with all men, but I know also I am bidden follow it with holiness; and since I could not obtain peace without prejudice to holiness, I thought myself obliged to let it go. And as for your commission, to intimate this sentence, Sir, I here declare I think myself called by the Lord to the work of the ministry, and did forsake my nearest relations in the world, and give up myself to the service of the gospel in this place, having received an unanimous call from the parish, and been tried and ordained by the presbytery; and I bless the Lord he hath given me some success, and a seal of my ministry upon the souls and consciences of not a few that are gone to heaven, and of some that are yet on their way to it. And now, Sir, if you will take it upon you to interrupt my work among this people, as I shall wish the Lord may forgive you the guilt of it, so I cannot but leave all the bad consequences that follow upon it, betwixt God and your own conscience. And here I do further declare before these gentlemen, that I am suspended from my ministry for adhering to the covenant and work of God, from which you and others have apostatized."

At this the curate interrupting him said, that the Lord had a work before that covenant had a being, and that he judged them apostates who adhered to that covenant; and that he wished that not only the Lord would forgive him (Mr. Guthrie,) but if it were lawful to pray for the dead—at which expression the officers and soldiers burst into laughter—that the Lord would forgive the sin of this church these hundred years bygone. "It is true," answered Mr. Guthrie, "the Lord had a work before the covenant had a beginning, but it is as true that it hath been more glorious since that covenant; and it is a small thing for us to be judged of you in adhering to that covenant, who have so deeply corrupted your ways, and seem to reflect on the whole work of reformation from popery these hundred years bygone, by intimating that the church had need of pardon for the same." Then directing himself to the soldiers —"As for you, gentlemen, I wish the Lord may pardon you for countenancing of this man in this business." "I wish we may never do a greater fault," answered one of them scoffing. "A little sin may damn a man's soul," Mr. Guthrie gravely replied. He then called for a glass of ale, and, after craving a blessing, drank to the officers, who, having been civilly entertained, quietly left the house and went to the church, where the curate executed his office without disturbance, except from a few boys, whom the soldiers easily chased away.*

Another instance was Andrew Donaldson of Dalgetty, described "as singular for a heavenly and spiritual temper," and one who had also been much blessed in his ministry. Through the interest of the Earl of Dunfermline, Lord Privy Seal, he had been allowed to continue in his parish till this year, when the Earl being called to London, Archbishop Sharpe urged the Bishop of Dunkeld to depose him. He accordingly summoned Mr. Donaldson to attend his clerical duty under pain of suspension; but for reasons similar to those of Mr. Guthrie, he declined

* This account of Mr. Guthrie's deposition is translated from a paper drawn up at the time by himself, and preserved by Wodrow; and it exemplifies a conduct in all respects becoming a Christian minister. Mr. Blackader's is of a similar description; and, had we equally authentic and particular relations of the proceedings in other cases, I have no doubt a majority would be found not less worthy of our cordial approbation. Obedience to lawful authority, where it did not interfere with duty to God, was both inculcated and exemplified by the Covenanters. Frequently the violent and outrageous conduct of the soldiers caused tumults, and sometimes the natural and honest feelings of the people got the better of their prudence, but all was charged upon the Covenanters; and when provoked past human endurance, if they expressed only a just resentment, they were seditious despisers of lawful authority! as if it had been impossible for lawful authority ever to become tyrannical, and so tyrannical, as to release men from their obligations to obey.

attending the presbyteries or owning the bishop's authority, and was in consequence (October 4th) formally deposed, "in the name, and by the authority of Jusus Christ, and with the consent of all his (*i. e.* the bishop's) brethren, not only from his charge at Dalgetty, but from all the parts of the ministerial function within any diocese of the kirk of Scotland." By his prudence, Mr. Donaldson prevented any disturbance—for his affectionate people were sufficiently disposed to have made resistance—and even prevailed upon the military deputation, who came with the curate to displace him, to suffer him to preach and take farewell of his weeping congregation who had assembled. Dunfermline, upon being apprised of the whole before he left London, applied personally to the king, and procured his warrant to present Mr. Donaldson to Dalgetty during life, which he brought to Scotland with him; and, showing it to the primate, complained that he had taken advantage of his absence to deprive him of a minister for whom he had so high a value. Sharpe, dissembling his anger, apologized, and, with many professions of regard for the Earl, promised obedience to his majesty's commands, only requesting, as a favour, that the Earl would do nothing in it for three weeks, till he got the young man now settled at Dalgetty provided for. To this his lordship consented, supposing, as a matter of course, that Mr. Donaldson would then be restored. But the archbishop in the interim, by his interest at court, got an order under the royal sign manual, forbidding all "outted" ministers to return to their charges, sent down express, long before the three weeks expired. Dunfermline felt sufficiently fretted at the cheat, but there was no remedy.

Field-preaching continuing on the increase in the west, in the south, and in Fife, several of the ministers, at the instigation of Archbishop Burnet, whose province they chiefly invaded, had been summoned before the council and endured vexatious and expensive prosecutions; others, who were more active and conspicuous, who knew that no defence they could offer would prove availing, chose rather to allow sentence to pass in absence than willingly to desist from proclaiming the gospel; and being determined in this to obey God rather than man, they persisted at their peril, in spite of acts of parliament and council, to exercise their ministry wherever they could find opportunity. Deprived of their livings and driven from their homes, they could furnish little spoil to the persecutor, but they were most affectionately received into the houses of their friends, who carefully provided for their safety; and their sermons, of which intelligence was easily communicated, were attended by numerous and attentive congregations. That they should thus elude the grasp of their persecutors, and be followed by the most respectable of the country population, was irritating to the managers and galling to the prelates. But many of those who protected them were possessed of property; and as they were now made liable by law for hearing the gospel, the council began to turn their attention to this lucrative branch of oppression.

William Gordon of Earlston soon attracted their attention. Descended from an ancient family, distinguished in the annals of the Reformation, he, from his childhood, had attached himself to the people of God, and in early life enjoyed the friendship of Rutherford, but does not appear to have courted notice till persecution dragged him into view. When the commission was sent to Galloway to inquire into the disturbances at Irongray, they wrote to him requiring him to take an active part in the settlement of a curate, presented by the Bishop of Galloway, to the church of Dalry. This he respectfully declined, because he could not do it with a good conscience, as what did not tend to God's glory and the edification of his scattered people; and, also, because he, as patron of the parish, had legally, and with the consent of the people, appointed already a truly worthy and qualified person and an actual minister to that charge. For this "seditious carriage" he was called before the council, but they do not appear to have found that his conduct amounted to a punishable crime, and therefore, on the 24th November 1663, he was summoned upon the more comprehensive accusation of keeping conventicles and private meetings in his house; and, on the 1st of March this year, he was found guilty, upon his own confession, of having been one at three several conventicles, when Mr. Gabriel Semple, a deposed minister, preached —one in Corsack wood, and two in the wood of Airds; of hearing Mr. Robert Paton, likewise a deposed minister, expound a text of Scripture, and perform divers acts of worship in his mother's house; and of allowing Mr. Thomas Thomson, another of the same kind, to lecture in his own house to his family on a Sabbath day—for these offences, and because he would not engage never to repeat them, he was banished forth of the kingdom, not to return under pain of death! Besides all these various me thods of harassing the Presbyterians, Sir James Tur ner, during this year, continued his missionary exer tions with uniform persevering diligence, only in creasing in severity, as an unlicensed, unresisted soldiery ever do.

Several political changes took place in the course of the year that required to be noticed, although they had no influence in stopping or altering the tide of persecution, which, being directed by the prelates, particularly the two archbishops, continued to roll on with accumulating violence. The Earl of Glencairn died on the anniversary of the king's restoration. He was carried off rapidly by a fever, believed to have been produced or exasperated by the treatment he received from Sharpe, and which he could find no opportunity to resent. In his last moments, he earnestly desired the assistance of some Presbyterian ministers; but before one could be procured, he was incapable of deriving any benefit or comfort from their spiritual instructions or devotional exercises—a circumstance neither uncommon among the noblemen of that time nor strange; for, when men who had been religiously educated, and had, for the sake of worldly ambition or licentious pleasure, apostatized from their early profession, came to encounter the solemnities of a deathbed, if the conscience had not been altogether seared—a still more awful state—the partial knowledge they had acquired would often awaken remorse for having forsaken the guides of their youth, and lead them, when perhaps too late, to seek those consolations they had despised, amid the hurry of business or in high-day of pleasure and of health. Rothes, about the end of the year, was made keeper of the great seal, which Sharpe, according to Burnet, had solicited. Sir John Fletcher was removed from the office of lord-advocate, and Sir John Nisbet appointed in his room. In the month of August, Sharpe and Rothes went to court, whence they returned in October—Rothes loaded with civil appointments, and in addition named commissioner for holding the national Synod—a council which the primate, who could bear no rival near the throne, continued effectually to prevent being ever assembled.

BOOK V.

JANUARY, A. D. 1665—1666.

Partial moderation of the King—Sir James Turner's campaign through Kirkcudbright and Galloway—Unpaid fines levied—Students' oaths—All meetings for religious purposes forbid—Quietude of the country—Proclamation of the Council—Apologetical relation—Sir James Turner's third campaign extended to Nithsdale—Visits Mr. Blackader at Troqueer—More troops raised—Rigorous acts more rigorously enforced—Rising of the persecuted—They gather strength—Their operations—Defeated at Pentland—Prelatic revenge—Testimony of the sufferers—Torture introduced—Nielson of Corsack—Hugh McKail—Executions in Edinburgh and the west country—William Sutherland—Executions at Ayr.

Prelacy, now fenced round with all the forms of law, and supported by all the civil and military authorities, wanted only the concurrence of the people to have become the permanent, as it was the predominant, religion of Scotland; and so fickle is the multitude—so little does real principle take hold on the minds of the mob of mankind—that a little moderation in the use of their power, by the prelates, seemed only wanting to have induced the bulk of the congregations to return to their parish churches, and to have sat down quietly under the ministrations of the curates and the form of Episcopacy. A contemporary Presbyterian writer says—"Truly, at this time the curates' auditories were reasonably throng: the body of the people, in most places of Scotland, waited upon their preachings; and if they would have been content with what they had, in the opinion of many, they might have stood longer than they did; but their pride vowed they would be more glorious and better followed than the Presbyterians, and because respect would not do it, force should."*

Much and justly as the king and courtiers have been blamed for the perfidious manner in which Episcopacy was re-introduced into Scotland, and for the establishment of despotism upon the ruins of a free constitution, solemnly approved and sanctioned both by his present majesty and his "martyred" father; yet in this year, at least at the commencement, softened perhaps by the state of the nations, they showed no disposition to proceed to extremities had they not been pushed on by the prelates.

Charles, by his mean subservience to France, had plunged the country into a ruinous war with Holland—an awful pestilence had almost desolated the city of London—while an unusually severe winter had interrupted all rural labour, till March threatened to add famine to the list of plagues. These judgments, calculated to solemnize the mind, and give weight to public instruction, were improved by the non-conforming ministers to rouse the attention of their hearers to their own sins, and the sins of the people among whom they dwelt; and the general open apostasy from God which had accompanied the general defection from the national religion, was too palpable to avoid being noticed in the catalogue of crimes that had drawn down divine vengeance. These national visitations were, in some degree, subservient to the preservation of the Presbyterian cause, by impressing the guilt of apostasy more deeply on the minds of the serious, and even recalling the attention of the careless, while the public calamities and disgrace occupied the attention of the king and English government, and perhaps softening their rancour for the time, rendering them less anxious about pursuing their labours of religious persecution.

Although, however, government did not actively interfere to urge on the prosecution of ministers or frequenters of conventicles, the curates and their assistants, the troopers, continued their exertions; and

* Kirkton, p. 221.

Sir James Turner opened another campaign in the south and west, scouring the country and besieging the churches with a success and renown not unworthy his former fame. But his commission this year was extended; for, dreading the desperation to which the insulted peasantry might be driven, orders were issued for disarming the south and west, under pretence that the fanatics had an intention of joining the Dutch! As these districts had been always the most zealous in the cause of the covenants, so they were likewise the best supplied with arms,* and were, in an especial manner, the objects of the prelates' aversion and dread. When they had got them deprived of arms, therefore, the next step was to deprive them of leaders; and this was effected by an arbitrary order from the Commissioner, to arrest the principal gentlemen in the country who were known to be unfriendly to Episcopacy, and, without accusation or trial, to confine them prisoners in the Castles of Edinburgh, Stirling, and Dumbarton. Among the gentlemen thus summarily proceeded with, were Major-General Robert Montgomerie, brother to the Earl of Eglinton; Sir William Cunningham of Cunningham-head; Sir George Maxwell of Nether Pollock; Sir Hugh Campbell of Cesnock; Sir William Muir of Rowallan; Major-General Holborne; Sir George Munro; Colonel Robert Halket; Sir James Stuart, late provost of Edinburgh; Sir John Chiesly of Carswell; and Dunlop of Dunlop, &c. Yet arbitrary though these proceedings were, perhaps, upon the whole, they may be deemed providential, as, had any insurrection taken place while their leaders were at liberty and the people armed, the struggle might have been protracted—much bloodshed ensued—and the final result been far less propitious to the country and cause of religious liberty.

* The Scottish peasantry had always been accustomed to keep arms, and when summoned to serve in the militia, each provided his own; so that, besides the indignity of being deprived of their weapons, the taking them away without compensation was an act of robbery.

A proclamation for levying the fines imposed by Middleton was immediately planned, with such modifications as evidently showed that not any disloyalty in the parties, but their sincere, tried attachment to the free constitution of their country in church and state, and their conscientious adherence to the religion in which they had been educated, were the delinquencies it was intended to punish. The term of payment for the first half was enlarged to such as had not already paid it, till the first of December; and the second moiety was to be remitted to all who, upon paying the first, should take the oath of allegiance and subscribe the declaration in the express words of the act of parliament—conditions which no true Presbyterian could comply with, and which therefore drew a distinctive line between those who disregarded, and those who feared, an oath; exposing the latter to all the penalties of the various enactments with the expenses of collecting them—a new and no trifling addition to the principal, and which was also intrusted to the military to exact.

Unnecessarily multiplying oaths is a deep species of criminality, of which the rulers of lands called Christian take little account, although nothing tends more to demoralize a people. The prelatic rulers of Scotland seemed to delight in it, and this year introduced a most pernicious practice, afterwards improved upon, of forcing students to take the oaths of allegiance and supremacy before they could obtain an university degree; and thus initiated them into the habit of taking oaths, about the propriety of which some of the wisest and best men in the land were divided, and concerning which they could not be supposed to be very accurately informed.

Towards the end of this year, the privy council resumed its cruel activity; and the primate being president, the High Commission was allowed quietly to demit, while its spirit was effectually transfused into the other. December 7th, an act was issued extending the severities of all former acts against Presbyterian ministers, to those who had been settled before 1649, who had relinquished their ministry or had been deposed; and all heritors were forbid to give them any countenance in their preaching or any part of their ministerial office. But, as the general opinion of the more moderate among the politicians was, that the change in the form of reli gion had been too sudden, that it ought to have been more gradual, to meet the prejudices of the older ministers, whose only crimes consisted in absenting themselves from the church courts—this act was accompanied by another, establishing a new kind of presbyteries, under the name of "meetings for exercise," which was intended to leave without excuse the adherents of the abrogated system, as men who chose to differ from the present establishment from motives of sedition, and who refusing the substance because it was enacted by the king, would fight for a shadow from mere humour. This species of mock-presbyteries was specially declared to emanate from the royal supremacy, and was to consist of such of the curates as the bishops should judge qualified, who were to convene for exercise and assist in discipline as they should direct them; but the whole power of ecclesiastical censure, except parochial rebukes, was reserved to the bishop, who alone could suspend, deprive, or excommunicate. A kind of caricature session was at the same time brought forward, which was afterwards turned into an instrument of persecution—the established ministers were empowered to make choice of proper persons to assist them in the exercise of discipline, who, if they refused to obey his summons, were to be reported to the bishop; and if they continued obstinate, given up to the secular arm to be prosecuted as the heinousness of the case might require.

The usual strain of the curate's pulpit services consisted of a quarter or half-hour's harangue upon those moral duties their lives set at defiance, or in abusing or distorting doctrines they did not understand. Such of the people, therefore, as had the least relish for gospel truth, and who preferred the faithful sermons and earnest manner of their late pastors, to the insipid discourses listlessly read by the present incumbents, continued to follow after the private meetings and public ministrations of the former. The council, in consequence, determined that all such seditious practices should be put down, and, in a virulent proclamation of the same date, strictly charged and commanded all public officers to disperse every meeting assembled under the pretence of the exercise of religion, of whatever number they might consist, except such as were allowed by authority, stigmatizing them as the ordinary seminaries of separation and rendezvouses of rebellion, and subjecting every person who should be present at or give the smallest countenance to them, to the highest pains inflicted by law upon seditious persons.

Enormous as the oppression and injustice which desolated the south and west of Scotland had been, the people had remained quiet. They had seen their civil and religious liberties swept away, the ministers they loved scattered, and hirelings they detested settled in their stead. They had groaned beneath the yoke of tyrannous enactments, the insolence of lordly prelacy, and the licentiousness of military exaction, and yet had abstained from any acts of rebellion. But their patient endurance only encouraged the perpetration of new mischief, and their unexampled loyalty was abused as the occasion of fresh aggression. For, notwithstanding all that has been said about the disloyalty, faction, and refractory spirit of the Scottish covenanters, they were men of thorough monarchical principles, and possessed a more than ordinary reverence and attachment for their royal family, under circumstances that would have justified resistance long before they had recourse to the last remedy. Affairs, however, had now reached that crisis in which their duty to their God and their duty to their king were placed in opposition, and as Christians no choice was left. To have deserted the assembling of themselves together for religious worship and edification, because their rulers forbade it, would

Mr. Welsh Baptizing Children.

have been to acknowledge a regal power over the conscience which neither Scripture nor nature allows; and as yet no disturbances had occurred at any of those meetings, which were peaceably conducted at a distance from places that could reasonably give offence—in the open air, on hills, and in woods, and sometimes under the covert of night, where the ordinances of the Lord were administered in the way of his appointment, and the word of his gospel preached in simplicity and truth. They therefore continued; and, in spite of the tyrannical edicts of their rulers, like the Israelites of old, did not only meet but multiply. John Welsh, minister of Irongray, from the first betook himself to the fields, and, with his co-presbyter Mr. Gabriel Semple, laboured constantly within the bounds of his presbytery, officiating alternately in Corsack-wood and the surrounding country, frequently acting as decoys to their persecutors, one of them being actively engaged in preaching, while the curates with their beagles were in full scent after the other in an opposite direction. For upwards of a year, Mr. Welsh is asserted to have "preached at least once every week in the parish of Irongray." Afterwards he extended his labours to the sheriffdom of Ayr; and on Galston moor and various other places, held large conventicles, where he baptized many children. Gabriel Semple was not less zealous. He held large "unlawful assemblages" at Achmannock, Labrochhill, besides many others, not only in the sheriffdom of Ayr, but in Nithsdale, and within the stewartry of Kirkcudbright. Mr. John Blackader ofttimes convened great numbers of the parish of Glencairn and the neighbouring parishes, sometimes to the number of a thousand. Mr. Alexander Peden—who had been expelled from New Glenluce, and was especially obnoxious for his exertions and popularity in the west—held meetings under cloud of night and in the winter season; these being now rendered imperative, as the increased diligence of the archbishop and his military satellites forbade more open assemblages. Encouraged by their example, many others ventured to the high places of the field; and their united active endeavours promised to supply, in the districts of Galloway, shire of Ayr, and stewartry of Kirkcudbright, in some degree, the want of a regular Presbyterian ministry.

The council, now entirely under the direction of the primate, on the 25th of January, 1666, promulgated another thundering proclamation, in which, reiterating their falsehoods, and re-asserting "that conventicles, and unwarrantable meetings, and conventions, under pretence and colour of religion and exercise thereof, being the ordinary seminaries of separation and rebellion, are altogether unlawful," they denounced the eminent servants of God mentioned before, who were said to convene, armed with swords and pistols, and some of them to ride in disguise up and down the country in gray clothes, together with Mr. John Crookshanks, who avowedly kept by him "that book called Buchanan De Jure Regni, which he had translated out of Latin into English;" and John Osburn in Keir, who acted as officer for giving notice to the people of these unlawful meetings; and in regard they were latent and kept themselves out of the way that they might not be apprehended, and had no certain dwelling-place. They were charged at the market-crosses of Kirkcudbright, Dumfries, and Edinburgh, and at the shore and pier of Leith, "to compear personally before the council to answer to the premises," which was, in other words, to surrender themselves and be silenced, or sent to join their brethren in exile.

A little before this the cause of the sufferers had been advocated in "An Apologetical Relation of the Particular Sufferings of the Faithful Ministers and Professors of the Church of Scotland, since August, 1660," attributed to John Brown, late minister of Wamphrey, and one of the banished—a performance written in a style of elegance superior to many of the publications of that day, and with a force of argument that defied reply, and which was peculiarly galling to the managers, as it convicted them of the most flagrant apostasy. The facts were too recent to admit of denial, while the cause which the persecuted suffered for defending, continued the same as when it had been pronounced by their persecutors themselves the cause of their king, their country, and their God! An exposure more complete was never perhaps exhibited to the world; and the sting was the more tormenting, because it was true. The council felt it, and answered it in a becoming manner by another proclamation, in the beginning of February, ordering it to be burned by the hands of the common hangman, "to vindicate," as they said, "the honour of this kingdom, and to witness and declare, that such principles and tenets as are contained in the said pamphlet, are detested and abhorred by them;" with certification, that whosoever should retain any copies in their possession, should be liable in the sum of two thousand pounds, Scots money, to be exacted without any favour or defalcation; and whoever should contribute to disperse it, were declared liable to the punishment due the venders of seditious libels! And still more strongly to mark their sense of its merit, on the very day this proclamation was issued, before the book had been declared seditious, or keeping it in possession a crime, the venerable relict of James Guthrie and her daughter were brought before the council, and because they refused to give any information respecting the author, they were sentenced to banishment to Zetland, and to be confined there during pleasure. But the sentence which, it is likely, clerical vengeance had dictated, was, upon a petition from the gentlewomen, referred to the Commissioner, and by him remitted.

Winter gave some short respite to the Presbyterians, who as yet were suffered, without much interruption, to attend their conventicles amid the inclemencies of the weather; but, with the return of spring, Sir James Turner was dispatched to commence his third campaign. Formerly, Kirkcudbright and Galloway had been the principal seat of his operations. now they stretched over Nithsdale; nor was his circuit more extended than were his severities increased The exactions in his former expeditions had been chiefly confined to the common people, now they were imposed upon the gentlemen of the country; and the curates, attended by files of soldiers, fined at their discretion all whom they considered inimical, and of such sums as they judged proper. The landlord was compelled to pay if his wife, children, servants, or tenantry, were not regular church-goers. The tenant was mulcted when his landlord withdrew from public worship—if the curate's services deserved the name—nor did it avail him, although both himself and family were as punctual as the parson. The aged and the sick, the poor, the widow, and the fatherless—all were compelled to liquidate the church-fines; and even the beggar was forced to lay down his pittance to satisfy the unhallowed demand. From mere wantonness, the ruffian soldiery would eject from their dwellings the non-compliants—driving husband from wife, and wife from husband—snatch the meat from their children to give it to their dogs—then quarter in their houses till they had wasted their substance, and finish by committing to the flames what they could not otherwise destroy. Thus many respectable families, reduced to utter indigence, were scattered over the country, not only robbed of their property, but deprived of the means of procuring subsistence. Complaints were useless or worse—they were either disregarded, or answered by additional outrage.

The following instances will give some faint idea of the nature of these visitations. John Nielson of Corsack was a proprietor to a considerable extent in the parish of Partan in Galloway—a gentleman of undoubted loyalty, whose only crime was non-conformity. When Sir James Turner came into that county last year, he was instantly delated by the curate for non-attendance—aggravated, however, by his having shown hospitality to Mr. Welsh—fined an hundred pounds Scots, and sent prisoner to Kirkcudbright, besides having four, six, or ten troopers quartered on him constantly, from the beginning of March to the end of May, to each of whom he paid half-a-crown per day, in addition to their board and what they might abuse. This year, for the same offence, he had six soldiers quartered upon him from March to the middle of June, when he was forced to leave his house and wander without any certain dwelling-place, while the villanous banditti demolished his household stuff, and rioted upon his provisions. When these were exhausted, they turned his lady and children out of doors, and forced his tenants to bring them sheep, lambs, oatmeal, and malt, till they also were nearly ruined, and then they drove the whole of the black cattle upon the estate to Glasgow and sold them!

Mr. Blackader being under hiding, the Bishop of Galloway ordered Turner to apprehend him. His second son, then a boy of ten years old, has left the following artless and affecting account of Sir James' visit to the manse:—

"About this time, winter 1666, Turner and his party of soldiers from Galloway came to search for my father, who had gone to Edinburgh to seek about where he might live in safety. These rascally ruffians besett our house round about two o'clock in the morning, then gave the cry—'Damned Whigs open the door,' upon which we all got up, young and old, excepting my sister, with the nurse and the child at her breast. When they came in, the fire was gone out: they roared out again, 'Light a candle immediately, and on with a fire quickly, or els we'l roast nurse, and bairn, and all, in the fire, and mak a braw bleeze.' When the candle was lighted, they drew out their swords, and went to the stools, and chairs, and clove them down to mak the fire withall; and they made me hold the candle to them, trembling all along, and fearing every moment to be thrown quick into the fire. Then they went to search the house for my father, running their swords down through the beds and bedclothes; and among the rest, they came where my sister was, then a child, and as yet fast asleep, and with their swords, stabbed down through the bed where she was lying, crying, 'Come out rebell dogs.' They made narrow search for him in all corners of the house, ransacking presses, chests, and flesh-stands. Then they went and threw down all his books from the press upon the floor, and caused poor me hold the candle all this while, till they had examined his books; and all they thought Whiggish, as they termed it—and brave judges they were!—they put into a great horse-creel and took away, among which were a number of written sermons and printed pamphlets. Then they ordered one of their fellow-ruffians to climb up into the hen-baulks where the cocks and hens were, and as they came to one, threw about its neck, and then down on the floor we't, and so on, till they had destroyed them all. Then they went to the meat-ambry and took out what was there; then to the meal and beef barrels, and left little or nothing there. All this I was an eyewitness to, trembling and shivering all the while, having nothing but my short shirt on me. So soon as I was relieved of my office, I begins to think, if possible, of my making my escape, rather than to be burned quick as I thought and they threatened. I goes to the door, where there was a sentry on every side standing with their swords drawn—for watches were set round to prevent escape. I approached nearer and nearer by small degrees, making as if I were playing myself. At last I gets out there, making still as if I were playing, till I came to the gate of the house; then, with all the little speed I had—looking behind me now and then to see if they were pursuing after me—I run the length of half-a-mile in the dark night, naked to the shirt—I got to a neighbouring toune, called the Brigend of Monnihyvie, when, thinking to creep into some house to save my life, I found all the doors shut and the people sleeping; upon which I went to the cross of the toune, and got up to the uppermost step of it, and there I sat me down and fell fast asleep till the morning. Between five and six a door opens and an old woman comes out, and seeing a white thing upon the cross comes near it; and when she found it was a little boy, cries out, 'Jesus save us, what art thou? 'With that I awaked and answered, I am Mr. Blackader's son.' 'O, my puir bairn, what brought thee here.' I answers, 'there's a hantle of fearful men wi' red coats has burnt all our house, my brother, and sister, and all the family.' 'O, puir thing,' says she, 'come in and lye down in my warm bed'—which I did, and it was the sweetest bed I ever met with."

After this the whole family was dispersed. "We all behoved," continues the narrator, "to scatter; one neighbour laird in the parish taking one child, and another another. I was sent to a place about a mile off, called the Peel-toune, who afterwards, likewise, were quite ruined and all taken from them—the poor mither begging but one lamb for meat to the bairns, but could not get it. The meat they were not able to eat they destroyed, threw down the butter-kirns, and hashed down the cheese with their swords among the horses' feet."

Besides all other exactions, the parliamentary fines which had hung so long suspended over the heads of the gentry, were ordered to be levied with the utmost rigour from all who would not take the oath of supremacy and subscribe the declaration; but to those who would, the one-half was remitted, as had been proposed the preceding year. This fine, like the rest, was collected by troopers, whose charges were always as much and frequently more than the original debt. The only consolation the sufferers had, was, that their plunder did not go to enrich those who were the authors of the robbery. Neither Middleton's party, who imposed, nor Lauderdale's, who uplifted, the mulct, were allowed to pocket a farthing of the proceeds, which were ultimately applied to support that worst and most dangerous instrument of tyranny—a standing body of household troops.

Sharpe, who assuredly was the cause of much of his country's calamity, and who was often execrated as almost the origin of the whole, has usually got the credit of this arrangement. It is well known that, although an imperious, he was by no means a fearless character, and it is therefore not unlikely he may have been the author of these precautionary measures which the country viewed with so much detestation. At any rate, about the time that he was in London, the affair was matured, and two regiments of foot and six troops of horse were ordered to be raised, of which Thomas Dalziel of Binns—a rude soldier who had once owned the covenant, and afterwards improved his manners in the Russian service—was appointed Lieutenant-General, with William Drummond, Lord Madderty's brother, who had gone through the same course of education, as Major-General. The troops of horse were disposed of among the nobility. This army was to be maintained from the fines, of whose application the General was to give an account; but from the manner in which they were collected, and the character of the gatherers, the public was little benefitted by this revenue, and the maintenance of the troops fell eventually upon the common exchequer.

Reinforced by these mercenaries, the council more strictly enjoined, by a fresh proclamation, (October 11,) submission to the acts of parliament against separation and resistance to ecclesiastical authority, requiring masters to oblige their servants, landlords their tenants, and magistrates the inhabitants of the several burghs, to attend diligently at the parish churches and partake regularly of the ordinances; and no one was to be retained as a servant, kept as a tenant, or suffered to dwell as a citizen, after the parish priest intimated his disobedience. Mandates so wantonly oppressive, which, without any rational object, were calculated to create crime by leading either to a violation of the consciences of the lieges or the laws of the land, seem to carry on their face an incitement to insurrection; and when the manner in which they were put in execution, among a sturdy peasantry, is remembered, it is truly astonishing that they did not excite a spirit of insubordination, general and deadly, and in truth produce those very outrages of which the calumniated Presbyterians were falsely accused. Many were driven from their homes and utterly ruined, who, merely from political motives, or from a desire to see something like decency in their clergymen, or from an aversion to have ministers forced upon them whom they did not like, had opposed the curates and subjected themselves to the fines; others, men of respectable rank in life who themselves had conformed, saw their estates ruined and their families dispersed, because some one, over whom they could have no possible control, would not attend the wretched sermonizing of a worthless parson, or take the sacrament from his polluted hands; besides those who, from a love to the truth and a sincere reverence for their tenets, deemed it a point of duty to withdraw from the ministration of men who neither understood nor preached the first principles of the gospel. Yet, notwithstanding all these terrible encroachments upon their liberty and property, notwithstanding these authorized violations of all that was dear or sacred to them as men or as Christians, they had suffered, they had complained, but they had not rebelled, when an incidental circumstance led to an insurrection, in perfect conformity with the spirit, and even authorized by the letter, of the ancient Scottish constitution before it was destroyed at the Restoration, which hardly deserves the name of rebellion.

Mr. Allan of Barscob, and three other of these unfortunate fugitives who had been forced by want from their places of retreat among the mountains or mosses of Galloway, had ventured, November 13th, to the Clachan of Dalry to procure some provisions. Upon the high road, a little from that place, they accidentally met some soldiers driving a few neighbours before them, to compel them to thresh out a poor man's corn for the payment of his church fines. They naturally sympathized with the sufferers, but passed on. While seated, however, at breakfast in the village, they were informed that the soldiers had seized the old man in his house—stripped him naked—and were threatening to place him on a redhot gridiron because he could not produce the money. Leaving their meal unfinished, immediately they repaired to the spot; and finding the poor man bound, desired the soldiers to let him alone. The soldiers in return demanded how they dared to challenge them, and drew their swords. A scuffle ensued, in which one of the others discharged a pistol and wounded a corporal with some pieces of a tobacco pipe—the only ball they had among them, when the military surrendered themselves prisoners, and the man was liberated.*

Thus fairly engaged, to retreat was as dangerous as to proceed. They knew they would be denounced as rebels and subjected to dreadful reprisals. A party of their friends at Balmaclellan, when they heard of the affair, knowing they too would be involved, seized and disarmed sixteen soldiers who were quartered there, one, who made resistance, being killed; and the whole country taking the alarm, their numbers soon swelled to about fifty horse tolerably mounted, and, perhaps, double that number of foot, miserably armed with pitchforks, scythes, cudgels, and a few pikes and swords. Turner's forces were scattered over the country; they therefore, without allowing them time to collect, marched direct to Dumfries, where, on the morning of the 15th, they surprised him, who having only heard some indistinct account of the scuffle, was preparing to go and chastise the culprits. The horse went straight up to head-quar-

* Sir James Turner says, that the corporal affirmed he was shot, "because he refused to sign the covenant." The corporal himself, in a petition to the privy council, says, "ten pieces of tobacco pipes were, by the surgeon's care, taken out of his bodie."—*Turner's Memoirs*, p. 148. *Kirkton's Hist.* note, p. 230.—Sir James in his account of the transactions which took place after his seizure, and till the battle of Pentland Hills, is frequently inaccurate, as might be expected, both from his situation, which prevented distinct information except about what he saw, and his prejudices and interest which led him to pervert even that. Some instances will be given afterwards in which he is palpably, if not designedly, at fault.

ters—the foot remaining without the town; and when Sir James appeared at the window, Nielson of Corsack told him, if he would quietly surrender he should receive no harm, with which he complied; and that gentleman preserved him from personal injury, which some of the party seemed anxious to inflict.*

The person who assumed the command was one Andrew Gray, said to be an Edinburgh merchant whom no body knew, but whose authority all obeyed without inquiry, so totally were they unprepared for any regular rising, and as little was he qualified for the situation into which he had thrust himself. They seized the General's papers and trunks, but found little money; himself they brought away in his night-gown and slippers, and placing him upon a little pony carried him to the cross, where, with much formality, they drank the king's health to evince their loyalty—a ceremony which some of their friends thought they might as well have omitted, and for which they received neither credit nor thanks. They then carried him back to his lodgings, and ordered him to make ready and go with them. That night they rested at Glencairn. Here they were alarmed by a report of the approach of the Earl of Annandale and Lord Drumlanrig, and set off hurriedly, carrying their prisoner with them under a strong guard. Next night they reached Carsphairn, where they remained; and here their redoubtable Captain Gray left them, not without violent suspicions of having carried a considerable sum of money along with him: yet more probably he retired from fear or a sense of his own utter incapacity;† but the numbers increas-

* "While they were speaking, the Commander comes up, and seizing Turner presented a pistol or carabine to have shot him, but Corsack interfered, saying, 'you shall as soon kill me, for I have given him quarters.'"—*Crichton's Life of Blackader*, p. 139.

† This was on the Friday. On the Monday following he was found by Colonel Wallace near Mauchline, in a situation very unlike that of a person possessed of much money. "About that house I saw two men, one whereof I perceived was Andrew Gray. He was in so uncouth a posture, with such a beggar-like habit, and looking with such an abashed countenance, I was astonished and could not

ed, and a kind of committee consisting of Maclellan of Barscob, Nielson of Corsack, and Mr. Alexander Robertson, a preacher, succeeded to the command.

Some days before the scuffle at Dalry, Rothes had taken his departure for London, and the chief cares of the government devolved upon the primate, as president of the council—thus called upon to discharge an important political duty at a very delicate conjuncture. One of the bailies of Dumfries who had witnessed the seizure of Turner, immediately proceeded to Edinburgh with information of the rising; and the members of council, who never calculated upon resistance, were surprised and alarmed beyond measure. Next day, they sent off an express to the king with the unpleasant intelligence, who, passing the Commissioner upon the road, furnished his majesty with very unexpected news to salute him with on his arrival. They ordered General Dalziel to march on the following day with as many men as he could muster to the west country, to establish his head-quarters at Glasgow, and thence to proceed to wherever his presence might be most urgently required—the various noblemen of those most interested in these districts, were, at the same time, required to use their every exertion to preserve the peace, and to receive and assist his majesty's forces; the guards of the town of Edinburgh were doubled, and the names of all strangers ordered to be registered. These measures, the most obvious and requisite, met of course the king's approval; but a proposal to enforce the subscription of the declaration respecting the covenant upon the heritors of the southern and western shires, was postponed by his

speak for a long time. Always he forbids me to be afraid. He tells me the Lord had favoured them with good success in that attempt upon Dumfries; and that, howbeit, after the business was done, many came and owned it that never appeared before, when it was but to be hazarded upon: yet all or most of these gentlemen and countrymen had left it and gone to their houses, as if there had been no more ado: whereupon he had left them to look to his own safety, being in a very insecure condition then, having been the chief actor in the business."—*Wallace's Narrative of the Rising at Pentland*, p. 391.

desire as unnecessarily exasperating an evil of which they did not yet know the extent. More effectually to protect the capital, the companies of the train-bands were ordered to be filled up by citizens who would willingly take the oath of allegiance, and further promise to maintain his majesty's authority with their lives and fortunes; such as would not, to be disarmed and their persons secured.

The noblemen of Fife, with their followers, were summoned, and an act of council was passed to put the country in a posture of defence, and all the lieges were ordered to assist the General with all their power. The ferries across the Forth were at the same time stopped, and even those who passed at Stirling Bridge were to be subjected to a rigid examination. A proclamation also was issued commanding the rebels to lay down their arms, but it was remarked that it contained no offer of pardon; and to desire them to surrender without security, was something like an invitation to confess and be hanged. Some of the nobility felt the degradation of being under an ecclesiastic, and murmured—"Have we none at such a juncture to give orders but a priest?" But they were too wofully spiritless to do more, and they only clanked, sulkily, the fetters themselves had forged.

Intelligence also had been sent by the insurgents to Edinburgh with equal expedition, and a few who were well-wishers to the cause met to consider what was their duty in the present juncture, when, at an adjourned meeting held in Mr. Alexander Robertson, a preacher's lodgings,* they resolved after deliberation and prayer, that it was their duty to assist their poor brethren so cruelly oppressed. One only dissented, Mr. Ferguson of Kaitloch, who was not convinced of the propriety of rising at that time. The rest were eager to engage immediately, and as

* *Kirkton,* p. 234. This was a different person from the Alexander Robertson formerly mentioned, though they have been sometimes confounded, owing to the surnames being spelled indifferently Robison or Robertson, both their first names being Alexander, and both being preachers.

soon as the meeting broke up, Colonel Wallace and Mr. Robertson set out for the west to see what could be effected there. Mr. Welsh went direct to the countrymen whom he found at Dalmellington; thence he proceeded to gather his friends in the south, while they, buoyed up with the expectation of being quickly and numerously joined, marched forward to Ayrshire, and on the 21st had their general rendezvous at the Bridge of Doon. Wallace's first disappointment was at Libberton, where, instead of forty stout horsemen, he only met eight; and on his journey by Linton, Dunsire, Mauchline, and Evondale, he found the country, in general, had been taken so completely unawares, that he arrived at the main body with a very slender accession of strength—the ministers remaining quietly in their houses, while the leading Whig gentlemen went to wait upon the General. He had by the way received notice from Cunninghame, that a reinforcement from thence might be procured if they had only a party to encourage and protect them till they got formed; and Captain John Arnott, accordingly, had been sent with forty horse to bring them up, and directed to join next day at Ochiltree.

Having received information of General Dalziel's arrival at Glasgow, they hastened to Ochiltree, where all their parties were ordered to meet, and where Mr. Semple preached while they were collecting.* After-

* *Wallace's Narrative*, p. 395. "Sir James Turner has a merrie fact, which he says occurred here. I was lodged that night at the principall alehouse of the toune, where I was indifferentlie well used, and visited by some of their officers and ministers. Most of their foot were lodged about the church and churchyard, and order given to ring bells next morning for a sermon to be preached by Mr. Welsh. Maxwell of Monreth and Major Mackulloch invited me to hear that phanatic sermon, for soe they merrilie call'd it. They said that preaching might prove ane effectuall meane to turn me, which they heartilie wished. I answered them that I was under guards, and that if they intended to heare that sermon, it was probable I might heare it likewise; for it was not like my guards would goe to church and leave me alone at my lodgings. Bot to what they spoke of my conversion, I said it wold be hard to turn a Turner. Bot because I found them in a merry humour, I said if I did not come to hear Mr. Welsh preach, then they might fine me in

wards they marshalled their army, named their officers,* and placed their guards. Sir John Cochrane was with Dalziel, and his lady received the leaders who were quartered at the mansion-house very coolly, although she expressed herself not unfriendly to the cause. Here they were joined by Mr. John Guthrie, minister of Tarbolton, with some of his parishioners, and Robert Chalmers, a brother of the Laird of Gadgirth's, who brought a report that the Duke of Hamilton was approaching with his troops, and that they had despatched John Ross with a small party to ascertain the fact. A council of war was then called, at which it was resolved that they should march eastward, as it was impossible to stay where they were, and there was no probability of farther help from the south or south-west districts, and Captain Arnott would bring with him whoever were well inclined in Cunninghame and Renfrew. Besides, they had an earnest invitation from Blackwood to come to Clydesdale, where he promised to meet them with one hundred men.

Next day they broke up for Cumnock, but were

fourtie shillings Scots, which was double the soume of what I had exacted from the phanatickes. Bot there was no sermon that day, which, undoubtedly, I would have heard, if there had been anie." Pp. 163–164. Afterwards, he has this passage—"This I shall say they were not to learn to plunder, and that I have not seene lesse of divine worship any where, than I saw in that armie of theirs; for thogh at their rendezvouses and halts they had opportunitie enough everie day for it, yet did I never heare any of their ministers (and as themselves told me there was not so few as two-and-threttie of them, whereof onlie five or sixe convers'd with me) either pray, preach, or sing psalms; neither could I learn that it was ever practised publicklie, except once by Mr. Robbison at Corsfairne, ane other time by Mr. Welsh at Damellington, and now the third time by Mr. Semple at Lanrick, where the lawful pastor was forced to resigne his pulpit to him." P. 169.

* The officers whose names have been preserved, were—Colonel Wallace, who left a written narrative of the rising at Pentland, and of whom some farther notice will be given; Major Joseph Learmont; Captains Andrew Arnott, John Paton, John Maclellan of Barscob, John Maxwell, younger of Monreith, and Robert Maclellan of Balmagachan; Cornet of Horse, Robert Gordon of Knockbreck; uncertain, Major John McCulloch of Barholme; Mr. George Cruikshanks had a command.

met on the road with the disagreeable intelligence that Ross and his party had been taken prisoners by the Duke, and that the enemy's whole force was at Kilmarnock; in consequence, they continued their route during a violent storm of rain and wind to Muirkirk. The night fell dark, and the road was detestable; yet the men marched forward with spirit, and even their enemy, Sir James Turner, gave them this credit—"I doe confesse, I never saw lustier fellows than these foot were, or better marchers; for though I was appointed to stay in the rear, and notwithstanding these inconveniences, I saw few or none of them straggle." When they arrived late at their quarters, wet as if they had been drenched in water, the poor foot were forced to lie all night in the cold church, without victuals and with but little fire. Here Mr. Andrew M'Cormack, a pious Irish minister, known by the name of the "Good-man," came to the Colonel and informed him it was the opinion of Mr. Robertson and Mr. Lockhart—that, as there was no appearance of any help either from Clydesdale or any other quarter, the business should be followed no farther, but the people dismissed as quietly as possible to their homes, to shift each for himself the best way he could, until the Lord gave some better opportunity. With this advice, which was not at all to the Colonel's liking, he could not of himself comply, but proposed to consult the other leaders who might join before or when they reached Douglas. Thither they arrived on Saturday night, November 24, without any of their expected reinforcements, excepting forty recruits brought by Captain Arnott.

Having quartered the troops, and, on account of an alarm, doubled their guards, a council of war was held, when, after earnest prayer to God, the question was proposed, whether they should disperse or continue in arms? On the one side was stated the strength of the enemy and the small number of their company, the total want of spirit discovered by the country and the tempestuous season of the year, which rendered it unfit for action. On the other, it was replied—that the coming forth to own the people of Galloway was clearly of the Lord, and in that they had done nothing but followed his call—that numbers had not only urged them, but had solemnly promised also to come forth, and if these should now desert the cause, between them and their Master let it be. As for themselves, they believed the Lord could work by few or by many. If he designed the present appearance should prosper, he would send men if necessary; or who could tell but he might honour them to accomplish this end? At all events, the cause they were assured was his; nor would they forsake it, but follow on whatever might be the consequence. Death was all they could endure; and, though they were only to bear their testimony to the the truth, that was well worth dying for. It was next proposed, whether they should renew the covenants? On this there was no dispute. They regretted they could not go about that work with the deliberate preparation they deemed necessary for entering into such solemn engagements; but, as the urgency of the case admitted of no delay, and they all under stood the nature of the transaction, they determined to prepare for the worst by again dedicating themselves to the Lord in the national bonds, whose obligation they believed to be perpetual, and the renunciation of which they considered as one of the deepest sins of the land. The disposal of their prisoner, as they had no safe place in which to confine him, was then considered. About this they were not so unanimous. Some were for putting him to death as a notorious murderer and bitter instrument of persecution, but others urged that he was a soldier of fortune, acting under a commission, also that he had been promised protection by one of themselves; and it appearing from his papers, though his conduct had been severe, yet that he had not even acted up to his instructions, it was carried to spare him.*

* "My guards, whereof David Scott, a weaver, was captain, carried me to Bathket, and took up for my quarters the best alehouse" *Turner's Mem.*

Hearing that Dalziel was at Strathaven, they decamped early next morning—Sabbath—and marched by Lesmahago, to Lanark, where they arrived in the evening, having been joined by Robert and John Gordon, the sons of Alexander Gordon of Knockbreck, with a few others from Galloway. Mr. Robertson refused to accompany them further. On their march, they completed the arranging of the troops, but found themselves wretchedly deficient in officers, there not being above four or five who had ever been in an army before, neither were they fully supplied with ammunition or arms; at Lanark, they caused a general search, but the country had been too well scourged before, and they found few or none. Notice, however, was given that the covenants would be renewed on the morrow.

When they assembled at the rendezvous for this purpose, they were told the enemy was within two miles, and it was proposed to delay; but as the public avowal of their cause and principles, besides being a solemn religious act of imperative obligation, was the best and only testimony they could exhibit in their circumstances, they determined that nothing but absolute necessity should prevent it. They therefore sent forward an advance of twelve horse, placed guards at the ford, and then deliberately went about the work of the day. The horse were drawn up at the head of the town, where Mr. Gabriel Semple and Mr. John Crookshanks presided. The foot were ranged in the street, near the tolbooth stairs, upon which Mr. John Guthrie stood and preached. Very few except the insurgents attended, so great was the universal terror and depression of the times; but the whole proceedings are said to have been deeply impressive, particularly the address of Mr. Semple, from Prov. xxiv. 11, 12: "If thou forbear to deliver them that are drawn unto death, and those that are ready to be slain; if thou sayest, Behold, we knew it not; doth not he that pondereth the heart consider it? and he that keepeth thy soul, doth he not know it? and shall not he render unto every man according to his works?" After sermon, the covenants were read, article by article, and the hearers, with uplifted hands, and apparently with much serious emotion, engaged and vowed to perform. Now in a situation of such peril, and pledged to their country and to their God, could they be other than deeply affected? It was no common ground these witnesses occupied.

About the same time, they emitted the following hurried but well-framed "declaration of those in arms for the covenant 1666," the effect of which was wonderfully, though sadly, impressed upon the religious part of the community, by the remembrance that these men had been allowed to stand alone, and to fall together in the righteous cause; and by the evils which overtook the adherents to the covenants and afflicted the nation for twenty-two succeeding years of persecution.

"The nature of religion doth sufficiently teach, and all men almost acknowledge, the lawfulness of sinless self-defence; yet we thought it duty at this time to give an account unto the world of the occasion and design of our being together in arms, since the rise and scope of actions, if faulty, may render a thing right upon the matter, sinful. It is known to all that the king's majesty, at his coronation, did engage to rule the nation according to the revealed word of God in Scripture—to prosecute the ends of the National and Solemn League and Covenants, and fully to establish Presbyterian government, with the Directory for Worship—and to approve all acts of parliament establishing the same; and thereupon the nobility and others of his subjects did swear allegiance: and so religion was committed unto him as a matter of trust, secured by most solemn indenture betwixt him and his people.

"Notwithstanding all this, it is soon ordered that the covenant be burned—the tie of it is declared void and null, and men forced to subscribe a declaration contrary to it—Episcopal government, in its height of tyranny, is established—and men obliged by law not to plead, witness, or petition against these things

Grievous fines, sudden imprisonments, vast quarterings of soldiers, and a cruel inquisition by the High Commission Court, were the reward of all such who could not comply with the government by lordly hierarchy, and abjure the covenants, and prove more monstrous to the wasting their conscience, than nature would have suffered heathens to be. These things, in part, have been all Scotland over, but chiefly in the poor country of Galloway at this day; and had not God prevented, it should have, in the same measures, undoubtedly befallen the rest of the nation ere long. The just sense whereof made us choose rather to betake ourselves to the fields for self-defence than to stay at home burdened daily with the calamities of others, and tortured with the fears of our own approaching misery. And considering our engagement to assist and defend all those who entered into this league and covenant with us; and to the end we may be more vigorous in the prosecution of this matter, and all men may know the true state of our cause, we have entered into the Solemn League and Covenant; and though it be hardly thought of, renewed the same, to the end we may be free of the apostasy of the times, and saved from the cruel usages persons resolved to adhere to this have met with; hoping that this will wipe off the reproach that is upon our nation, because of the avowed perjury it lies under; and being fully persuaded that this league, however misrepresented, contains nothing in it sinful before God, derogatory to the king's just authority, the privileges of the parliament, or the liberty of the people; but, on the contrary, is the surest bond whereby all these are secured, since a threefold cord is not easily broken, as we shall make appear in our next and larger declaration, which shall contain more fully the proofs of the lawfulness of entering into covenant, and necessity of our taking arms at this time for the defence of it, with a full and true account of our grief and sorrow for our swerving from it, and suffering ourselves to be divided to the reproach of our common cause, and saddening the hearts of the godly—a thing we sorrowfully remember and firmly resolve against in all time coming."

At this period the number of the insurgents had reached its maximum—more having joined on that day than for three before—supposed to amount to nearly three thousand; and the opinion of many among them was, if they did intend to fight, it would be better to do it in that quarter, where, if defeated, they were among friends, and could more easily find the means of escape, than in the east, where every thing would be against them; but their want of discipline, and want of arms, did not warrant a trial of strength with the king's forces, who were equal if not superior in numbers and in a complete state of equipment. They were likewise the more encouraged to try the Lothians, as, at this critical moment, they received from Edinburgh pressing letters of invitation to come thither. They chose what eventually proved the most unfortunate for themselves, and that same evening took the road for Bathgate. Before they left Lanark, Lawrie of Blackwood paid them a visit. He said he had come by desire of the Duke of Hamilton to learn what were their intentions and to endeavour to prevail upon them to lay down their arms and save the effusion of blood; but he produced no written commission, and only spoke in general terms to some of the ministers, which induced in the mind of the Colonel a suspicion that he came merely to spy out their nakedness; and he afterwards blamed his own simplicity in allowing a person of such dubious character to pass between them and the enemy without restraint. Hardly were they in motion when Dalziel made his appearance; but he contented himself with sending a body of horse after them, who, when they found the countrymen prepared for an assault, returned to the general, with whom they remained for the night in the quarters the others had left. The night was deplorable; it rained incessantly, blew a hurricane, and the road across the moors was deep, "plashy," and broken. When they arrived at their destination, two hours after night-fall, they could get no accommodation, not even a covert from the tempest; and their leaders retired to a wretched hovel to consult about their further operations. After prayer, they discussed the subject. To return was now impracticable, for the enemy was at their heels; but they still expected some assistance from Edinburgh, and thitherwards they resolved to continue their route, convinced that they would at least hear from their friends before they were entirely within the jaws of Leviathan.

But never were poor men more completely deceived, disappointed, and entangled. On every side was danger. The whole spasmodic energy of government had been forced into action by the fearful throes of the primate; almost all Scotland south of the Tay, had been set in motion, while the capital was fortified more in proportion to his ecclesiastical terrors than to the band that was approaching. Sir Andrew Ramsay, the provost, had barricaded the gates and planted them with cannon—Lord Kingston was stationed on Burntsfield Links with an advanced guard of horse and foot—the advocates were accoutred and the citizens in arms—and all the array of the Lothians, Merse, and Teviotdale, were ordered to hold themselves in readiness. Yet such was their want of intelligence, that the covenanters, upon an alarm being given, broke up about twelve o'clock in this dark and foul night—"One of the darkest," says Wallace in his Narrative, "I am persuaded that ever any in that company saw. Except we had been tied together, it was impossible to keep together; and every little burn was a river." During this disastrous march, which many were unable to accomplish —as "they stuck in the clay and fainted by the road" —the army diminished wofully; and the remainder who arrived in the morning at the New Bridge, within eight miles of Edinburgh, "looked rather like dying men than fighting soldiers—weary, worn-out, half-drowned, half-starved creatures." Yet, beyond expectation, in an hour or two, they mustered nearly a thousand men, only officers were sorely lacking; and now when the enemy was within five miles in their rear, they first learned that all Edinburgh and Leith were in arms against them.

Dreadfully perplexed—without directors, without intelligence, without food—they knew not what to do, but they resolved to march to Colinton. On their way thither, Blackwood again came to them with a verbal requisition from the Duke for them to lay down their arms, and he would endeavour to procure an indemnity; but desperate as their situation was, had they had no other aim than their own personal safety, they could not have listened to so vague an arrangement with such men as they had to deal with; and when Blackwood urged their compliance, they dismissed him with a caution to beware how he behaved himself, and see well that he walked straightly and uprightly between the parties. Having had so little rest, and scarcely tasted any thing since they left Lanark, a few horsemen were sent out to try and procure some provision and forage in the neighbouring farms, as they intended, if possible, to take some repose and refreshment in their quarters that night, which, continuing tempestuous, seemed to promise them, for some hours at least, security from any hostile incursion. Accordingly, having provided in the best manner they could for the foot in the village, and sent the horse to the neighbouring farms, they set their guards, and the officers were retiring to rest, when Blackwood came to them again, accompanied by Richards, the laird of Barskimming, and repeated the proposal he had formerly made; telling them at the same time, he had the General's parole for a cessation of arms till to-morrow morning, having given in return the same for them. Wallace, who was little pleased with the officious presumption of "the tutor," told him, "he did not understand this paroling of his, but he believed neither would break the truce in such a night." Upon this they parted, and Barskimming, without taking leave, set off early next morning, but Blackwood waited till day-break, and requested to know what answer was to be returned The leaders upon calmly considering their situation—their men now hardly nine hundred, the greater part without arms—their spirits broken by the apparent want of heart in the country—their bodies worn out by fatigue, hunger, want of sleep, and exposure to the weather—the utter hopelessness of any rein forcements—and their great inferiority in numbers to Dalziel's troops—were strongly induced to attempt coming to some terms not incompatible with the object for which they had ventured to the field; they therefore proposed sending one of their number along with Blackwood to represent to the General their grievances, and the grounds of their appearance in arms; but the only person they had to whom they could intrust such a message being objected to as an outlaw, Wallace sent a letter by Blackwood to Dalziel, stating—"That, on account of the intolerable insolences of the prelates and their insupportable oppressions, and being deprived of every usual method of remonstrating or petitioning, they were necessitated to assemble together, in order that, jointly, they might the more securely petition his majesty and council for redress; they therefore requested of his excellency a pass for a person whom they might send with their petition, and begged an answer might be returned by Blackwood who had promised to fetch it."

Trusting, however, very little to this negotiation, they commenced a retreat, and turning the west end of the Pentland Hills, took the Biggar road. As their men were straggling, they drew up near the House of Muir, on a spot now well known—Rullion Green. The ground rises from the south towards the north, where the Hill terminates abruptly. Here the poor fatigued remnant were posted in three bodies. Upon the south, a small body of horse, under Barscob and the Galloway gentlemen—in the centre, the foot commanded by Wallace himself—and upon the north, the greater part of the horse along with Major Learmont. Hardly had this small company got arranged, when an alarm was given that the enemy was approaching; and upon moving towards the ridge of the hill, they observed their horse under Major-General Drummond upon an opposite hill, within a quarter of a mile—for their foot had not arrived. The little band of Covenanters being so posted that the enemy could not attack them from the north, about fifty picked troopers marched along the ridge to the westward, evidently with a design to approach from that quarter. Observing this, a party of about the same strength, under Captain Arnott, was dispatched by Wallace to meet them, which they did in the glen, at no great distance. Having fired their pistols, they instantly closed, and a sharp contest ensued in sight of both armies, which lasted for a considerable time, when the troopers gave way and fled in confusion to their own body. In this rencounter, Mr. John Crookshanks and Andrew McCormack fell;* and several were killed and wounded on both sides.

The nature of the ground preventing pursuit by cavalry, a part of the Covenanters' foot was ordered to support their horse, but the enemy moved to another and safer eminence, farther to the east, where they waited until their own foot came forward; and then descending from the hill, drew up upon Rullion Green, in front of their opponents, in order to provoke them to leave their ground and engage. But seeing that they were not inclined to leave their vantage ground, they pushed forward a squadron of their horse, flanked by foot, upon the south, which the others observing, consulted whether they should give them a second meeting, when considering that, although they might be able to defer an engagement for that night, they must inevitably be forced to fight on the morrow, and under much greater disadvantage—as the enemy would be certainly increased in

* "Two main instruments of the attempt, two Ireland ministers." *Wallace's Narrative*, p. 416. It appears doubtful if ministers in any case may lawfully take arms—Peter was reproved for drawing his sword in defence of his master. Matt. xxvi. 52.

numbers—they, after prayer, resolved that they would not decline the combat—"they would quit themselves of their duty, though it should serve for no more than to give a testimony by leaving their corpses on the field." A party of Learmont's horse, also supported by foot, was then sent forth, whose onset the regulars were unable to sustain, and staggered and fled. Each now endeavoured to support their own men by successive detachments.

While the combatants were at all equal, the Covenanters successfully maintained the honour of the day, till Dalziel, about night-fall, brought up the whole of his force, and, with one simultaneous and vigorous charge, broke their array. Overwhelmed by numbers, they found it impossible to rally, and every one shifted for himself as he best could. The slaughter was not great, for the countrymen made to the hills, and their flight was covered by the darkness; nor were the horsemen very eager in their pursuit, for, being chiefly gentlemen, they sympathized in the sufferings, and many approved of the cause of the vanquished. About a hundred were killed and taken prisoners at the time, and about fifty were brought in afterwards. Of Dalziel's troops, the casualties never appear to have been fairly reported They acknowledged some half-dozen, but the allowed valour of the Covenanters, and the obstinacy and nature of the skirmishing, forbid our accepting this as any thing like an accurate return. Some of the neighbouring rustics, more cruel even than the military, probably expecting money, are said to have murdered several of the fugitives, but the crime was held in deserved execration; and the popular tradition, that these "accursed spots" were the scenes of foul nocturnal visions, sufficiently marks the general opinion of the country. Sir James Turner, who had accompanied the insurgents in all their movements, when the battle was about to commence, bargained with his guards that, if they would save his life from the vengeance of their friends, if defeated, he would secure their safety from the conquerors, which was agreed to, and was one of the few agreements which appears to have been faithfully kept. Those who were slain on the field were stripped where they fell, and lay naked and unburied till next day, when some godly women from Edinburgh brought winding sheets and interred them; but such is the brutality of avarice, that the bodies were afterwards taken out of their graves by some miscreants for the sake of the linen!

The victors entered the capital shouting with their prisoners.* "A sight," says a contemporary, "the saddest that ever Edinburgh had seen, which drew tears in abundance from the eyes of all that feared God, considering what vast difference there was between the persons and the cause on the one side and the other: and surely a most astonishing dispensation it was to see a company of holy men—for such were the greatest part, yea, but few otherwise—and that in a good cause, given up into the hands of a most desperate crew of scoffing, profane atheists. But God had called them together, it seems, to have a testimony at their hands, and that he missed not, for he helped them to glorify him in their sufferings, which made their cause more lovely throughout all parts of the land, even in the eyes of enemies, than victory would have done!" They were imprisoned, the common men in the kirk, called Haddo's-Hole†—those of superior rank were sent to the common

* "Mr. Arthur Murray, an honest 'outted' minister (from Orkney,) dwelling in a suburb of Edinburgh, by which Dalziel's men entered the city after the victory,—he, hearing they were passing by, opened his window to view them, where he saw them display their banners tainted in the blood of these innocent people, and heard them shout victory, upon which he took his bed and died within a few days."—*Kirkton* p. 247.

† It received this name from Gordon of Haddo having been confined there previous to his execution in the civil war in the reign of Charles I. Burnet tells us that Wiseheart, Bishop of Edinburgh and indeed the whole town, were so liberal to the prisoners, that they were in danger from repletion. Wallace, with an appearance of more accuracy, says, "the charity of the godly people of the town appeared in furnishing them with all necessaries, both for maintenance and the healing of their wounds." P. 428.

jail. In the height of their exultation, the privy council sent off their despatches announcing the victory, and breathing a spirit of the most implacable hatred against the Presbyterians. "Although," said they, "this rabble be totally dissipated for the time, yet we conceive ourselves obliged, in the discharge of our duty, to represent unto your majesty that those principles which are pretended as the ground of this rebellion, are so rooted in many several places through the kingdom, and there be such just ground of apprehension of dangers from persons disaffected to your majesty's government, as it is now established by law, as will require more vigorous application for such an extirpation of it as may secure the peace of the kingdom and due obedience to the laws." Orders were immediately given by the council to sequestrate the property of all who had been at Pentland, and to apprehend all who were suspected of having been with them, or of having aided or abetted them before or since.

Priestly resentment is proverbially implacable; but if those priests happen to be infidels, or apostates, such as the generality of the Episcopalian-restoration-church of Scotland were, their revenge assumes a degree of rancour bordering on the diabolical, of which the punishments that followed the suppression of this feeble and ill-supported insurrection, afford afflicting examples. There cannot be a stronger proof that the rising was unpremeditated and accidental, than that, notwithstanding the enormous oppression the country had endured, and the universal discontent both in the south and west, so few attempted to join the insurgents. In Renfrew, only one small company assembled; but before they were ready, Dalziel had interposed between them and the Covenanters, and they retired without doing more than showing good will and incurring punishment. William Muir of Caldwell was their leader; and among them were, Ker of Kersland, Caldwell of Caldwell, Cunningham of Bedland, Porterfield of Quarrelton, with Mr. Gabriel Maxwell, minister of Dundonald,

George Ramsay, minister of Kilmaurs—and John Carstairs, minister of Glasgow, unwillingly forced out by the entreaties of his friends, with several others, who all afterwards suffered confiscation, fining, or banishment. What was, perhaps, not the least galling part of the trial; they were denounced by John Maxwell of Blackston, one of themselves, who either through treachery or terror was induced to become an informer and witness against them.

It was natural, and followed as a matter of course, that, of men taken with arms in their hands, some examples should be made by the government against whom they were alleged to have rebelled. But what gave to the executions in this case their peculiar features of atrocity, was, their victims had surrendered upon a promise of quarter, and the more appalling fact of a letter from the king to the council, forbidding any more to be put to death, having been kept up by one or both of the archbishops,* till they were satiated with the blood of some obnoxious victims. When the question, whether the prisoners should be sent to trial, was first agitated at the privy council board, Sharpe violently urged the prosecution. Sir John Gilmour, esteemed one of the best lawyers of his day, pusillanimously shrunk from giving any decided opinion, and the rest seemed inclined to be silent, when, unhappily, Lord Lee started the vile jesuitical distinction, not, however, unmatched in later times, that men may be granted quarter on the field as soldiers, yet only be spared to die on a scaffold as citizens—a distinction which General Dalziel, notwithstanding his little respect for the lives of the Covenanters, could not by any means be brought to comprehend.

Eleven of the prisoners were accordingly picked out for trial, and, on the 4th of December, Captain Andrew Arnott; Major John McCulloch; John Gor-

* Kirkton asserts it of Sharpe, p. 255. Burnet says that his namesake, Burnet of Glasgow, kept up the letter, pretending that there was no council-day between and the day of execution, vol. i, p. 348.

don of Knockbreck, and his brother Robert; Gavin Hamilton, Mauldslie, Carluke; Christ. Strang; John Parker, Kilbride; John Ross, Mauchline; James Hamilton, Killiemuir; and John Shiels, Titwood, appeared before the Court of Justiciary. Thomas Patterson, merchant in Glasgow, died in prison of his wounds. The objections to the relevancy of the indictment were argued with great ability, and, in particular, that one arising from the quarter granted by the General, which, if we may judge from the pleadings, he appears to have himself considered a point of honour. It was alleged, that being in the form of an army, and as such assaulted by his majesty's forces, and as such having accepted quarter, and in consequence delivered up their arms, and that that quarter being *publica fides*, and offered and granted, should be inviolably observed. To this it was answered, that their presumption in appearing in arms against their sovereign lord was an aggravation of their rebellion; that unless his majesty had given a special commission for the purpose, the General had no right to grant a pardon to rebels, whatever he might have done in fair and honourable war. In return, it was replied, that without debating the justness of the war, the pannels being then in arms, might have defended their own lives and reached the lives of the greatest that opposed them. In laying aside these arms, they in effect ransomed their lives; and soldiers who may defend their own lives, are not obliged, nor is it in use, nor would the urgency of the case permit it to them, to seek the granter's commission, common soldiers being accustomed to grant quarter, which their superiors never annulled; and this had been the practice, not only between the contending parties in France, but likewise practised by his majesty's own forces in the hills, and with the rebellious English, which, unless it were adhered to, a method of martial massacre would be introduced, and rebels of necessity would become desperate and indomitable traitors. The court repelled the objections; and as none of the pannels denied the facts of which they were accused, they were unanimously found guilty, and sentenced to suffer the doom of traitors on the 7th of December.

Previous to their execution, they drew up a united testimony, which stands upon record, an evidence of the purity of their motives and the justice of their cause—a cause which, however defamed by the advocates of passive obedience, or oppugned by more modern objections, was in their hands the sacred cause of civil and religious liberty, only these patriots were driven by enormous oppression prematurely to assert it. "We are condemned," say they, "by men, and esteemed as rebels against the king, whose authority we acknowledge; but this is the testimony of our conscience, that we suffer not as evil-doers, but for righteousness, for the word of God and testimony of Jesus Christ--particularly for renewing the covenant,* and, in conformity with its obligations, for defending ourselves by arms against the usurpation and insupportable tyranny of the prelates, and against the most unchristian and inhuman oppression and persecution that ever was enjoined and practised by rulers upon free, innocent, and peaceable subjects! The laws establishing prelacy, and the acts, orders, and proclamations made for compliance therewith, being executed against us by military force and violence—and we with others, for our simple forbearance, being fined, confined, imprisoned, exiled, scourged, stigmatized, beaten, bound as beasts, and driven unto the mountains for our lives, and thereby hundreds of families being beggared, several parishes, and some

* *On the binding obligation of the Covenants.*—How far the vows of a parent are obligatory on a child, is a question both delicate and difficult to determine. That, in certain circumstances, they are imperative, is perfectly clear; and national compacts, vows, or covenants—by whatever name they may be called—entered into by the heads of the people, are, in Scripture, considered as binding upon the succeeding generations, even when the parties have rashly entered into them, under circumstances of ignorance, delusion, or deceit, provided they contain nothing in opposition to the moral law of God, which is unchangeable in its enactments, though they should contravene extraordinary enunciations of the divine will, as in the case of the covenant between Joshua and the Gibeonites.

whole country sides, exceedingly impoverished; and all this either arbitrarily, and without any law or respect had to guilt or innocency, or unjustly contrary to all conscience, justice, and reason, though under the pretence of iniquitous law, and without any regard to the penalty specified in the law; while all remonstrating against grievances, were they ever so just and many, and petitions for redress being restrained by laws—there was no other remedy left us but that last of necessary self-preservation and defence. And this being one of the greatest principles of nature, warranted by the law of God, scriptural instances, and the consent and practice of all reformed churches and Christian states abroad, and of our own famous predecessors at home—it cannot, in reason or justice, be reputed a crime, or condemned as rebellion, by any human authority." Then, after lamenting the perjury, backsliding, and breach of covenant throughout the land, the overturning of the work of reformation, the obtrusion of mercenary hirelings into the ministry, the universal flood of profanity and apostasy from participating in the guilt of which they ardently prayed to be cleansed, they exhort their countrymen and fellow-christians to remember the example of their noble and renowned ancestors, and warn them not to be offended with the cross of Christ on account of their sufferings, and conclude in a strain of exhilarating, animated, and believing anticipation, almost prophetical—"Though this be the day of Jacob's trouble, yet are we assured that when the Lord hath accomplished the trial of his own, and filled up the cup of his adversaries, He will awake for judgment, plead his own cause, avenge the quarrel of his covenant, make inquiry for blood, vindicate his people, break the arm of the wicked, and establish the just, for to him belongeth judgment and vengeance; and though our eyes shall not see it, yet we believe that the Sun of Righteousness shall arise with healing under his wings—that he will revive his work, repair his breaches, build the old wastes, and raise up the desolations."

Ten were executed together; and, on the scaffold, their dying speeches, containing similar sentiments, were delivered with a high and elevated courage, that excited no common emotion among the spectators, while their kindlier feelings were melted into tenderness when the two brothers—the Gordons—were thrown off locked in each other's arms, and whose last agonies were expressed by the convulsive clasp of a fraternal embrace. The heads of the sufferers were sent to various parts of the country, but the right hands which they had uplifted at the oath of the covenant, were sent in derision to be affixed to the top of Lanark jail.

Enraged to find that no appearance of any premeditated scheme of rebellion could be traced in the confessions of the late sufferers, who all agreed in assigning as the cause of the rising, the intolerable oppression they endured in soul, body, and estate, they determined to elicit by torture, if possible, some plausible confession that might afford a colouring of justification for the cruelties they were perpetrating and determined to perpetrate. Accordingly, Nielson of Corsack, whose enormous oppression we have already seen, and Hugh McKail, a preacher, were brought before the council on the 4th of December; and the boots, an instrument which had not been used in Scotland for a century, was again put in requisition. This "infernal machine" was a kind of box, strongly hooped with iron, into which the leg of the prisoner was put, where it was compressed by wedges, driven frequently till the bone was crushed, and even the marrow sometimes extruded. Nielson was fearfully tormented; but his cries, which were most piercing, had no effect upon Rothes, before whom he was examined, who frequently called for "the other touch." Hugh McKail, whose fate produced a stronger and more indelible impression than any that occurred during this period, was a young man of great promise. He had been tutor in the family of Sir James Stewart of Coltness, some time before the Restoration, when Sir James was provost of Edinburgh. He was licensed to preach at the early age of twenty-one, and soon became so deservedly popular, that he eminently attracted the hatred of the prelates, particularly Sharpe, and was forced to keep under hiding. During this time, he went to Holland, and for four years attended one of the Dutch Universities, then distinguished for theological literature. In 1664–5, he returned secretly to his father's house, where he remained, till, hearing of the appearance made by the people of God for the cause of the covenants, he joined them in the west; but his tender constitution was unable to bear the fatigue of their severe toil and privations, and he was, finally, obliged to leave them near Cramond Water. On his return home to Libberton, he was seized at Braid's Hills and brought to Edinburgh. His limb, also, was shattered by repeated strokes of the mallet; but from neither of the two could torture extort any other fact than their confessions contained.

Nielson, notwithstanding the treatment he had undergone, was indicted to stand trial on the 10th of December. When he was placed at the bar along with other four—Mr. Alexander Robertson, preacher, who had been basely betrayed by the Laird of Morton, his friend, to whose protection he had committed himself; George Crawford, in Cumnock; John Gordon, Irongray; and John Lindsay, Edinburgh—they were found guilty upon their own confessions, and were executed on the 14th, except Lindsay, who was pardoned. They all left testimonies in similar terms to those who went before, lamenting the defection of the times, but rejoicing in the hope that God would return and bless his church and people. They all pointedly refused the appellation of rebels, avouched their loyalty to the king and the constitution of their country before it was illegally overturned, and warned their friends not to be discouraged because the few who had taken their lives in their hands had fallen before their adversaries, but to abound more in holiness, prayer, and steadfastness, nothing doubting, but that the Lord would arise in due time and plead the cause which is his own.

McKail having fevered from the torture, had not been tried along with Nielson, and it was thought his youth and the torments he had already endured would have been deemed sufficient punishment; but they knew little the mortal strife of ecclesiastics, when power is the object, who thus calculated, although the highest interest was made for him. He had insinuated a likeness between the primate and Judas—a crime never to be forgiven, for it was true; and being recovered so far as to allow his being moved, he was carried to court, December the 18th, and, together with seven others, indicted for rebellion, found guilty, and condemned. When allowed to answer for himself, he pled the obligations that were laid upon the land, and the oath of God under which they were bound. The last words of the National Covenant, he said, had always had great weight on his spirit; upon which the Lord Advocate interrupted him, and desired him to answer to his own particular charge. His answer was, "that he acted under a solemn impression of the saying of our Lord Jesus—'Whosoever shall confess me before men, him shall the Son of Man also confess before the angels of God.'" When the sentence was pronounced, he cheerfully said, with meek resignation—"The Lord giveth, and the Lord taketh away; blessed be the name of the Lord."

His prison hours were enviable, not composed merely, but full of joy. "Oh, how good news!" said he to a friend, "to be within four days' journey of enjoying the sight of Jesus Christ." When some women were weeping over him—"Mourn not for me," was his cheering exhortation; "though but young, and cut down in the budding of my hopes and labour of the ministry, yet my death may do more good than many years' sermons might have done." On the last night of his life, after having supped with his father, some friends, and his fellow-prisoners, he burst forth in a strain of animated queries; among others, "How they who were hastening to heaven should conceive of the glories of the place, seeing it was written, 'Eye hath not seen, nor ear heard, neither have entered into the heart of man, the things which God hath prepared for them that love him!' It is termed a glorious city and a bride; but, oh, how insufficient, how vastly disproportionate, must all similitudes be! therefore the Scripture furnishes yet a more excellent way, by conceiving of the love of Christ to us; that love which passeth knowledge, the highest and sweetest motive of praise —'Unto him that loved us, and washed us from our sins in his own blood, and hath made us kings and priests unto God and his Father; to him be glory, and dominion, for ever and ever, amen!'—by holding forth the love of the saints to Christ, and teaching us to love him in sincerity. This, this, forms the very joy and exultation of heaven!—'Worthy is the Lamb that was slain, to receive power, and riches, and wisdom, and strength, and honour, and glory, and blessing!' Nothing less than the soul breathing love to Jesus can rightly apprehend the joys of heaven." Then, after a while, he added, "Oh! but notions of knowledge, without love, are of small worth, evanishing into nothing, and very dangerous."

His great delight was in the Bible. Having read the sixteenth Psalm before going to bed, he observed, "If there were any thing in the world sadly and unwillingly to be left, it were the reading of the Scriptures—'I said, I shall not see the Lord in the land of the living;' but this needs not make us sad, for wherever we go, the Lamb is the book of Scripture and the light of that city, and there is life, even the river of the water of life, and living springs to delight its inhabitants." He laid him down in peace, and slept sweetly from ten o'clock till five next morning. When he arose, he called his companion, John Wo drow, in a tone of pleasantry—"Up, John, you are too long in bed—you and I look not like men going to be hanged this day, seeing we lie so long." Some time after, he made a striking and peculiarly happy allusion to his own situation, and that of his fellow-sufferers—"Earthly kings' thrones have advocates against poor rebels; thy throne, O God, hath Jesus an advocate for us." He early requested his father to take leave, lest their parting afterwards might discompose him, and to retire and pray earnestly that the Lord might be with him to strengthen him, that he might endure to the end. On the scaffold, a heavenly serenity beamed in his countenance. He ascended the ladder with alacrity, saying, "Every step of this ladder is a degree nearer heaven." Then looking down to his friends, he said, "Ye need neither be ashamed nor lament for me in this condition, for I can say, in the words of Christ, I go to your Father and my Father, to your God and my God." Just before he was turned off, he burst out into this rapturous exclamation—"This is my comfort, that my soul is to come to Christ's hand, and he will present it blameless and faultless to the Father, and then shall I be ever with the Lord! And now I leave off to speak any more to creatures, and begin my intercourse with God, which shall never be broken off. Farewell, father and mother, friends and relatives—farewell, the world and all delights—farewell, sun, moon, and stars. Welcome—welcome, God and Father—welcome, sweet Jesus Christ, the mediator of the new covenant—welcome, blessed Spirit of grace and God of all consolation—welcome, glory—welcome, eternal life—welcome, death!" Then, after praying a little within himself, he said aloud, "O Lord, into thy hands I commit my spirit, for thou hast redeemed my soul, Lord God of truth!" And thus leaving time, was joyfully launched into the boundless ocean of eternity.

The crowd of spectators was immense; and, "when he died," Kirkton tells us, "there was such a lamentation as was never known in Scotland before, not one dry cheek upon all the street, or in all the numberless windows in the mercate place. He was a proper youth, learned, travelled, and extraordinarily pious. He fasted every week one day, and signified, frequently, his apprehension of such a death as he died; and heavy were the groans of the spectators when he spoke his joys in death. Then all cursed the bishops who used to curse; then all prayed who used to pray, entreating God to judge righteous judgment. Never was there such a mournful day seen in Edinburgh—never such a mournful season seen in Scotland, in any man's memory."

The others were equally supported in the last trying hour, and cheerfully laid down their lives for a cause which they believed to be the cause of God and of their country, and which they never doubted would ultimately and gloriously triumph. Their names were, John Wodrow, a merchant in Glasgow—Ralph Shields, a merchant in Ayr, but an Englishman by birth—a Humphry Colquhoun, of whom Kirkton testifies, "that he spoke not like ane ordinary citizen, but, like an heavenly minister relating his comfortable Christian experiences, called for his Bible, and laid it on his wounded arm, and read John iii. 8, and spoke upon it most sweetly to the admiration of all"—John Wilson, of the parish of Kilmaurs, in Ayrshire—and Mungo Kaipo, from Evandale. Three of little note, and who agreed to some partial compliances, were pardoned.

While these bloody transactions were going forward in the capital, a commission was issued for the Earls of Linlithgow and Winton, Lord Montgomerie, and Mungo Murray, to hold a Justiciary Court in Glasgow, and Sir William Purves, solicitor-general, despatched to prosecute. Four of the Covenanters were accordingly brought before them, Monday, December 17th, all men in humble life—Robert Buntine, in Fenwick; John Hart, in Glassford; Robert Scott, in Dalserf; and Matthew Paton, in Newmills—found guilty that same day, and ordered to be hanged on Wednesday. They went to the gibbet with the same Christian fortitude, and evinced, by their deportment, that the same peace of God which had comforted the martyrs in the capital, dwelt also in them. But the impression which the dying declarations of the martyrs had made, especially of those last murdered in Edinburgh, forbade that they should be allowed the privilege of addressing the spectators in a quarter where their solemn testimonies might have deeper effect; and when the sufferers attempted to address the crowd, the drums were ordered to beat and drown their voices—a detestable practice, which proclaimed their dread of the truth they were vainly attempting to stifle. Rothes himself took a tour to the south-west, accompanied by the Earl of Kellie, Lieutenant General Drummond, Charles Maitland of Hatton, and James Crichton, brother to the Earl of Dumfries, as a Justiciary commission. At Ayr, twelve were tried and ordered for execution; eight in that town, two at Irvine, and two at Dumfries. When those at Ayr were to be executed, the executioner fleeing, and none being willing to perform the hated office, in this dilemma, the Provost had recourse to the shocking expedient of offering any of the prisoners pardon, upon condition of his hanging the rest of his brethren; and one Anderson was found, who purchased a few days' miserable existence at this expense; yet even he had to be filled half drunk with brandy to enable him to perform the dreadful ceremony, while the sufferers, more to be envied than he, courageously met that death which he basely inflicted.

The conduct of William Sutherland, the executioner of Irvine, stands out in fine contrast with that of Anderson. This man, who had been born of poor parents in the wildest part of the Highlands, had been seized with an uncommon desire to learn the English language, which, with much difficulty, he acquired so well, as to be able to read the Scriptures in that tongue. He had acted as common hangman in the town of Irvine for some time; when, having been converted to God through the reading of the Bible, and the instructions of the persecuted, he scrupled about executing any person whom he was not convinced deserved to die. When the Ayr hangman fled, he was sent for, but would not move till carried by force to that town, and peremptorily refused to execute the prisoners, because he had heard they were godly men, who had been oppressed by the bishops; upon which he was committed to prison, and flattered, and threatened—first promised money, then told he would be hanged himself, if he persisted; yet nothing could either terrify or induce him to comply. When they called for the boots, "You may bring the spurs too," said William, "ye shall not prevail." The provost offered him fifty dollars, and told him he might go to the Highlands and live. "Aye, but where can I flee from my conscience?" was the pointed query of the honest mountaineer. He was then placed in the stocks, and four musketeers stood ready with lighted matches, but the dauntless man bared his bosom, and told them he was willing to die; and they finding him immovable, dismissed him.* Anderson was also obliged to execute those condemned to be hung at Irvine. Uni-

* Some curious interviews took place with Sutherland and one White, a curate, of which he afterwards published an account. The following is a specimen:—"Then came one Mr. White, a curate, to persuade me, who said to me, 'What are you doing? Do you not know that these men are guilty of the sin of rebellion, and rebellion in Scripture is as the sin of witchcraft?' 'I answered, I know the Scripture, it is in 1 Sam. xv. 28. That was Saul's rebellion against the immediate revealed will of God, in sparing Agog and the best of the flocks; and that it was like that rebellion spoken of in the Israelites when they rebelled and refused to go to the land of Canaan, according to God's command, but would have chosen a captain and gone back again to Egypt. He then instanced Shemei, who cursed David and flang earth and stones at him; yet David forgave him, and much more should the king forgive the Galaway men who respect and pray for him, and would not let a hair of his head fall to the ground if he were among them.' 'But,' says Mr. White, 'David was a prophet and a merciful man!' 'Ho!' says I, 'ye will not take a good man for your example, but an ill man; what divinity is that?' At which, the soldiers laughing, he said in his anger, the devil was in me, and that I had to do with a familiar spirit. I said, than he was an unnatural devil, for he was not like the rest of the devils who desire the destruction of many, that he may get many souls, but the spirit that is in me, will not suffer me to take good men's lives; so at that time Mr. White went away as ashamed." *Life and Declaration of William Sutherland*, pp. 4, 5. Wodrow says of this declaration, I am well assured it is genuine, and formed by himself, vol. i. p. 260.

versally detested, he left the country soon after and settled in Ireland, near Dublin, where his cottage was burned, and he perished in the flames. The others were, pursuant to their sentence, hung at Dumfries, whither the Commissioner went to endeavour to trace the conspiracy; but no other discovery was made than that the rising had been accidental, and that oppression had been the cause. Upwards of thirty-four had now been put to death by the hands of the executioner; yet these executions did more harm to the cause of prelacy than almost any other circumstance could have done, for the universal detestation of the people was heightened in proportion to the fortitude and composure of the sufferers, whose dying testimonies possessed a power and energy beyond that of a thousand sermons.

BOOK VI.

JANUARY, A. D. 1667—1669

Dalziel sent to the South and West—His cruelty, and that of the inferior officers—Sir Mungo Murray—Sir William Bannantyne—Arrival of the Dutch fleet—Crusade abates—Forfeitures increase—Standing army proposed—Convention of estates—Cess—King's letter—West country disarmed—Sir Robert Murray sent to Scotland—Army partially disbanded—Political changes—Bond of peace—Trials of Sir James Turner and Sir William Bannantyne—Field-preaching proscribed—Michael Bruce—John Blackader—Attempt upon Sharpe's life—Search for the assassin—Remarkable escape of Maxwell of Monreith—Case of Mr. Robert Gray, merchant—Mrs. Kelso and Mrs. Duncan—Death of Mr. Gillon, minister of Cavers—Field-preaching and family worship punished—Mr. Fullarton of Quivox before the Council—Mr. Blackader patrols his "diocese" untouched safely—Mr. Hamilton, minister of Blantyre.

The army followed fast upon the heels of the justiciary, and the devoted west and south were again subjected to military oppression. Dalziel established his head-quarters at Kilmarnock, and, in a few months, extorted from that impoverished district, the sum of fifty thousand merks, besides what was destroyed by the soldiers in their quarterings through mere wantonness and a love of mischief. Whoever was suspected of favouring Presbyterianism, was apprehended and brought before the General. If he possessed money, the process was short. A private examination was generally terminated by a heavy fine or loathsome imprisonment in a vile dungeon, where men and women were so crowded together, that they could neither sit nor lie, and where decency and humanity were at once violated. An instance of the summary mode in which Dalziel exercised his authority will show, better than any general description, the miseries of military rule. David Findlay at Newmilns, a plain country man, who had accidentally been at Lanark when the Covenanters were there, but had not joined, was brought before him; and, because he either would not, or could not, name any of the rich Whigs who were with the army, he was instantly ordered, without further ceremony, to be shot. When the poor man was carried out to die, neither he nor the lieutenant who was to superintend the execution, could believe that the general was in earnest, but the soldiers told him their orders were positive. He then earnestly entreated only for one night's delay, that he might prepare for eternity; and the officer went to Dalziel to request this short respite, when the ruffian threatened him for his contumacy, and told him that "he would teach him to obey without scruple." In consequence, there was no further delay; Findlay was shot, stripped, and his naked body left upon the spot.

Nor were the inferior officers unworthy of their commander. Sir Mungo Murray having heard that two cottar tenants had lodged for a night two of the men who had escaped from Pentland, bound them together with cords, and then suspending them by their arms from a tree, went to bed, and left them to hang for the night in this torture, which, in all probability, would have finished them before morning, had not some of the soldiers, more merciful than he, relieved them from their painful situation at their own peril. Sir William Bannantyne, in Galloway, caused even the removal of Turner to be regretted. He took possession of Earlston House, which he garrisoned, and thence sent out his parties, who plundered indiscriminately the suspected and those who had given no cause for suspicion, whose only crime was their property. Some, who could not purchase forbearance, they stripped almost naked—then thrust them into the most abominable holes in the garrison, where they were kept till nearly dead, before they were suffered to depart; and one woman, whom they alleged to have been accessory to her husband's escape, they tortured, by burning matches between her fingers with such protracted cruelty, that she fevered, and shortly after died; and so great was the universal consternation produced in these quarters among the conscientious Presbyterians, that such as could get out of the country, fled to foreign parts; and those who remained, lurked during a severe winter, in caves, pits, or remote unfrequented places of the land.

The arrival of a Dutch fleet in the Frith of Forth (April) relieved the afflicted west a little. This squadron, which had threatened Leith, and fired a few shots at Burntisland, occasioned the collecting of the whole troops in Scotland to defend the east, while the success that attended an attack upon the shipping in the Thames, obliged the government to suspend their crusades against the Presbyterian heretics, in order to guard their coasts from foreign insult. At the same time, the exasperation of the English, on account of their national disgrace, enabled the king to get rid of Lord Clarendon, a troublesome minister, whose habits of business, and ideas of economy, ill suited the beloved indolence and unmeaning, and worse than useless, profusion of his master, and whose regard for the decencies of life were opposed to the utter shamelessness of his profligate court.

But though relieved, in some measure, from military execution, the property of the Presbyterians was reached by a more base and cowardly mode of rapine. Heretofore, in cases of treason, the estates of rebels could not be confiscated, as the rebels themselves could not be tried in absence; and so express was the law on this subject that, in a former reign, it was deemed necessary to bring the mouldering bones of a traitor from his grave, and produce them in court, before he could be legally forfeited. The Lord Advocate, however, judged it proper to procure the authority of the court, previously to proceeding in opposition both to the statutes and common practice; and, therefore, proposed to the judges the following query—"Whether or not a person guilty of high-treason might be pursued before the justices, albeit they be absent and contumacious, so that the justices, upon citation and sufficient probation and evidence, might pronounce sentence and doom of forfeiture, if the dittay be proven?" The lords answered in the affirmative, and established a precedent, which was afterwards improved, for forwarding the severe measures of a party already sufficiently disposed to disregard all the ordinary forms of justice. All the gentlemen of property who had gone into exile, were in consequence forfeited, and their estates divided between the rulers and their friends.

Continual dissensions among the Scottish politicians had been the bane of Scotland almost ever since the nation existed. At this period they proved of some small service, by diverting, for a short space, the attention of the persecutors to their own personal affairs. Sharpe, by his duplicity, had incurred the displeasure of the king; and a strong party in the Scottish council, consisting of the military officers and a majority of the prelates, were opposed to Lauderdale, whom they still suspected of being too much attached to his old friends, and envied for enjoying so much of the favour of the king. This party, to secure their ascendancy, proposed to continue and increase the standing army, and to enforce the declaration, under pains of forfeiture, upon all the Presbyterians, fanatics, or Whigs, whom it was necessary to extirpate as incorrigible rebels, whose principles were hostile to all good government, and Lieutenant-General Drummond, with Burnet, archbishop of Glasgow, had been sent to London to procure the king's concurrence.

A convention of estates, held at Edinburgh in the month of January in order to further these objects, voted a cess of sixty-four thousand pounds a month, and, besides, offered to maintain all the forces the king should think proper to raise.* Lauderdale instantly perceived that this would give his enemies an overwhelming power in Scotland, by throwing into their hands the disposal of the forfeitures and the army commissions, and he obtained from the king a letter which, although it authorized very arbitrary proceedings, yet effectually counteracted the scheme of his opponents. It empowered them to tender the oath of allegiance and declaration, and to incarcerate in case of refusal; it authorized disarming the gentlemen in the disaffected shires—seizing all serviceable horses in possession of suspected persons—ordered the militia to be modeled—arms and ammunition to be provided—the legal parish ministers to be protected from violence—and all engaged in the late rebellion, to be criminally pursued without further delay. Proclamations were in consequence issued for again disarming the west and seizing the horses; and no person in future, who did not regularly attend his parish church, was to be allowed to keep a horse above one hundred merks value; but as nothing had been said by his majesty about forfeitures, the declaration was little heard of, and the leading men being changed shortly after, the afflicted country obtained a brief glimpse of repose.

Lest, however, it might be supposed that any relaxation was meant to be shown in supporting prelacy, a letter was transmitted from court, early in May, expressing the royal determination not only to encourage and protect the bishops in the exercise of their callings, and all the orthodox clergy under them, but also to discountenance all, of what quality soever, who should show any disrespect or disaffection to that order or government; and earnestly recommending to those in power, to give the utmost countenance to the orthodox clergy, and to punish

* A convention of estates differed from a parliament, in being convened for one specific purpose, commonly like those for raising money.

severely any affronts put upon them, "to the end," it is added, "that they may be the more endeared to their people, when they see how careful we, and all in authority under us, are of their protection in the due exercise of their calling." The council in consequence issued a proclamation, rendering heritors and parishioners liable for all the damages that might be done to their ministers, which, in the sequel, was most rigorously enforced, although it had certainly little tendency or effect in producing any sentiments of endearment in the breasts of the people towards pastors who required such eminent exertions of royal and magisterial care.

Not long after, Sir Robert Murray, distinguished for his love of science and his moderation of temper, was sent down to Scotland to procure, if possible, an accurate account of the state of the country. He was at this time high in the confidence of Lauderdale, whose interest he assiduously promoted, and whose party he essentially strengthened by the mighty accession of character he brought them. The bishops and their party were extremely anxious to have, above all things, the army continued, and used every method to induce Sir Robert Murray to coincide with them in opinion. Burnet, archbishop of Glasgow, protested that, if the army were disbanded, the gospel would depart out of his diocese; and the Duke of Hamilton said he did not think his life would be secure even in following his sport in the west; when Tweeddale, with many professions of care for his Grace's life, proposed a squadron of the life-guard might be sent to quarter on his premises—a mode of protection with which the Duke did not appear very highly enraptured. But their guardian, Hyde, was in disgrace—an unfavourable peace had terminated an unsuccessful Dutch war—and a show of temporary moderation, at least, was required by the circumstances of the nation. Peremptory orders were therefore sent to Scotland to disband the whole army, except two troops of horse and one (Linlithgow's) regiment of foot guards, which was accordingly done to the great joy of the country, but much to the distress of many idlers who had lately bought their commissions for the purposes of plunder, and considered a captaincy equal to an estate, although numbers, especially of the higher ranks, had their losses more than compensated by their shares of the forfeited estates.

Lauderdale was too good a politician to allow the present humiliation of his opponents to pass unimproved. The indolence and dissipation of Rothes had laid him open to the charges of inattention and neglect of duty during the Dutch visit. He was therefore, as an honourable dismissal, made Lord Chancellor preparatory to losing the Commissionership. The Earl of Tweeddale's eldest son, Lord Yester, having been married to Lauderdale's only daughter and presumptive heiress, his father was named one of the commissioners of the treasury along with Kincardine and Sir Robert Murray, who had also been appointed Lord Justice-Clerk; and his party in the privy council had been still further augmented by the admission of the Earl of Airly, Lord Cochrane, and others. The first trial of strength between the factions, was upon the important question, how the peace of the country was to be secured when the army was disbanded? As the same vile and mischievous system of forcing a hated hierarchy upon the people was determined to be persisted in, the prelates and military were for pressing the declaration according to the king's letter; for although they had now no immediate prospect of touching the money, yet they always had a kind of natural propensity to urge the harshest measures, and those which would promote, rather than appease, the troubles of the land. The Lauderdale party proposed a general pardon and a bond of peace, so moderate in its terms, as that it would be either cheerfully taken, or render those who refused it inexcusable. The contest was long and hotly maintained; and when the council divided, their clerk, Sir Peter Wedderburn, affirmed that the declaration was carried; this,

Sir Robert Murray denied, and the vote was again put, and again the clerk affirmed a majority was for the declaration; Sir Robert still contended that this was not the case, and the Chancellor warmly asking, if he doubted the clerk's fidelity, Sir Robert replied he would trust the evidences of his own senses before any clerk in the world, and insisted that the names should be distinctly called, and the votes accurately marked; when it plainly appeared that a majority was for the bond, which, but for his firmness, by an impudent shameless falsehood would have inevitably been lost.

Pursuant to these resolutions, a pardon was proclaimed; but the exceptions were so numerous, that it was of no avail to any person who possessed either influence or property, and it was remarked that already more than half the number of those who had been at Pentland, were either executed or forfeited; and those who were pardoned, were only the persons whom from their obscurity it would have been impossible to discover, or from their poverty, fruitless to forfeit. The bond was short, and ran thus:—"I, *A. B.*, do bind and oblige me to keep the public peace, and not to rise in arms without the king's authority, and that if I fail I shall pay a year's rent: likewise, that my tenants and men-servants shall keep the public peace; and in case they fail, I oblige myself to pay for every tenant his year's rent, and for every servant his year's fee. And for more security, I am content thir presents be registrate in the books of council." Excepting, perhaps, the hardship of obliging a landlord to bind himself for his tenant and servant, there does not appear, at first sight, any thing objectionable in this obligation. But the government had entirely lost the confidence of the upright Presbyterians, by their uniform endeavours to ensnare their consciences with oaths and obligations, conceived in general terms, to which a double meaning was attached; and which, when any dispute arose, they insisted should always be understood according to the sense the administrators of the oath imposed upon it. Now this bond was constructed in the usual manner, and the expressions—"keep the public peace, and not rising in arms"—were the ambiguous phrases; and numbers refused to sign, unless allowed to explain that by these expressions they were not to be understood as binding themselves to support the prelatical religion, to attend their churches, and desert the preaching of the gospel by their own ministers, or acknowledge the doctrine of passive obedience. Many pamphlets were printed, and much discussion took place upon the subject; but the bond being soon laid aside, the controversy became unimportant, except in so far as succeeding events plainly showed that the objections to the bond were not unmeaning scruples, and that those who refused to sign, acted from a complete knowledge of the persons with whom they were dealing, who would allow of no interpretation inconsistent with entire, implicit, unconditional submission. The proclamation for disarming the west was also in part recalled, and orders issued for restraining the irregularities of such soldiers as were kept in pay—a number of gentlemen who had been imprisoned in 1665 were liberated—and the year closed with the illusive prospect of a deceitful calm.*

[1668.] Great expectations were entertained that some legal protection might be again enjoyed by the harassed Presbyterians, as during last year a commission had arrived from the king to bring Sir James Turner to trial for his tyranny and oppression in the south. But it soon appeared that whatever might have caused the act of justice, it was no sympathy for the sufferings of the "Fanatics." The extortions, harassings, imprisonments, and other charges against

* In December, "Naphtali, or the Wrestlings of the Church of Scotland," written by Sir James Stuart of Goodtrees, and Mr. James Stirling, minister of Paisley, was ordered to be burned by the hands of the hangman, and all who had copies of it after that date to be severely fined—a very foolish but not uncommon mode of publicly confessing that a book is unanswerable. Honeyman, bishop of Orkney, attempted to answer it, which produced an able reply by Sir James—"Jus populi vindicatum."

Sir James, were easily established; but it did not appear that he had either acted without or beyond his instructions, or appropriated much of the spoil for himself, and he was only dismissed the service, while those he had robbed received no compensation. Sir William Bannantyne's trial followed. The accusations against him were more atrocious, torturing and rape being offered to be proved in addition to plunder and rapine. But, perhaps, what was his most indefensible crime, he could not account for the moneys he had received. He was therefore banished and fined in two hundred pounds sterling—a gentle sentence for such conduct.* Little real relief was however afforded to Presbyterians, whose principles would not bend to the times, or to those who, at the risk of reputation, property, liberty, or life itself, refused to abstain from preaching the gospel to their fellow-sinners, or those who would not consent to forsake the worship of God, or leave his ordinances dispensed by his ministers—to attend on a profanation of all sacred service by hirelings who were—scarcely even the disguised—enemies of the cross of Christ. In proportion as lenity was exercised to others, so much the more was hatred evinced towards ministers and those who frequented conventicles.

Hitherto there had been but few field-meetings, yet preaching and exhortation in private houses, barns, and other convenient places, had been very common and well attended; and, from the concurring testimony of all who were accustomed to frequent them, who have left any record, the Spirit of God seems in an eminent manner to have blessed these calumniated, despised, and persecuted assemblies.† In a letter from the king, January 16, which settles the meaning of "the public peace," these meetings, which were peculiarly obnoxious to the bishops and

* He went afterwards to the low country, and was killed by a cannon-ball at the siege of Grave, which drove his heart out of his body—a mode of death he had been accustomed to imprecate upon himself.

† Memoir of Fraser of Brae, p. 126-7.

curates, are thus pointed out to the notice of the council:—"We most especially recommend to you to use all possible means and endeavours for preserving the public peace under our authority, and with special care to countenance and maintain Episcopal government, which in all the kingdom we will most inviolably protect and defend. You must by all means restrain the gatherings of the people to conventicles, which are indeed *rendezvouses of rebellion*, and execute the laws severely against the ringleaders of such faction and schism." The council, with prompt obedience, appointed any of their number to grant warrants for seizing and haling to prison all "outted" ministers and others who should keep unlawful convocations; and the Earl of Linlithgow, commander of the few forces, was directed to distribute them over the country in such manner as might be calculated most easily to dissipate these illicit concerns. A company of foot was, in consequence, ordered to lie at Dumfries; another with fifteen horse, at Strathaven, in Clydesdale; forty troopers at Kilsyth; two companies and fifteen horse at Glasgow; one company at Dalmellington; and a last at Cumnock, in Ayrshire.

To stimulate their exertions, and still further "to endear" his beloved prelates to the lieges, the king, on the 25th July, requires them to rid the kingdom of all seditious preachers or pretended ministers who had kept conventicles or gathered people to the fields since January last; "for we look on such," he adds, "as the great disturbers of the peace and perverters of the people." And the council urged their officers to be upon the alert; even Tweeddale, who was generally supposed friendly to the Presbyterians, or at least moderate, was not less anxious than his associates to prevent or extinguish the light of the gospel which from these conventicles was spreading over the country. In writing to the Earl of Linlithgow, he says—"Your lordship knows the counsel's design reachith furder then to make them peaceable when the rod is over their head, which I believe your lordship will follow as far as possible; for, iff ther be not som of thes turbulent peopel catched, all is in vayn: when they are chassed out of one place, they will flie to another: for God's sake, therefor, endeavour by all means possible to learn wher they haunt and whither they are gon;" and then he advises the commander colonel-commandant to send parties "to catch them wher they can be had, wer it one hundred mils off, especially Mr. Michael Bruce."

Michael Bruce, thus denounced, was of the fami ly of Airth, so highly and deservedly esteemed in the annals of the Reformation, himself, a worthy, useful, and affectionate preacher." He had been driven from Ireland, where he had been settled, and was now zealously and boldly preaching in Stirlingshire to large auditories, generally in houses, but occasionally in the fields, and had "presumed also to baptize and administrate the sacraments without any lawful warrant," he was therefore pursued by the soldiers as a wild beast, and at last surprised, wounded, and taken prisoner. After his wounds would allow of his being moved, he was brought to Edinburgh and sentenced to banishment, but, on his being sent to London, his sentence was altered, and he was ordered to be carried to Tangiers in Africa. He, however, obtained the favour of being permitted to retire secretly to Ireland. Several of the other "outted" ministers were likewise ordered to prison, and some fined for similar misdemeanours; numbers, however, in Fife, in the north, and even in Edinburgh,* laboured with much success, while "Mr. Blackader and his accomplices" were not less assiduous in their visits to the west and in the south. Professions of greater indulgence to the Presbyterian ministers were, notwithstanding these proceedings, held out to them by Tweeddale, who had had interviews and made proposals to several of the most eminent then under hiding, when an unfortunate

* Kirkton, Welsh, Blackader, Donald Cargil, and many others, at this time resided in the capital for months together, and secretly exercised their ministry.

circumstance put an end to all hope of favour for the present.

James Mitchell, a preacher, who had been at Pentland, and was by name exempted from the indemnity, considering Sharpe the prime instigator of all the calamities his country had endured, and was enduring, as well as the author of his own exclusion from pardon, and having heard of his keeping up the king's letter till the last six were executed at Edinburgh, determined to free the land from such a monster, whom he viewed in the light of an enemy whose life he had a right to take in self-defence, as well as in the service of his country.* In pursuance of this resolution, he waited for the primate, July 11th, at the head of Blackfriar's Wynd, where his house was, on purpose to effect it; and having allowed him to be seated in his coach, deliberately walked up and fired at him, but Honeyman, bishop of Orkney, who was in the act of getting up, received the shot, by which his arm was shattered, and Sharpe, for the present, escaped. Mitchell, after firing, walked away coolly, and turning down Niddry's Wynd, went thence to Stevenlaw's Close, shifted his clothes, and returning to the High Street, without being discovered, mixed with the multitude who had collected, but who were giving themselves very little concern about the matter, when they heard that it was only a bishop that had been shot.

Immediately the hue and cry was raised—the city gates were shut—the magistrates were ordered to make strict search after Whigs in the city or suburbs —the constables were called out, and a hundred soldiers sent to assist them. The town being considered a place where those who were proscribed could best conceal themselves, several of this description were then secretly residing there, and had narrow escapes, none of the least remarkable of which was that of Maxwell of Monreith.

Being unacquainted with the town when the search began, he came running to Nicol Moffat, a

* Vide Testimony, Naphtali.

stabler in the Horse Wynd, and begged him to conceal him, for he knew of no shelter. "Alas!" answered Nicol, "there is not a safe corner in my house." But there was an empty meal-barrel that stood at the head of a table in his public room, and he added, if he chose to go in there, he would put something over and cover him. There was no alternative, and in Mr. Maxwell went. Scarcely was he out of sight, when a constable arrived, with a band of soldiers, and demanded if there were any Whigs there? "Ye may look an' see," replied Nicol carelessly, and the constable, deceived by his manner, proceeded no further; but, being thirsty, called for some ale for his party, and they sat down at the table. While drinking, they began talking about their fruitless search, when one said he knew there were many Whigs in town, and he did not doubt but there were some not far distant, to which another answered with an oath, knocking at the same time on the head of the barrel, "there may be one below this;" but they were restrained from lifting the lid; and when they had finished their potations, they went quietly away.

Others were not, however, so fortunate. The servant girl of a Mr. Robert Gray, a merchant in Edinburgh and a godly man, having quarrelled with her mistress, out of revenge went to Sharpe, and told him that there they would find a receptacle of Whigs, and might discover the assassin, on which Mr. Gray was brought before the council. Conjecturing what his servant might have told, he at once informed them that Major Learmont, Mr. Welsh, and a Mrs. Duncan, a minister's widow, had dined with him not long before; but with regard to the assassin he knew nothing. The advocate then going up familiarly, after a short conversation, took the ring off his finger, telling him he had use for it, and dispatched a messenger of his own with it to Mrs. Gray to tell her that her husband had discovered all, and sent this as a token that she might do the same. Deceived by this trick, worthy of the Inquisition, she acquainted them that Mr. Welsh sometimes lodged with Mrs. Kelso, a rich widow, and preached in her house, and also where Mrs. Duncan was to be found. Mrs. Gray and her two female friends were immediately sent to prison, and soon after brought before the council, when Mrs. Kelso was fined five thousand merks and banished to the plantations. Mrs. Duncan also was sentenced to banishment, and only escaped torture by Rothes observing, it was not customary for gentlewomen to wear boots." After a long confinement, the sentence of banishment was relaxed; but Mr. Gray felt so keenly, from having been the innocent cause of so much suffering, that he sickened and died within a few days. Mr. Gillon, the "outted" minister ot Cavers, likewise met his death upon this occasion in a very inhuman manner. He had retired to Currie, a few miles from Edinburgh, for the benefit of his health, where, being apprehended about midnight by two or three rascally soldiers, who pretended to be searching for the bishop's assassin, he was forced, in sport, to run before them a distance of nearly four miles to the West Port, where, after he had arrived, he was kept standing for some hours in the open air before he could obtain admission, and then was sent to lodge in a cold jail. Next day, on being brought before the council, he was recognized and dismissed, but he did not survive the treatment he had received above forty-eight hours. During this year, to compensate for the loss of the regulars, the militia were modelled, properly officered, and prepared for service—a circumstance which, as it was a time of profound peace, might have created some misgivings respecting any alteration in the plans of government.

[1669.] Flattering themselves still with the returning favour of government, the ministers pursued their prohibited labours, and conventicles continued to increase, while the council, impelled on by the repeated injunctions from the king and solicitations of the prelates, not unfrequently forgot their professions of moderation, and proceeded to acts, which might have dispelled the delusion. Conventicles found no mercy. The magistrates of burghs were now made responsible for any that might be held within their bounds; and early this year, the civic rulers of the capital were fined fifty pounds sterling, because "Mr. David Hume, late minister of Coldingham, took upon him to preach in the house of Widow Paton on the last Sunday of February"—a circumstance, it is highly probable, the worthy provost and bailies had never heard of till they were summoned to pay for the exercise. An act of council immediately followed, prohibiting every person from having their children baptized by any other than the Episcopal clergy, under the penalty, to an heritor, of the fourth part of his valued rent—a tenant one hundred pounds Scots and six weeks' imprisonment—and a cottar twenty, and the same. To enforce this decree, the militia were to be employed in seizing the disobedient, and ordered to be supported by them, while on this service, at the rate of one shilling and sixpence sterling each man, and three shillings each officer per day; at the same time, collectors of fines were appointed to take care that the whole penalty was exacted; and among these, it is somewhat ludicrous to observe the Earl of Nithsdale, a papist, required to see a measure faithfully executed, the professed intention of which was, to prevent the growth of popery, then it seems lamentably on the increase—an increase the council had the effrontery to aver, was owing to the frequency of field-preaching.

The archbishop of Glasgow, whose jurisdiction was grievously annoyed by these pests, was peculiarly virulent in his opposition, prevailed upon Lord Cochrane (created Earl of Dundonald next year) to bring before a committee at Ayr, eleven ministers of that district who had been guilty of preaching and baptizing irregularly. Upon examination, the committee were inclined to dismiss them, but his lordship insisted upon their being sent to Edinburgh. There they were examined before a committee of the privy council, and acknowledged that they had allowed others, besides those of their own households, to attend when they worshipped God in their families and expounded the Scriptures, but none of them had been guilty of the enormity of field-preaching, and all promised to demean themselves peaceably, as they had hitherto done, and to give no just ground of offence. Their brethren, who were aware that temporizing would serve little purpose, were dissatisfied that they had not asserted their indefeasible right as ministers of Christ to preach his gospel; and they appear to have been convinced that they had acted too faintly in his cause, for when they were called to receive sentence, Mr. Fullarton, the "outted" minister of St. Quivox, in name of the rest, addressed the Chancellor. After reminding him of the unshaken loyalty which the Presbyterian ministers had displayed towards his majesty in his lowest estate, and the unlooked for return they had met with, he added—"But now seeing we have received our ministry from Jesus Christ, and must one day give an account to our Master how we have performed the same, we dare have no hand in the least to unminister ourselves; yea, the word is like a fire in our bosoms seeking for vent; and seeing, under the force of a command for authority, we have hitherto ceased from the public exercise of our ministry, and are wearied with forbearing, we therefore humbly supplicate your lordship, that you would deal with the king's majesty on our behalf, that at least the indulgence granted to others in our way within his dominions, may be granted to us." Then, after requesting to be delivered from the oppressive tyranny of their collector of the fines, a Mr. Nathaniel Fyfe, whom Kirkton styles "a poor advocate, and alleyed to one of the bishops," he concluded by telling him it would be no matter of regret when he entered eternity and stood before Christ's tribunal, that he had acted as a repairer of breaches in his church. The council was crowded and very attentive, but the ministers were only excused for the time, and straitly charged in future to abstain from similar practices, on pain of being visited not only for any new, but likewise for their old transgressions; and the same day a proclamation was issued, strictly forbidding all conventicles, and rendering all the heritors in the western shires liable to a fine of fifty pounds sterling for every such meeting, on pretence of religious worship, as should be kept in any houses or lands pertaining to them.

How Mr. Blackader escaped, is astonishing, for during this year he seems to have been the most active of all the ministers, as well as the boldest. In the month of January, he preached publicly at Fenwick, and continued labouring in the west, till his over-exertions, more suited to the earnest desires of the people than his bodily strength, produced an illness which confined him for several weeks.* When recovered (June) he went again to his "diocese," round by Borrowstownness, where he established a congregation and secured to them the freedom of undisturbed worship, through the interest of his relation Major Hamilton, who was the Duke's bailie of regality, and lived at Kinniel House. At the request of the Ladies Blantyre, Pollock, and Dundonald, he preached to large auditories, sometimes not fewer than two thousand. In Livingstone, he administered the Sacrament of the Lord's Supper, and the example was followed in fifteen or sixteen adjacent parishes. The preaching of the gospel and dispensation of the ordinances were attended with such blessed effects, that it was no wonder the enemy raged. Upon a humiliation day, in the muir of Livingstone, the four ministers who were to preach called aside several of the gravest and most sagacious men of the bounds, and inquired at them what were the most reprovable sins they observed as necessary to be confessed unto God in these bounds, and where-

* "Money frequently was offered him for bearing accidental expenses. Several gentlemen contributed sums, and collections were made on purpose, but he uniformly declined receiving any donation, 'lest his ministry might bear the imputation of a covetous and mercenary spirit, or the enemy have occasion to reproach their cause as if money made them eager to preach.' "—*Crichton's Mem. of Blackader*, p. 148.

of the people were to be admonished that they might the better know how to carry on the following work of the day; the men, after a deliberate pause, answered, as to public scandals and every kind of profanity, they could not say much, for they had not heard of any outbreakings of fornication, adultery, or drunkenness, scarce these seven years past, in that parish or in several parishes about, since the public preaching of the gospel had broke up among them.

About the same time, Mr. Hamilton, the "outted" minister of Blantyre, was apprehended and sent to Edinburgh to answer to the council for holding a conventicle in his own house in Glasgow. Being asked how many hearers were in use to attend his meeting, he archly answered, that for these several years past the poor ministers of Christ who were forced from their flocks, could with difficulty support themselves and families, and could neither hire palaces nor castles. They might then easily judge what kind of houses they were able to rent, and whether they could hold large companies. His reply to whether others than his family were present, was equally pointed—"My lords, I have neither halberts nor guards to keep any out." One of the members who thought his sarcasms bore hard on the archbishop, reminded him of the favour he had got from his lordship, in being permitted to remain so long in Glasgow. "Not so much," retorted the prisoner, "as Paul got from a heathen persecuting Emperor, for he dwelt two whole years in his own hired house, and received all that came in unto him, preaching the kingdom of God, and teaching those things that concern the Lord Jesus Christ with all confidence, no man forbidding him; but both the honest people of Glasgow and myself have been often threatened with violence if we did not forbear." Finding themselves no match at this species of interrogation, the council demanded if he was willing to give bond to preach no more in that way. He replied, he had got his commission from Christ, and would not voluntarily restrict himself, whatever he might be forced to do. "An' where got you that commission?" asked the Chancellor. "In Matthew 28th chapter and 19th verse, Go teach and baptize." "That is the apostles' commission," rejoined Rothes; "an' do you set up for an apostle?" "No, my lord," said Mr. Hamilton, "nor for any extraordinary person either; but that place contains the commission of ordinary ministers as well as of extraordinary ambassadors." When again asked, if he would give assurance that he would neither preach nor exercise worship any where but in his own house, he repeated his refusal, and was sent to prison, where he lay till his health became so much impaired that his brother, Sir Robert Hamilton of Silvertoun Hill, made interest and got him released, he giving bond of a thousand merks to compear when called.

BOOK VII

JULY, A. D. 1669—1670.

An indulgence proposed—Partially accepted by the ministers—Mr. Hutchison's address—Proclamation against those who refused it —Archbishop of Glasgow's remonstrance—Parliament assert the king's supremacy—Vote the militia, and a security for orthodox ministers—Field-meeting in Fife—Difference between Presbyterians and prelatists in doctrine and teaching—Curates disturbed —Lecturing forbid—Compromising ministers—Success of the gospel—Remarkable meetings at the Hill of Bath, &c.—Rage of the Primate—Strange escape of four prisoners.

A STATE of things so incongruous could not long exist. An immense majority of the population, including almost all who had any pretensions to religion, were decidedly inimical to the Episcopalian mode of worship. The churches of the curates were deserted, and themselves despised, while the exercises of the Presbyterian ministers were attended by crowds. Harsh methods had been used, and had but exasperated the evil. It was, therefore, now proposed to try what more lenient measures would produce, and an insidious indulgence was resorted to, by which it was hoped that the "fanatics" might be divided among themselves, or cheated into compliance with a modified Episcopacy. Accordingly, Tweeddale having privately consulted with Messrs. Robert Douglas and John Stirling, late ministers of Edinburgh, prevailed with them to draw up a letter or petition, which he carried with him to London,*

* Burnet claims this service for a letter of his own. "I being there (summer 1669) at Hamilton, and having got the best information of the state of the country that I could, with a long account of all I had heard, to the Lord Tweeddale, and concluded it with

where a similar system of cozenage was carrying on by Charles himself with the non-conformists, and easily obtained from the king a letter of indulgence. By it the council were authorized to appoint so many of the ministers ejected by the Glasgow act, 1662, as had lived peaceably, to return to their former charges, if unfilled up, and to allow patrons to present to other vacant parishes such as they should approve. Those of them who should take collocation from the bishop, and keep presbyteries and synods, to be entitled to their full stipends; those who would not take collocation to have only the glebe, manse, and a moderate allowance; and such as refused to attend the presbyteries and synods, to be confined within the bounds of their parishes. But none were to admit as hearers in their congregations, nor as participators of the ordinances, any persons from the neighbouring parishes, without the consent of their own parson. The ministers not thus provided for, were to be allowed, out of the stipends of the vacant churches, an annual pension of four hundred merks, so long as they continued to behave themselves peaceably. This indulgence limited as it was, was by no means acceptable to the prelate's party. The counsellors long contested it at the board, and the bishops, with some of "the orthodox clergy," had private meetings to oppose it; but Sharpe, who understood the subject better, is said to have advised to make no objections to its publication, but to throw every obstacle in the way of its success, by clogging it in every possible manner with requirements, to which he knew the Presbyterians could not consistently submit—a line of conduct which his party followed, and which ultimately gained its object.

an advice to put some of the more moderate of the Presbyterians into the vacant churches, Sir Robert Murray told me the letter was so well liked that it was read to the king. Such a letter would have signified nothing if Lord Tweeddale had not been fixed in the same notion. So my principles and zeal for the church, and I know not what besides, were raised to make my advice signify somewhat."—*Hist.* vol. i. p. 413.

Meanwhile, it was referred to a committee, composed of the two archbishops, the Duke of Hamilton, the Earls of Argyle, Tweeddale, Kincardine, and Dundonald, with the officers of the Crown, and the Lord of Lee, to carry his majesty's pleasure into effect, and on the 27th July, ten ministers were nominated to various places.

At first the treacherous boon was not perceived by many excellent "outted" ministers in its naked deformity. They thought that it opened for them a door to preach the gospel, of which they were anxious to avail themselves, and imagined that by explicitly avowing their sentiments when they accepted their appointments, they would exonerate their consciences and satisfy their brethren. Accordingly, when these ten were brought before the council, and received their allotments, accompanied with injunctions, Mr. George Hutchison, late one of the ministers of Edinburgh, transported to Irvine, thus spoke:—"My lords, I am desired in the name of my brethren present, to acknowledge in all humility and thankfulness, his majesty's royal favour, in granting us liberty and the public exercise of our ministry, after so long a restraint, and to return thanks to your lordships for having been pleased to make us, the unworthiest of many of our brethren, so early partakers of the same. We having received our ministry from Jesus Christ, with full prescriptions from him for regulating us therein, must, in the discharge thereof, be accountable to him; and as there can be nothing more desirable or refreshing to us upon earth, than to have free liberty of the exercise of our ministry, under the protection of lawful authority—the excellent ordinance of God, and to us most dear and precious—so we purpose and resolve to behave ourselves, in the discharge of the ministry, with that wisdom and prudence which becomes faithful ministers of Jesus Christ, and to demean ourselves towards lawful authority—notwithstanding of our own judgment in church affairs—as well becomes loyal subjects, and that from a principle of conscience. And now, my lords, our prayer to God is, that the Lord may bless his majesty in his person and government, and your lordships in your public administrations; and especially, in pursuance of his majesty's mind, testified in his letter, wherein his singular moderation eminently appears, that others of our brethren may in due time be made sharers of the liberty, that, through his majesty's favour, we now enjoy."

Mr. Hutchison's address neither pleased the council nor satisfied his brethren. The latter thought it did not assert with sufficient plainness the sole kingship of Christ in his church, nor bear an honest enough testimony against the usurpation of Charles and his council. The rest, who were selected for a similar favour, had therefore resolved to be more downright, but they were never allowed an opportunity. The council, who wished to hear no more upon the subject, sent their appointments to them. The whole number under the first indulgence amounted to forty-three. They were willingly received by the people, and as they abstained from controversial subjects and confined themselves to the pure doctrines of the gospel, it was remarked that they were eminently countenanced of the Lord in their labours.

As had, however, always been anticipated by the more unbending part of the ministry, this partial relaxation to a few was accompanied by harsher measures against the rest, especially those who, choosing to obey God rather than man, could not in conscience comply with the mandates of those rulers, and desist from declaring the glad tidings of salvation as He, in his providence, gave them opportunity. A fresh proclamation was issued, (August 3,) commanding all heritors to delate to the next magistrates, any who, within their bounds, should take upon them to preach and carry on worship in any unwarrantable meetings, that they might be thrown into prison—the magistrates of burghs were required to detain them till further orders—and the lieges were likewise informed, that the laws would be rigidly put in execution against all withdrawers from public worship in their respective congregations. These, however, were only preparatory to severer parliamentary enactments, which confirmed the worst suspicions of those who uniformly distrusted the equivocal toleration of their rulers, and justified their refusal to come to any compromise as a matter of sound policy, even had it not been a point of conscience. In the interim, the prelates pursued their own measures, to render abortive the provision intended for the unindulged, but quiet, part of the brethren. They procured that the act of parliament which allotted all vacant stipends, since 1664, to the support of the universities, should be examined into; nor does it appear that any one of the sufferers ever received a farthing from that fund. Mr. John Park, one of the ten, late minister of Stranraer, was reponed to his own parish, but the bishop of Galloway, three days after the council's nomination, admitted one Nasmith to the charge; and notwithstanding, or perhaps rather because the people were unanimous in favour of their late pastor, the council rather chose to submit to the insult done their authority, than disoblige the prelate, and confirmed the intruder in his office.

A project of an union between the two kingdoms was the ostensible reason for assembling the Scottish parliament after six years' interval. The project came to nothing; but, in the meanwhile, it subserved the ambition of Lauderdale, who was appointed Commissioner. The elections went entirely in favour of his party, and he was received in Scotland with little less pomp than if he had been the sovereign, for his opponents were eager to deprecate his anger; and the Presbyterians, the dupes of their own wishes, fondly believed that he was still in heart with them, though he had been forced by circumstances to act otherwise, in which they were the more confirmed by an incident that occurred two days before the parliament sat down, which yet was only a political fracas. Burnet, archbishop of Glasgow, who was one of the stoutest assertors of the king's absolute supremacy, when it overturned Presbyterianism and settled Episcopacy, was by no means so clear about his majesty's right to set aside the laws when he trenched upon the functions of the bishops, and granted relief to the persecuted ministers. He, therefore, in the Episcopal synod of Glasgow, caused, or allowed, a remonstrance to be drawn up against the indulgence, representing it as an illegal stretch of power, and likely to be destructive to the church. Unfortunately for the right reverend father, he stood opposed both to Lauderdale and Sharpe, and the affair being brought before the council, his lordship was ordered to produce the paper, which was forwarded to the king; and James Ramsay, dean of Glasgow, and Arthur Ross, parson, who had drawn it up, were severely reprimanded—the paper suppressed—and "all his majesty's lieges, of what function or quality soever, discharged from countenancing or owning the same." Lauderdale did not, however, long allow the Presbyterians to remain in doubt as to his real sentiments. In his speech to parliament, which met on the 19th, he assured them of the king's unalterable determination to support Episcopacy—avowed his own attachment to it—and inveighed against conventicles, whose entire suppression he urged, as his majesty having granted an indulgence, would never now consent to tolerate them.

The parliament, like their predecessors, showed every inclination to comply with whatever was required; and in their first act asserted and declared, that his majesty had the supreme authority and supremacy over all persons and in all causes ecclesiastical within the kingdom, and that the ordering and disposal of the external government and policy of the church did properly belong to the king and his successors, as an inherent right of the crown, who might emit such orders concerning the external government of the church—the persons employed in it—their meetings, and the subjects to be discussed there, as in their royal wisdom they should think fit, which, when entered in the books of council and duly published, were to be obeyed by all his majesty's subjects, any law, act, or custom, to the contrary notwithstanding. Even the bishops themselves were not greatly delighted with this act, and such of the nobility as retained any lingering respect for the religious liberties of their country, were only induced to support it by the representations of Lauderdale, that it was necessary to have some check upon the bishops, whose insolence was intolerable; but the consistent Presbyterians saw in it nothing but the assumption of an anti-christian power, which no magistrate on earth had any right to possess, and it afforded to them another and a stronger objection than they previously had, to accepting any indulgence from the king. The conduct of the council in embodying the militia, and thus, under another name, establishing a standing army in Scotland, was next approved of by an *ex post facto* act, empowering his majesty to do what had been already done, and declaring this also an inherent right of the crown. Then followed an act for the security of the persons of the orthodox ministers.

It seems three women, or men in womens' clothes, most probably the former, had, during the summer, on one night about nine or ten o'clock, come into the house of John Row, curate of Balmaclellan, in Galloway—who afterwards turned a papist—and taking him out of his "naked bed," had inflicted upon his carcass a very irreverent flagellation, after which, it is said, they opened his trunk and took away what they had a mind; for this, the heritors of the parish were fined one thousand two hundred pounds Scots. Mr. Lyon, curate at Orr, was searched for, but missed; and, it was reported, his house was spoiled; for which his parishioners were assessed in the sum of six hundred merks. These sums having been levied by order of the privy council, this act was procured to legitimate all similar exaction in future, and, like almost every other enactment of this period, added a new link to the chain of despotism. The forfeitures inflicted by the Court of

Justiciary were, in like manner, legalized by an act of this congregation of sycophants, whose session ended on the 23d of December.

Towards the close of the year, the first field meeting was held in Fife. Mr. John Blackader having gone to visit his two friends, Sir James Stewart and Sir John Chiesly, who were then imprisoned in Dundee, Lady Balcanquhal invited him to preach in her house—the only species of conventicle yet known in that district; but he fearlessly caused public advertisement to be made, that all that were athirst might come without money and without price. "Let all the world," said he, "see that you do not huddle up so profitable and honest a work, or keep it to yourselves; for my part, I am not ashamed to avow, in the face of danger or death, I came not to call the righteous, but sinners to repentance." A multitude in consequence assembled, too numerous for the house to contain, and they betook themselves to the fields. Many were much affected; and some, who were present, when asked, what they thought of the work, answered with tears, that they had never seen such a day, and were eager to know when such an opportunity might occur again.

[1670.] Under whatever figure of speech it might be disguised, it was now no longer a matter of doubt what was the dispute between the Presbyterians and the Episcopalians. It was not a mere form of church government—it was not a question about obedience to lawful rulers. It was a contest between light and darkness—it was, whether the gospel of the grace of God was to be freely preached to the poor inhabitants of Scotland, or was not. Historians, or men styling themselves historians, in overlooking this circumstance, either do not understand or wilfully avert their eyes from the fundamental cause of the persecution, from this date till Bothwell Bridge, when it again became mingled with political matters. Had there been any doubt upon the subject, the proceedings of the privy council and of parliament this year, would have sufficiently cleared it.

Mr. Andrew Boyd, minister of Carmunnock, was, in the month of January, committed to close confinement in Stirling Castle, for having preached to, and met, for the purpose of worshipping God, with his former parishioners. Nor would his defence be listened to, although he pled the necessity of preaching the gospel when ignorance and profanity so much abounded, and so many souls were perishing for lack of knowledge. The ministers of Newbattle, Strathaven, and Symington, were similarly treated, although they appear only to have followed the apostolic practice, and "ceased not in every house to teach and preach Jesus Christ." Some fines were at the same time levied upon those who attended. One lady (Helderston) was fined four hundred merks for having had a conventicle in her house in Edinburgh—a merchant, for having had his child baptized, was mulcted in two hundred—and four citizens, for being present, paid each one hundred pounds—although, as a venerable minister observed before the council, there was as yet no law of Scotland forbidding the worship of God, which was the only crime laid to their charge.

While the "outted" ministers were forbid to exercise their ministry in any shape, those who were indulged soon began to experience that their liberty was by no means perfect freedom. The first link that was added to their chain, was a prohibition from explaining the Scriptures to their people in the manner they thought best fitted to convey instruction. It is evident that, in stated congregations, an exposition of connected passages of Scripture, or what is generally known in Scotland as "lecturing,"* is eminently calculated to improve and edify the church; and this had been an old method employed by the most distinguished and successful of the Presbyterian ministers. The indulged continued the practice; but for this the uneducated and worth-

* There is not a more delightful example of this mode of teaching than Leighton's exposition of the First Epistle of Peter.

less crew who had been thrust into their charges were totally unfit, and their pulpit exhibitions only encountered the scorn of their hearers—sometimes perhaps too rudely expressed.

Complaints were therefore made to the privy council, and their superior ability and mode of teaching were imputed as crimes to the indulged, whose favour with the people, by the same reasoning, was considered the cause of their hatred to the curates. They were in consequence forbid to lecture, and a commission was granted to the Duke of Hamilton, the Earls of Linlithgow, Dumfries, Kincardine, and Dundonald, the Lord Clerk Register, and Lieutenant-General Drummond, or any four of them, to "put to due and rigorous execution the acts of parliament and councils" respecting "pretended" religious meetings, the security of the orthodox clergy, and to examine into the conduct of the indulged ministers. The charges of outrage brought forward by the legal incumbents against their parishioners, were in some cases villanously false, and in others ridiculously exaggerated. One Jeffray, curate of Maybole, accused the Whigs of having attempted to shoot him, and produced a volume contused by a ball, which he said had saved his life, having been in his bosom when he was fired at; but, upon examination, it was found that the clothes he wore at the time were untouched, the blockhead having forgot to perforate his garments when he wounded his book. This precious evangelist was, in consequence, dismissed; but when there happened to be any ground for complaint, the case was remitted to Edinburgh, and the punishment was extravagant. Some idle boys had thrown a bit of rotten wood at the curate of Kilmacomb while he was holding forth; and when he left the pulpit in terror, they followed the fugitive, huzzaing and shouting, till he reached the manse. For this boyish insolence, which probably merited a whipping, four of the offenders were sentenced to be transported to the plantations! and the heritors of the parish were fined one hundred pounds sterling, which Mr. John

Irvine, the said curate, received as a solatium. The parson of Glasford's house was robbed by common thieves, one of whom being afterwards executed for another crime, confessed the fact. The Whigs, however, were accused, and the parish paid one thousand pounds Scots for having maltreated a man they had only despised.

These instances may serve to show the spirit of the times which all our historians agree in representing as mild and moderate, and certainly the managers were so, in comparison of those who succeeded them. The indulged ministers were examined by the commissioners as to whether they had desisted from lecturing; but the equivocal shifts to which they had recourse, exposed them to the animadversions of their stricter brethren, and did not exalt their characters with the prelatical party. Some read a whole chapter, naming one verse only as a text. Others read two chapters, and offered a few observations; and in this part of the service they, in general, never exceeded the length of half an hour, which seems to have been a redeeming qualification, for the visiting committee neither silenced nor removed any of them. They contrived also to celebrate the 29th of May in a manner equally illusive, by contriving to have a baptism, a diet of catechizing, or their week-day sermon, upon that anniversary day; but the jealousy of the people was kept alive by the exiled ministers. Mr. John Brown, late minister of Wamphray, and Mr. John Livingston, both wrote, condemning such duplicity in practice, and exposing its danger, thoug at the same time they expressed themselves affectionately with respect to their brethren, the men whose conduct they condemned. Nor did the visiting committee fulfil the expectation of their employers. Gilbert Burnet, afterwards bishop of Sarum, was at this period professor of divinity in the University of Glasgow; and as he was respectable both for his talents and conduct—moderate in his principles regarding church government, and a friend to toleration, the commission were considerably influenced by his advice, which, from his first outset in life, was uniformly opposed to all persecution; and also by that of the amiable Leighton, who with much reluctance had been prevailed upon to hold the archbishopric of Glasgow, *in commendam*, upon the resignation of Alexander Burnet, whose conduct in the remonstrance being offensive to his majesty, had rendered it requisite for him to demit. They therefore, though they imprisoned and harassed a number of the Presbyterians for not attending the church, and for attending conventicles, yet, because they did not execute in their full rigour the instructions and proclamations of the privy council, were reckoned unfriendly to the cause of Episcopacy.

A great desire to hear continued to increase and to prevail during this period; and these servants of Christ—who could not consent that the word of God should be bound, followed by vast multitudes, when they could not find accommodation within any common house—imitating the example of their Lord, chose the field for their cathedral, and, with the heavens for their canopy, and the mountain side for their benches, preached boldly the gospel of salvation. The most remarkable assemblage of this kind which had yet occurred, was that held, 18th June, on the Hill of Beath, near Dunfermline, of which one of the presiding ministers has left an account, and which I insert in his own language. They could not now, however, be held with the same security as formerly, for the council had offered a reward to the soldiery for dispersing these meetings and apprehending the minister, or such as could give information concerning him, with the most considerable heritors and tenants, who were all rendered liable to imprisonment and fine. It was therefore necessary to appoint watches and take precautions for their personal security; and as people of that rank generally went armed, they did not lay their arms aside when their attendance on gospel ordinances was threatened to be interrupted by violence. Upon this occasion, Burnet says, as a matter of course, "many of these came in their ordinary arms, that gave a handle to call them rendezvouses of rebellion," vol. i. p. 430. Though the spot was not distinctly marked out, it was, during the preceding week, pretty generally understood, and a vast congregation gathered from almost every quarter of the country.

"On Saturday afternoon," says the narrator, "people had begun to assemble. Many lay on the hill all night; some stayed about a constable's house, near the middle of the hill; several others were lodged near about, among whom was Barscob and nine or ten Galloway men. The minister, Mr. Blackader, came privately from Edinburgh on the Saturday night, with a single gentleman in his company. At Inverkeithing, he slept all night in his clothes, and got up very early expecting word where the place of meeting was to be, which the other minister (Mr. John Dickson) was to advertise him of. However, he got no information, and so set forward in uncertainty. Near the hill, he met one sent by the minister to conduct him to a house hard by, where he resolved, with the advice of the people, to go up the hill for the more security and the better seeing about them. When they came, they found the people gathered and gathering, and lighting at the constable's house, who seemed to make them welcome. While they were in the house, a gentleman was espied coming to the constable's door and talking friendly with him, who went away down the hill. This gave occasion of new suspicion and to be more on their guard. However, they resolved to proceed to the work, and commit the event to the Lord.

"When a fit place for the meeting and setting up of the tent was provided—which the constable concurred in—Mr. Dickson lectured and preached the forenoon of the day. Mr. Blackader lay at the outside within hearing, having care to order matters and see how the watch was kept. In time of lecture he perceived fellows driving the people's horses down the brae, which he supposed was a design to carry them away. He rising quietly from his place, asked them what they meant? They answered, it was to drive them to better grass. However, he caused them bring them all back again within sight. After Mr. Dickson had lectured for a considerable space, he took to his discourse, and preached on 1 Cor. xv. 25. 'For he must reign till he hath put all his enemies under his feet.' In time of service, some ill-affected country people dropped in among them, which being observed by Mr. Blackader and those appointed to watch, he resolved to suffer all to come and hear, but intended to hinder the going away of any with as little noise as might be. Among others came two youths, the curate's sons, and about fourteen or fifteen fellows at their back, who looked sturdily; but after they heard, they looked more soberly. The two young men were heard to say they would go near the tent and walk about to the backside of it, which some who were appointed to watch seeing, followed quickly, so they halted on their way. The man that came to the constable's house in the morning was seen at the meeting, and kept a special eye upon; essaying to go away to his horse at the constable's, two able men of the watch went after, and asked why he went away? He answered, he was but going to take a drink. They told him they would go with him, and desired him to haste and not hinder them from the rest of the preaching; so he came back; but he was intending to go and inform the lieutenant of the militia who was at the foot of the hill and gathering his men. However the sermon closed without disturbance, about eleven hours in the foreday, the work having begun about eight.

"Mr. Blackader was to preach in the afternoon. He retired to be private for a little meditation. Hearing a noise, he observed some bringing back the curate's two sons with some violence, which he seeing, rebuked them who were leading them, and bade let them come back freely without hurt; and he engaged for them they would not go away; so they staid quietly, and within a quarter of an hour he returned and entered into the tent. After some preface, which was countenanced with much influence, not only on professed friends, but on those also who came with ill intentions, so that they stood as men astonished with great seeming gravity and attention, particularly the two young men; it was indeed a composing and gaining discourse, holding forth the great design of the gospel to invite and make welcome all sorts of sinners without exception. After prayer, he read for text, 1 Cor. ix. 16. 'For though I preach the gospel, I have nothing to glory of, for necessity is laid upon me; yea, wo is unto me if I preach not the gospel.'

"After he had begun, a gentleman on horseback came to the meeting and some few with him. He was the lieutenant of the militia on that part of the country, who lighting, gave his horse to hold, and came in among the people on the minister's left hand, stood there a space, and heard peaceably. Then essaying to get to his horse, some of the watch did greatly desire he would stay till the preaching was ended, telling him his abrupt departure would offend and alarm the people. But he refusing to stay, began to threaten, drawing his staff. They fearing he was going to bring a party to trouble them, did grip and hold him by force as he was putting his foot in the stirrup. Upon this Barscob and another young man, who were on the opposite side, seeing him drawing his staff, which they thought to be a sword, presently ran each with a bent pistol, crying out—'Rogue, are you drawing?' Though they raised a little commotion on that side, yet the bulk of the people were very composed. The minister seeing Barscob and the other so hastening to be at him, fearing they should have killed him, did immediately break off to step aside for composing the business, and desired the people to sit still till he returned, for he was going to prevent mischief. Some not willing he should venture himself, laboured to hinder him. He thrust himself from them, and pressing forward, cried—'I charge and obtest you not to meddle with him or do him any hurt,' which had such influence on them, that they professed afterwards they had no more power to meddle with him. The lieutenant seeing it was like to draw to good earnest, was exceeding afraid and all the men he had; but hearing the minister discharging the people to hurt him, he thrust near to be at the minister who had cried—'What is the matter, gentlemen?' Whereon the lieutenant said, 'I cannot get leave, sir, to stand on my own ground for thir men.' The minister said, 'Let me see, sir, who will offer to wrong you; they shall as soon wrong myself; for we came here to offer violence to no man, but to preach the gospel of peace; and, sir, if you be pleased to stay in peace, you shall be as welcome as any here; but if you will not, you may go, we shall compel no man.' 'But,' said he, 'they have taken my horse from me.' Then the minister called to restore his horse, seeing he would not stay willingly. Then he was dismissed without harm at the minister's entreaty, who judged it most convenient that the gentlemen and others to whom he should report it, might have more occasion of conviction that both ministers and people who used to meet at such meetings, were peaceable, not set on revenge, but only endeavouring to keep up the free preaching of the gospel in purity and power, in as harmless and inoffensive a way as was possible. Some of the company, indeed, would have compelled and bound him to stay if he had not been peaceable; but they were convinced afterwards that it was better to let him go in peace. The whole time of this alarm on that quarter, all the rest of the people sat still composedly—which was observed more than ordinary in any meeting either before or after—seeing such a stir. As in many other things the mighty power and hand of the Lord was to be seen in that day's work, and the fruit that followed thereon.

"When the lieutenant was gone, the rest that dropped in through the day, with the curate's two sons, stayed still, not offering to follow. After the composing that stir, which lasted about half an hour, the minister returned to the tent, and followed out the rest of his work, preaching about three quarters of an hour with singular countenance, especially after composing the tumult. All the time there were several horse riding hither and thither on the foot of the hill, in view of the people, but none offered to come near; for a terror had seized on them, as was heard afterwards and confessed by some of themselves. The minister, apprehending the people might be alarmed with fear, that they could not hear with composure—though none did appear—did for their cause close sooner than he intended, though the people professed afterwards, and said they would rather he had continued longer, for they found none either wearied or afraid.

"The minister that preached in the afternoon, with about sixteen or twenty of the ablest men, went to to the constable's house, where they had prepared dinner, and would have him and his company come in to dine; but he calling for a little drink and bread on horseback, the rest also taking something without doors, and missing the other minister, feared lest some of the enemy in dismissing had apprehended him. So, leaving the rest at the house, he rode up the hill again, with some others who were on horseback, to seek him; for he said he would not go without the other minister, but resolved to cause rescue him if he had been taken; and coming to the place where the meeting had been, some of the people told him the minister had taken horse with another gentleman a little before the close; upon which he returned again to the company at the house, who desired him to ride away, they being on foot. He told them he would stay, and also desired them to stay, till they should see all the people get safe from the hill; and when all were peaceably dismissed, he with another on horseback, rode to the Queensferry. The rest being able men and on foot, were to follow. When he came thither, none of the boats would go over at that time, the country being ill set and in such a stir. It was not thought fit he should stay on that side of the water, therefore he rode up three or four miles, expecting to get boat at Limekilns; but that being gone over with others at the meeting before, he rode forward towards Kingcairn, where they again essayed at Hoggin's-neuk; but the boat being on the other side, they were forced to ride on towards Stirling. He came thither about nine at night; and after they had crossed the bridge, and rode through some back lanes of the town, they came at the port they should go out at, but it was shut, only a wicket open, through which they led their horses, and so escaped the alarm which arose in the town a little after they were gone. They rode that night about four miles to Torwoodside, where they lighted at an honest man's house, took a little refreshment for man and horse, till break of day, and then rode for Edinburgh. They went hard by the gate of the place of Callander, where the Chancellor and other noblemen were at the time, they not knowing till afterwards. They rode also by the back of the town of Linlithgow, where many ill set people were. About seven o'clock on Monday morning, he came to Edinburgh, where the noise was come before; therefore he retired to another chamber, and, after taking breakfast, he lay down and slept six hours' space, being much wearied, having not cast off his clothes and ridden forty-eight miles from Sabbath about twelve o'clock. The gentlemen and the rest whom he left on the hill, came over at the Ferry, and returned to Edinburgh in safety that night."

Reports of this meeting quickly spread to the remotest corner of the land; and the evident tokens of the divine presence which had accompanied the exercises of the day, stirred up a holy emulation in the other ministers, who thanked God and took courage, and excited and kept alive among the people an attention to the concerns of their souls, which too often languishes in the days of ease and amid the undisturbed enjoyment of gospel privileges, while to many the word came in the demonstration of the Spirit and with power; so that even some who were unfriendly to these irregular proceedings, were constrained to ac knowledge that in their sermons, in houses and fields, the "outted" ministers were remarkably countenanced of the Lord and blessed with many seals of their ministry, in the conversion of many, and edifying those who were brought in. It was followed in about a fortnight by another not less numerous at Livingseat, in West Calder, where Mr. John Welsh presided; and, in the beginning of July, a large conventicle was held at Torwood-head, for which a Mr. Charles Campbell, in Airth, was imprisoned and fined; but who was the minister on this occasion, I have not learned. Grievous was the rage of the prelates; but the invasion of the primate's more immediate territories behoved to be visited with signal vengeance, as a horrid insult had been offered so near the place where he had his seat. The two ministers were denounced and put to the horn—"multitudes" were imprisoned, fined in large sums, and otherwise harassed—James Dundas, the brother of the Laird of Dundas, was sentenced to transportation, under pain of death if he returned—and others, equally respectable, were brought to no little trouble, although but few were actually sent to the plantations.

The case of "four Borrowstownness-men," is too remarkable to be passed over. Their names were, John Sloss, a residenter in the town; David Mather, elder in Bridgeness; John Ranken, in Bonhard; and James Duncan, in Grange. These having been apprehended, were brought before the council, and refusing to give any information, or turn informers against their brethren, were fined each five hundred merks, and sent back to prison to remain during the council's pleasure. They were afterwards brought before the council, and, along with other six, condemned upon an *ex post facto* statute to be sent as slaves to the plantations; and when one of them only entreated to be allowed to take farewell of his wife and small family, Lauderdale furiously replied—"You shall never see your home more," adding, with a malignant sneer, "this will be a testimony for the cause."

In this, however, he proved a false prophet. Mr. Blackader tells us, the four got their liberty, which fell out by a singular cast of providence. The guard that conducted them from the Canongate jail brought them to the outer council-house, and leaving them there with the guards who waited on their neighbours from the high town tolbooth; and thinking themselves exonered, they went their way, expecting that the guard that waited on the prisoners from the town tolbooth would notice them. After they had gotten their sentence, command was given to carry the whole to their respective prisons; upon which those who guarded the prisoners of the town carried them to the tolbooth, the rest were left without a guard. Notwithstanding, at the dismissing of the council, and the throng of people, they went on, supposing their guard to be following. One of them never knowing, went the whole length, and entered the prison again. Other two went the length of the Cross, till a friend came and asked, whither they were going? They said, "to their prison." He said, "Will you prison yourselves, seeing there is none waiting to take you to it?" which they perceiving, made their escape. Other two went the length of the Netherbow, then looking behind, and seeing none guarding them, made their escape also. The other five, together with him who went back inadvertently, were afterwards, through the interest of the Chancellor's secretary, and perhaps owing to the ludicrous appearance the council cut by the escape of the four, also granted their liberty.* A pious youth, who was at the Beath Hill and Livingseat, was committed close prisoner, ordered to be put in irons, and fed on bread and water during pleasure; and although great interest was made for him, he obtained no release, till the iron had gangrened his legs, which eventually, according to Kirkton, cost him his life.

Previous to the meeting of parliament, Lauderdale, wishing to ingratiate himself with the prelatic party, urged on the persecution of the non-conform

* Blackader's Mem. MSS. quoted in his life.

ist Presbyterians. They had in the beginning of the year been banished the capital. Immediately upon his arrival, he issued a proclamation forbidding any of them to come to Edinburgh without a license, upon pain of death; but summonses were issued to the most zealous who had been guilty of preaching, requiring them to appear before the council. The latter came privately to town, to ascertain the temper of their rulers and their own probable fate, when finding that imprisonment or exile would be the consequence of their attending, they resolved to decline. Before separating they drew up an affecting letter to their brethren, bemoaning the desolations of Zion and the rod of wickedness lying upon the lot of the righteous, but chiefly lamenting the little kindliness and melting of heart among professors—their little sympathy with the Lord's dear servants and people, now bearing the heat and burden of the day, made wanderers and chased from mountain to hill, not having where to lay their head—and the readiness of some rather to censure than partake of affliction with those who were suffering for the sake of the gospel;—beseeching them to stir up that great mean and duty—all that seemed left to them—of serious prayer, supplication, and wrestling with the Lord, both alone and together—an exercise which Christ himself had so much recommended, "that we ought always to pray, and not to faint;" so much practised by the saints, especially in particular exigencies, as Acts xii. 5; "Prayer was made of the church without ceasing;" and ever followed with a blessed success when seriously gone about—"They called upon the Lord and he answered them." Psal. xcix. 6. Jas. v. 16—18; while it carried with it a sweet reward in its own bosom, even "the peace of God, which passeth all understanding, keeping and guiding both heart and mind through Christ Jesus." Phil. iv. 7.

This letter was attended with the best effects. Many of the godly ministers throughout the land—men of prayer—were stirred up by it, and set apart stated seasons for solemn fasting and supplication for the church and country, which God answered to themselves by terrible things in righteousness. He caused men to ride over their heads; they went through fire and through water, but he brought them out into a wealthy place. Their wordly circumstances were straitened, but the gospel had free course and was glorified. Some lived to see his gracious interposition in the glorious Revolution, 1688; numbers never did, but were favoured to go by a shorter road from a scaffold to a throne; yet their posterity have reaped and are reaping the benefit of their prayers.

BOOK VIII.

JULY, A. D. 1670—1674.

Parliament—Act against conventicles—Bond—Leighton's efforts to reform the Episcopate—Council appoint a committee—Leighton attempts an accommodation—Conference—Rigid treatment of indulged ministers—Conventicles increase—Implacability of the Prelates—Lady Dysart—Ascendency of Lauderdale—Parliament —Finings—Indulgence—Dissensions of the ministers—Sufferings of the indulged—Mr. Forrester and Mr. Burnet abandon Prelacy —Their testimony—Proceedings at the meeting of estates—Mr. Blackader's tour in Fife—Ministers' widows' petition—Its consequences—Sharpe's troubles.

Parliament commenced a short session, July 28, ostensibly for the purpose of forwarding an union between the two kingdoms; and their first bill empowered the king to name commissioners for this purpose, but the scheme, if ever seriously entertained, proved abortive. Their other proceedings were of more deplorable efficacy. Men of principle, who were accustomed to attend upon the preaching of the gospel, or the worship of God in unauthorized places, and who seldom or never refused to acknowledge their own participation in such misdemeanours, yet, as they considered it a crime to discover the minister or their fellow-worshippers, uniformly refused to turn informers; and this which, in any other case, would have been extolled as an high and honourable feeling, was in them to be treated as a felony. An act was therefore introduced against "such who should refuse to depone against delinquents," ordaining that all of what degree, sex, or quality soever, who should refuse to declare upon oath their knowledge of any unlawful meetings, the several circumstances of the persons present, and things done therein, to any having authority from his majesty, or who should conceal or reset any who were or might be declared rebels—should be punished by fining, imprisonment, or transportation as slaves to the plantations. To ensure the safety of the orthodox clergy, any attempt upon their houses or persons was declared punishable by death and confiscation of goods; and a reward of five hundred merks was offered to any person who should discover and seize such "robbers or attempters;" or, if one should inform, and another seize, the first was to have two, and the other three hundred merks of the same.

The most atrocious measure, however, of this assembly, was their "act against conventicles," by which it was statute and commanded that the "outted" ministers, who were not licensed by the council, and no other persons not authorized nor tolerated by the bishop of the diocese, should presume to preach, expound Scripture, or pray in any meeting, except in their own houses, and to those of their own family, "under pain of imprisonment till they should find security to the amount of five thousand merks never again to trespass in a similar manner, or to remove out of the kingdom and never to return without his majesty's license; every person present was to be fined—an heritor, a fourth part of his yearly rent—a tenant, twenty-five pound Scots—a cottar, twelve pounds—and each servant, a fourth part of his yearly fee; and if accompanied by wives or children, half the sum for each. The master or mistress of the house to pay double. Besides which, the magistrates of any burgh where a conventicle was kept, were rendered liable to a fine at the pleasure of the privy council, they having recourse upon the persons present, who were thus subjected to be twice mulcted for the same crime; and in addition, punished with imprisonment as long as the council should see fit."

Field conventicles, denominated "rendezvouses of

rebellion," but explained to be meetings for hearing the Scriptures expounded, or for prayer, were punishable—the minister by death and confiscation—the attenders by double penalties to those of house conventicles; and every meeting was declared to be a field conventicle, although held in a house, if there were any persons standing without at the door or at the windows. The execution of this act was entrusted to the sheriffs, stewards, lords of regalities, and their deputies, who were to account to the privy council for the fines of the heritors; but all others, to stimulate their activity, they were allowed to retain. Persons having their children baptized by any minister except their own parish priest, were rendered liable to additional fines, to be levied in the same manner, and, to complete the tyranny with the most cruel insult, by enforcing a principle which Lauderdale well knew the Presbyterians acknowledged—the king's right to regulate the externals of religion.

His majesty conceiving himself bound in conscience and duty to interpose his authority, that the public exercises of God's worship be countenanced by all his good subjects, and that such as upon any pretext do disorderly withdraw, be by the censures of the law made sensible of their miscarriage, and by the authority of the law drawn to a dutiful obedience of it—with advice and consent of his estates in parliament, ordained and commanded all his good subjects of the reformed religion, to attend and frequent the ordinary meetings for divine worship in their own parish churches; and whoever should absent themselves three Lord's days, without a reasonable excuse for every time, were to be fined—an heritor an eighth of his yearly rent—a tenant six pounds Scots—a cottar or servant forty shillings. So sensible, however, did the framers of the act appear to be, that such care for the religious improvement of the people, instead of being likely to produce reformation, was more likely to produce rebellion, that they ordained if any person, after being fined, should persist in still absenting himself from the means of instruction which the government had so kindly provided, he should be required to sign a bond to the following purport:—" I, ——, oblige myself that I shall not, upon any pretext or colour whatsoever, rise in arms against the king's majesty, or any having his authority or commission; nor shall assist nor countenance any who shall rise in arms." And if any person refused, he was to be imprisoned or banished, and his single escheat or life-rent escheat was to fall to his majesty.

Acts so immeasurably rigorous, which passed without one dissenting voice except that of the young Earl of Cassils, so vile was that crouching assembly, grieved the soul of the amiable Leighton—whose first coldness towards the Presbyterian profession had arisen from what he conceived to be a persecuting spirit in the manner they forced the covenants to be sworn—and he declared he would never consent to propagate Christianity itself by such means, far less a form of church government.* Tweeddale told him they were never intended to be put in execution, but were merely hung out, *in terrorem*, to induce the Presbyterians to comply with the advances of government, and meet them on a plan of equitable moderation. Duped by these false and hollow professions, he strenuously set himself to endeavour accomplishing so desirable an end; and, as a first step, immediately on his entry into the archiepiscopal office, he made an effort to rid his district of the incapable and scandalous underlings who degraded their function, and rendered it contemptible in the eyes of the people. He appointed a committee to inquire into the complaints made against the curates, of whose

* The conduct of Leighton has always appeared to me inexplicable; and, although I willingly give him credit for the best of motives, yet I have never met with any very satisfactory apology for his accepting a then bishopric. It must not, however, be forgotten, that he repeatedly tendered his resignation to the king, who personally urged him to retain it; and that he did so upon the faith of the royal promise that milder measures would be pursued, and that when he found himself deceived, he left the archiepiscopate.

21*

proceedings we have no authentic record. From the testimony, however, of the Presbyterian writers, it appears that several had been removed; that others who feared a similar sentence, compounded with their parishes for a little money, and voluntarily went back to the north and east, whence they had come; and that the archbishop, at least in one instance, had personally interposed, where his committee were inclined to be partial, and dismissed the noted curate of Maybole, against whom the crimes of swearing, fighting, and drunkenness, were proved. But I apprehend his exertions in this had been cramped by the interference of the civil power; for "the council, upon being informed that the synod of Glasgow had appointed a committee of their number to hear and take trial of such complaints as should be given in to them against scandalous ministers; and considering it expedient that they should have all encouragement, appointed Sir John Cochran of Ochiltree, Sir Thomas Wallace, Sir John Cunninghame, Sir John Harper, and the provosts of Glasgow and Ayr, to meet with them and assist them." The nature of all such assistance is sufficiently plain; and if less was accomplished than expected, the cause of the failure may be easily accounted for without any fault on the part of the bishop.

Another scheme which he tried at the same time to elevate the Episcopalian character, proved even still more abortive. He employed several of the most learned and decorous of their preachers, who were also reckoned pious, Dr. Gilbert Burnet, Mr. James Nairn, Mr. Laurence Charteris, men of superior abilities and unblamable lives, with some others of more obscure name, as missionaries to preach in the west. They were received by the people with scorn, and contemptuously styled the bishop's evangelists; few could be persuaded to hear them, and of those who did, they did not appear to have made many converts. Burnet himself gives this candid account—"The people of the country came generally to hear us, though not in great crowds. We were mdeed amazed to see a poor commonalty so capable to argue upon points of government, and on the bounds to be set to the power of princes in matters of religion. Upon all these topics they had texts of Scripture at hand, and were ready with their answers to any thing that was said to them. This measure of knowledge was spread even among the meanest of them, their cottagers and their servants."

Neither did the grand object to which these were preliminary, succeed any better. After several conferences, the accommodation was given up. The first was held at Holyrood House before Lauderdale, Rothes, Tweeddale, and Kincardine, in the month of August, between Messrs. G. Hutchison, A. Wedderburn, John Baird, and John Gemble—indulged ministers who had been invited to Edinburgh by Lauderdale—and Bishop Leighton and Professor Gilbert Burnet. Sharpe would not be present. Lauderdale opened the business by an eulogium on the king's condescension and clemency—his wishes for a complete unity and harmony—and recommended an agreement upon joint measures which might tend to the peace of the church. Leighton followed. He deplored the mischief their divisions had occasioned, the many souls that had been lost, and the many more that were in danger, while they were wasting their strength in contention, and exhorted every one to do what he could to heal a breach that had let in so many evils. For his own part, he said, he was persuaded that Episcopacy, as an order distinct from Presbytery, had existed in the church ever since the days of the apostles; that the world had every where received the Christian religion from bishops; and that a parity among clergymen was never thought of in the church before the middle of the last century, and was then set up rather by accident than design; still, how much soever he was persuaded of this, as they were of a different judgment, he had a proposal to make by which they might both preserve their opinions, and yet unite in carrying on the preaching of the gospel and the end of their ministry; and that was, merely to recognise the bishops as the presidents of their synods and presbyteries, with liberty to dissent from any measure they did not approve of.

The ministers made no reply; but next day, in the bishop's chamber, Mr. Hutchison, in name of the rest, answered his observations respecting Episcopacy:—Parity among the ministers of the gospel, he affirmed to be the original apostolic institution, that a perpetual presidency had made way for a lordly dominion in the church; and that however inconsiderable the thing might seem to be in itself, it both had been and would be of great and mischievous consequence. Those present, however, he said, could come to no agreement without consulting their brethren, and therefore desired that the project might be submitted to them, which was accordingly done in the following form:—"Presbyteries being set up by law, as they were established before the year 1638, and the bishop passing from his negative voice, and we having liberty to protest and declare against any remainder of prelatic power, retained or that may happen at any time to be exercised by him, for a salvo for our consciences from homologation thereof—your opinion is required, as to whether we can with safety to our principles join in these presbyteries? or what else is it that we will desire to do for peace in the church and an accommodation—Episcopacy being always preserved?"

Upon these queries, the ministers in the south and west had a very numerous meeting, when, after long reasoning, it was unanimously agreed, that to sit in ecclesiastical courts called by bishops, whose only right emanated from the supremacy of the crown, was virtually acknowledging that supremacy—a thing very different from meeting in the presbyteries which were indicted, A. D. 1638, by the intrinsic power of the church, and therefore could not be complied with; and as to the salvo of a protest, it would be a protestation contrary to the fact, and so no salvo to an honest man's conscience. For the sake of peace, they had no objection to join in public worship with a bishop, or such as were ordained by him; but as to acknowledging their office, by sitting in courts with them, they could not see how that could at all be reconciled with their principles.

Several conferences took place between Leighton and Mr. Hutchison's small party; but the utmost the latter could be brought to concede, was, to consent to the appointment of the bishops as perpetual presidents or constant moderators in their Synods and presbyteries, which being no divine institution, it was thought the king might be allowed to appoint, but they required the resumption of assemblies and the legal recognition of all the essential parts of Presbyterian Church government—a proposal which met the approbation of no party. The prelates saw in the loss of their negative voice in the courts, a relinquishing of a main pillar of Episcopacy; while the more consistent Presbyterians affirmed that, to allow the royal nomination of a perpetual president, was laying a foundation for again rearing, when times should prove more propitious, the prelatic power.

Thus the conferences broke up; and as usual in all such cases, the ineffectual endeavours to procure peace, tended greatly to imbitter the war. Some, however, refused to conform to the present establishment upon higher and more scriptural grounds. They had observed that popery and profanity always increased where conformity prevailed, and that the Lord had stamped this mark of his displeasure upon prelacy, that under it truth and godliness had ever sensibly decayed. They therefore rejected all fellowship with it, as a plant which man, and not God, had planted; and they refused to hold communion in church government with those who, by their carelessness and negligence, were the destroyers of his holy mountain, and laid his vineyard waste—who had been thrust into the oversight of charges whence many had been cast out, whom the Lord had made polished shafts in his own right hand for gaining souls to Christ.*

[1671.] Where the fundamental principles of parties in religion are opposite, it is vain to expect that public disputation will reconcile them. The Presbyterians have ever held that Jesus Christ is the supreme Head, King, and Lawgiver of his church, with whose statutes, ordinances, and appointments no earthly power has a right to interfere; and however this principle may have been obscured by circumstances, or how much soever it may have been misrepresented by enemies, or misunderstood by ill-informed friends, it was the principle for which these excellent men, who were now accounted too rigid, earnestly contended, and which, when they came to die, they were anxious should be fully cleared as the ground of their sufferings. The Scottish Episcopalians owned the supremacy of the king, their whole system was based upon his prerogative, and they acknowledged his power to model the government of the house of God according to his pleasure.

Leighton had attempted a compromise between these two abhorrent opinions, and, had not their self-interest opposed, it is evident the latter could offer no argument for non-compliance with a royal mandate for conciliation; while the former, without violating their conscience, could not advance a step upon such ground. When they separated, however, upon this distinct, palpable, and, so long as each retained their principles, irremediable cause of difference, the Presbyterians were represented as obstinate, unreasonable men, full of an entangled scrupulosity; and the privy council, immediately ordered their act requiring all the indulged ministers to attend the bishops' presbyterial meetings, under the penalty of being straitly confined within the limits of the parishes where they preached, to be strictly enforced; nor dared they visit a dying parent, although not a

* Mr. Menzies, minister of Carlaverock, who had conformed, withdrew this year from the bishop's presbytery of Dumfries, and gave in a testimony to this effect.

mile distant, without special leave asked and granted from that arbitrary court. To add to the hardship of this imprisonment, their salaries were very irregularly paid, and their applications so violently opposed by the primate, that it was with difficulty, and after in some cases a twelvemonth's delay, an order could be obtained upon the collector of the vacant stipends.

The observation of the anniversary of the king's birth-day was anew rigidly enjoined, and the sheriffs required to see that the council's act forbidding lecturing was obeyed, and that the names of such as contravened should be sent to them. A committee, at the head of which stood the Archbishop of St. Andrews, was next appointed, to consider what further could be done to suppress conventicles, and to see that the militia did not neglect their duty in preventing or dispersing these hated assemblies, or in apprehending and bringing to condign punishment all who should contenance such atrocities! In order to render offenders still more inexcusable, the patrons in the west were recommended to use all diligence to get their churches planted with able and godly ministers, but they were either unable or unwilling to comply; and, in the month of July, the affair was turned over to the bishops, who provided incumbents, which inflamed the evil; for, instead of decreasing, the obnoxious meetings multiplied.

Linlithgowshire, Fife, and the Lothians were especially infected; and, during the present year, the most remarkable conventicles appear to have been held immediately in the vicinity of the primate's dwelling, not far distant from Linlithgow Palace, and in the muirs of Livingstone, Bathgate, Calder, and Torphichen. The Duke of Hamilton's factor at Kinniel, who acted likewise as baron-bailie, was favourable, and by his connivance Mr. Blackader frequently visited the seaport town of Borrowstownness or its vicinity, where, many years after, the effects of his and his brethrens' preaching were felt.

Implacably bent against the "outted" ministers,

the prelates would neither allow them to obey their consciences actively nor passively. If they preached, prayed, or exhorted, beyond the bounds of their own families, they were persecuted as the most obnoxious pests of society. If they remained at home and refrained from these duties, if they did not attend the parish church regularly with their families, they were complained of as disobedient, and the sheriffs were ordered by the council to commit them to prison. Yet, notwithstanding, "at that time," Mr. Fraser of Brae remarks, "the church of Christ had great rest and liberty from persecution, through variance among the statesmen;" so highly was a short respite from actual suffering then esteemed, though loaded with heavy, and what would now be reckoned intolerable, burdens.

The variance referred to was a quarrel between Lauderdale and those who had assisted him in overturning his former opponents, whom he now rewarded with the usual gratitude of politicians, by procuring their dismissal from office as soon as he found them stand in the way of his own advancement. When he sacrificed his religion upon the altar of ambition, he threw his morality into the same fire; and, according to the fashion of the court, lived in open adultery. Lady Dysart, his paramour, whom, upon the death of his lady, soon after [1672] he married, was remarkable in her day for personal beauty and fascinating manners, joined to unfeeling rapacity and cruel extravagance; and her influence completed a dreadful revolution in his character, already depraved by his prosperous career as a courtier. She caused him to separate from the only portion of his confidential friends who had the courage to oppose his violence, or the virtue to attempt it; and when Sir Robert Murray and Tweeddale were now removed from the direction of public affairs, all decency and moderation soon followed. Together with a few of his devoted creatures, he engrossed every place of importance in the country In his own person he held the offices of Commis sioner, President of the Council, a Lord of the Treasury and of the Session, Agent at Court for the royal burghs, Captain of the Castle, and Captain of the Bass*—a high insulated rock at the mouth of the

* "The Bass is a very high rock in the sea, two miles distant from the nearest point of the land which is south of it; covered it is with grass on the uppermost parts thereof, where is a garden where herbs grow, with some cherrytrees, of the fruit of which I several times tasted, below which garden there is a chapel for divine service; but, in regard no minister was allowed for it, the ammunition of the garrison was kept therein. Landing here is very difficult and dangerous; for, if any storm blow, ye cannot enter because of the violence of the swelling waves, which beat with a wonderful noise upon the rock, and sometimes in such a violent manner, that the broken waves reverberating on the rock with a mighty force, have come up over the walls of the garrison on the court before the prisoners' chambers, which is above twenty cubits height. And with a full sea must you land; or, if it be ebb, you must be either craned up, or climb with hands and feet up some steps artificially made on the rock, and must have helps besides of those who are on the top of the rock, who pull you up by the hand. Nor is there any place of landing but one about the whole rock, which is of circumference some three quarters of a mile; here you may land in a fair day and full sea without great hazard, the rest of it on every side being so high and steep. Only on the south side thereof, the rock falls a little level, where you ascend several steps till you come to the Governor's house, and from that some steps higher you ascend to a level court, where a house for prisoners and soldiers is; whence likewise, by windings cut out of the rock, there is a path which leads you to the top of the rock, whose height doth bear off all north, east, and west storms, lying open only to the south; and on the uppermost parts of the rock there is grass sufficient to feed twenty or twenty-four sheep, who are there very fat and good. In these uppermost parts of the rock were sundry walks of some threescore feet length, and some very solitary, where we sometimes entertained ourselves. The accessible places were defended with several walls and cannon placed on them, which compassed only the south parts. The rest of the rock is defended by nature, by the huge height and steepness of the rock, being some forty cubits high in the lowest place. It was a part of a country gentleman's inheritance, which falling from hand to hand, and changing many masters, it was at last bought by the king, who repaired the old houses and walls, and built some new houses for prisoners; and a garrison of twenty or twenty-four soldiers therein are sufficient, if courageous, to defend it from millions of men, and only expugnable by hunger. 'Tis commanded by a Lieutenant, who does reap thereby some considerable profit, which, besides his pay, may be one hundred pounds a year and better. There is no fountain-water therein, and they are only served with rain that falls out of the clouds, and is preserved in some hollow caverns digged out of the rock. Their drink and provisions are

Frith of Forth, now converted into a state prison. His brother, Hatton, was Treasurer, Depute-General of the Mint, and Lord of Session; Atholl, Justice-General and Privy Seal; Kincardine, Admiral of Scotland; Sir James Dalrymple of Stair, President of the Court of Session; and Lockhart of Lee, Lord Justice-Clerk.

Influenced by French counsels, Charles in the beginning of the year, suddenly commenced against the Dutch the most unprovoked hostilities, by a piratical but unsuccessful attack upon their Smyrna fleet, which was followed by a declaration of war, founded upon pretexts either false or ridiculous.* The whole line of his policy went to destroy liberty and religion at home and abroad—to fetter his people, though at the expense of being himself as much the despicable pensioner of France, as he was the degraded slave of his own licentious passions. Lauderdale aptly ministered to all his iniquity; and his management of Scotland was in unison with the traitorous band of conspirators, of whom he was one, against English freedom, known by the name of the "Cabal," and in entire subservience to the king's designs against his subjects. Being created a duke, he came down to his vice-royalty with his duchess, in great pomp, and made a tour with her Grace throughout the country, the nobles vieing with each other in the magnificence of their entertainments to the noble pair.

Parliament met in June, and was opened in great state by the Commissioner, whose lady, seated within

carried from the other side by a boat, which only waits on the garrison, and hath a salary of six pounds yearly for keeping up the same, besides what they get of these persons that come either to see the prisoners, or are curious to see the garrison. Here fowls of every sort are to be found, who build in the clifts of the rock, the most considerable of which is the solan goose, whose young, well fledged, ready to fly, are taken, and yield near one hundred pounds yearly, and might be much more, were they carefully improved."—*Mem. of Fraser of Brea*, pp. 298—300.

* One of the reasons for involving the nation in blood, was, that the Dutch had insulted the king by allowing a caricature to be sold, in which he was exhibited as receiving a quantity of money in a "discrowned" hat, which fell as fast into the lap of his mistress!

the bar, heard her lord deliver his speech—a mark of honour none even of the kings of Scotland had ever bestowed upon their queens, and which the very doubtful character of the duchess did not in public opinion seem to merit. All the severe acts against conventicles were confirmed and extended. To shut every avenue to power or place against Presbyterians, none but those well affected to the religion and government of the church as established, were to be appointed officers of the militia; and both officers and men were ordered to take the oath of allegiance and the declaration, under pain of banishment; and to prevent the continuance of that detested religion, the whole of those who professed it were forbid to license or ordain any person to the ministerial office; all ordinations since 1661 were declared null and void, the ordainers and ordained subjected to banishment, and their goods to confiscation; persons married by non-conformists forfeited their legal matrimonial rights; and those who did not bring their children to the parish minister to be baptized within thirty days after their birth, were to be punished by fining—heritors in a fourth part of their rent, and merchants by a pecuniary mulct.

Good laws are too often dead letters in the statute-book; but it is seldom that cruel, persecuting enactments are allowed to slumber; and if these enactments are rendered sources of gain to the wretches who are to enforce them, wo to the subjects their fangs can reach. Believe their pretences and preambles, never was a kingdom blessed as was Scotland at this time with excellent legislative measures, passed for the preservation of religion, for ensuring attendance on the ordinances, the protection of an orthodox ministry, the prevention of schism, and the promotion of Christianity in a regular orderly manner. There were, also, admirable laws for suppressing profanity and all manner of immorality. These stand enrolled among our records; and were we to judge from the preambles of the printed acts of parliament, no nation was ever so happy in an establishment for the furtherance of the gospel—that so strenuously watched over its interest by seeing all the churches filled by able pastors, and these pastors properly supported by legal contributions. In fine, judge from the profession of her rulers, representatives, and clergy, the people were too happy in a pious, beneficent, and fatherly government, but did not know their own mercies. Now look at the fact. The churches were deserted because the clergy were incapable, and the gospel was banished to the wilds of the country, and even there persecuted. I subjoin an instance.

"At or near Bathgate a great multitude had assembled to hear the word of God preached by Mr. Riddell. This being known, a party of dragoons, commanded by one Lieutenant Inglis, who kept garrison in Mid Calder, made search for them on the muirs. The meeting had notice of this; but hearing they were at a distance, and, as some reported, returning to their quarters again, they were the more secure and continued their worship; but within a little, they appeared in sight and that near, ere they knew. Upon which the most part got over a bog and that hard by, where horse and foot could not follow, but many stood on the other side, thinking themselves safe. Mean time, the dragoons came up and apprehended several on the spot; among others, Sandilands, Lady Helderston's brother. Then they approached to the side of the bog, and shot on among the people, as they usually basely did on such occasions to shoot bullets among such a promiscuous multitude of men, women, and children, though they found them without arms. One of their shot lighted on ane honest man, an heritor in Bathgate parish, and killed him dead on the spot. They carried their prisoners to the garrison at Calder, with a great booty of cloaks, plaids, bibles, and what else they could lay their hands on, spoiling the poor people, as they had got the victory over a foreign enemy."

Fining was too fertile a source of emolument to be relinquished by an administration so extravagant as the Duke of Lauderdale's. Exorbitant sums were thus extorted from the most respectable gentlemen and substantial tenants, which were lavished upon the retainers of government or the private friends of the Commissioner. It would be idle to attempt even guessing the amount of money raised this year by small exactions, but some of the larger may be mentioned. Hay of Balhousie, or Boussi, as Kirkton styles him, afterwards Earl of Kinnoull, then a very young man, but newly left school, was fined one thousand pounds sterling for having heard his own chaplain officiate in situations that brought him under the penalties of the conventicle act. Drummond of Meggins, because his wife had been guilty of attending some field-preaching, was tabled for five hundred; and their convictions were aggravated by the insulting raillery of Lauderdale, who told them when their bonds were signed—"Gentlemen, now ye know the rate of a conventicle, and shame fall them first fails." A house conventicle cost Ann Countess Dowager of Wigton, four thousand merks. A Mr. James Duncan at Duplin, got off for half the sum. The general rate for those of lower rank seems to have been five hundred each.

Yet, while thus actively urging this lucrative persecution, his Grace had brought with him powers for granting a new and more comprehensive indulgence. It was not, however, till the month of August that any thing was done in the matter, when about twenty of the "outted" ministers met at Edinburgh, and deputed two of their number, Mr. James Kirkton and Gabriel Cunningham, to wait upon Sir James Dalrymple of Stair, to learn the certainty of the report and entreat his good offices. These he readily promised, but, from whatever reason, they proved ineffectual; and on the 3d September, Lord's day, an act of council was agreed to, that was in fact rather an act of confinement than one of indulgence. By it the Presbyterian ministers, "outted" since 1662, were ordered to repair to certain parishes, there to remain—some two together, some three—and to ex ercise their functions, nor pass their limits, without a license from the bishop of the diocese. They were not to preach any where but in the parish church—to administer the Lord's Supper on the same day in all the parishes—and to admit no person from a neighbouring parish to any church privilege without a line from their minister, unless the parish kirk were vacant. And all ministers not mentioned by name in this act, if they presumed to exercise any part of the ministerial duty, were to be punished according to the pleasure of the council.

An indulgence so miserably clogged did not, and perhaps was not intended to, meet the views of any of the Presbyterians; but whilst they almost unanimously disapproved of the act, they divided as to the propriety of accepting the offer of government under protest; or, in other language, of entering upon the office of the ministry under any restriction, after presenting to the council an enumeration of their grievances, and praying for a relaxation. This mode of procedure some thought would exonerate their consciences, and be a testimony against the Erastian proceedings of government. The more consistent agreed that the testimony would be right provided they acted up to it by refusing to accept the indulgence, else it would only be affording an excuse for ministers who wished one, to accept what they otherwise were not in their minds clear about accepting.

The dispute ran high; and, at this distance of time, and living as we do, untried by the perilous assailments to which these good men were exposed, it would ill become us to pronounce harshly upon the conduct of either party; yet it is impossible not to approve, and that highly, of the noble, intrepid, and disinterested proceedings of the latter, who chose rather to suffer for a good conscience, than accept of deliverance under such circumstances. The proposal for emitting a testimony was accordingly dropped, and a number of ministers accepted of parishes without further dispute. A few, on entering upon their charges, disavowed from their pulpits giving countenance to Erastianism, making a wretched compromise with their professions and consciences, which neither gained them credit with the people nor secured them from molestation by their rulers. Those who could not comply were in consequence exposed to the increased fury of the persecutor; but that was a small matter compared to the heart-burnings and melancholy divisions these debates caused among the brethren. The exiles in Holland, who were suffering for their consistency, published against it; and the common people, who entered keenly into every question, began to doubt of the propriety of hearing ministers who departed from the purity of Presbyterian principle and practice, and became cold even to the ministers who, though they had not accepted of the indulgence themselves, did not in their public discourses bear testimony against it; and a spirit of distrust arose which afterwards led to most unhappy consequences.

[1673.] Early next year, upon the Duke of Hamilton's coming to Edinburgh, a council was held to learn the success of the indulgence in the west, when he gave it as his opinion, that, had the whole of the Presbyterian ministers accepted, the country might have been quiet; but, as so many refused themselves and dissuaded their brethren, he believed the schism, as he termed it, would still continue to distract the church and disturb the land. He complained chiefly of five who were exceedingly active in their meetings, James Kirkton, author of the History of the Church of Scotland; Alexander Moncrief; Robert Lockhart; George Campbell; and Robert Fleeming.

Some of these residing in Edinburgh, the council determined that they should either be silent or proceed to the parishes allotted as their places of confinement. By an order of the 7th March, all "outted" ministers were enjoined to remove to a distance of five miles from the city, unless they gave bond to keep no conventicles; and on the 12th, those of the indulged who had not entered upon their parishes, were called before them, and peremptorily commanded to show their obedience before the 1st of June Kirkton thanked them for allowing him so much time to consider, and said "he should desire to advise with the Lord and his conscience;" and was dismissed till then, together with Mr. Matthew McKail, Robert Lockhart, James Donaldson, and some others.

These injunctions were shortly after followed by another fierce proclamation against conventicles, requiring all heritors and others to give prompt information respecting such meetings to the council under pain of being fined at least in a fourth part of their rents. Still the activity of the respectable part of the population not meeting the wishes of the council, the higher ranks, Hamilton, Eglinton, and Cassilis, were ordered to undertake the hated office of hunting out conventicles and report to Edinburgh. The reason alleged was, that the king being at war with the Dutch, the latter designed to raise troubles in Scotland, and the conventicles behoved to be dispersed as holding communication with the enemy. The council now also commenced sending ministers to that horrible prison, the Bass: and Mr. Robert Gillespie, for conducting the worship of God in a house at Falkland, was the first who had that honour, because he would not consent to inform upon those who were present, and whose fines might have been more profitable than his imprisonment. He was followed in the month of June by Alexander Peden, an eminent servant of the Lord Jesus Christ, whose character has suffered little less from the credulity of his admirers, than from the ridicule of his enemies. He appears to have sprung from persons in humble life, and, previously to being licensed, had been schoolmaster, precentor, and session-clerk to Mr. John Guthrie, at Tarbolton.* He was three years minister at New Glenluce, in Galloway, whence he was ejected soon after the Restoration, and was among the first of the field-preachers. In the beginning of

* Wodrow says Fenwick, evidently a mistake, for William Guthrie, author of the well known excellent treatise, the "Trial of a Saving Interest in Christ," was minister at Fenwick.

1666, he was denounced by proclamation, and next year declared a rebel and forfeited both in life and fortune. He continued from that time wandering and exercising his ministry to great numbers, and with much success, alternately in Scotland and Ireland, till June this year, when he was seized by Major Cockburn in the house of Hugh Ferguson of Knockdow, in Carrick, and sent together with his landlord to Edinburgh. On the 26th he was examined before the council and committed to the Bass. Mr. Ferguson was fined a thousand merks for affording him a night's lodgings. And so highly did the managers estimate the capture, that they ordered fifty pounds sterling to be paid to the Major—twenty-five to be distributed among the soldiers, to stimulate to new service.

All proving ineffectual, Lauderdale sent down a letter, May 31, in his arrogant style of rude bantering jocularity, telling the council that if any of the indulged were still unwilling to accept of that favour upon the terms upon which it was granted, they should not at all press them to it; but instead of that, require sufficient assurance of their forbearing conventicles, going regularly to church, and behaving orderly in the places where they resided, adding, "because some of them are displeased, forsooth! with the late indulgence, you shall secure them from the fear of any more of that kind! and let them know that if after all the lenity used toward them, they still continue refractory and untractable, the whole of the royal power shall be employed for securing the peace of the church and kingdom from their seditious practices."

Money and blood are the fundamental principles of all false religions; and love of the world is not a more absolute criterion by which to judge of an individual's Christianity, than a sure and certain rule by which to judge whether a church be a church of Christ or no. Attachment to the temporalities of an ecclesiastical establishment is as clear and distinct a feature of antichrist, wherever it is found, as any given in the word of God, by whatever name that establishment be called, whether a Protestant Episcopacy or the Hierarchy of Rome. These were prominent features of the prelacy of Scotland. I subjoin an example of their extortion. The whole succeeding years will bear evidence to their lust of blood. In Renfrew alone the following sums were awarded against eleven gentlemen, and only not levied to their full extent because a compromise could be readily procured by the ecclesiastical robbers, while it might have been doubtful whether, if the whole had been sued for, they might not have been forced to share the produce with the legal ruffians:—Sir George Maxwell of Newark, for three years' absence from church, 31,200 pounds Scots; for weekly conventicles, 62,-400; and for disorderly baptisms, 1200, making a total of 94,800 pounds Scots, or £7800. 1s. 6d. sterling—the Laird of Douchal, afterwards Porterfield, 84,400 Scots, or £7032 sterling—Sir George Maxwell, Netherpollock, in 93,600 Scots, or £7500 sterling—Cunningham of Carncurran, 15,833. 6s. 8d., Scots—John Maxwell of Dargarvel, 18,900 Scots—Walkinshaw of Walkinshaw, 12,600 Scots—and five others in different sums, making a total of 368,031. 3s. 4d., Scots.

Partial compliances did not secure the indulged from trouble, nor were they less the objects of the bishops' hatred than their more resolute brethren. When the anniversary of the king's birth-day return ed, they were summoned to appear before the council to give an account of the manner in which they cele brated it; and the "reverend fathers in God" appear ed as their most violent accusers. As upon former occasions, their answers were respecting their past practice. When required to promise obedience for the future, the majority answered they could not keep any day holy but the Sabbath, and were fined in the one half of their stipends, which does not appear, however, to have been rigorously exacted. Unfortunately, however, some excused themselves by not having seen the council's instructions; immediately the instructions were tendered them, but Mr. Alexander Blair, minister in Galston, told them that though in politeness he would not refuse receiving the paper, yet he could accept of no instructions from them for regulating his ministry, otherwise he should be their ambassador, not Christ's. For his insolence, as they termed it, he was cast into prison, where he remained till December, when he was allowed, on account of sickness, to be carried to a private house, till death unloosed his fetters. In the month of January, he departed in much joy and in full assurance of faith.

This incident tended to increase the coolness between the people and the indulged; for they did not think that the other ministers had been sufficiently explicit in their testimony; and when they returned to their parishes, "they were to their great grief," says Kirkton, "treated with no less reproach than the nickname of Council Curates." "Outted" ministers who had no particular parishes allowed them, were required to repair to such as the council should name; but as they could not see it consistent with any moral or Christian duty to present themselves for the purpose of being punished without a crime, Robert Fleeming, Thomas Hogg, John Lidderdale, and Alexander Hutchison, were ordered to be apprehended and brought before the council, wherever they could be found. Instead of reconciling the Presbyterians to the domination of bishops, such proceedings added to the number of recusants, and these always from the most conscientious. Mr. Forrester, minister at Alva, and Mr. John Burnet, indulged at Kilbride, both abandoned prelacy towards the end of this year, and both bore explicit testimony against the civil power of the magistrate in the church of God. Mr. Forrester, in a letter to the prelatical presbytery of Stirling, disclaimed their jurisdiction, "because it was fountained in, derived from, or referrible to, the magistrates," which says he, "I judge to be contrary to the word of God, the confession of reformed churches, and our own church's government; for the two powers, civil and ecclesiastic, are distinct *toto genere* both as to the original, the subject matter, the manner of working, and the end designed, distinct limits being put betwixt them, both in the Old and New Testament. Under the law, a standing priesthood were to meddle with matters of the Lord distinct from matters of the king. The judgments on Saul and Uzziah, show the Lord's displeasure at magistrates intermeddling with spiritual matters. Under the New Testament, the Lord Jesus, the King, Head, and Lawgiver of his church, hath a visible kingdom which he exerciseth in and over the church visible by its spiritual office-bearers, given to it as a church, and therefore distinct from, and independent upon, the civil power—the keys of the kingdom of heaven being by him committed, not to the magistrates, but to the apostles' successors in the work of the ministry." He therefore quitted the Established Church, betook himself to the fields, and shared in the labours and obloquy of the persecuted. Mr. Burnet was prevented by sickness from personally bearing witness to the same high prerogatives of Christ; but he left his reasons for refusing to submit to any temporal supremacy in writing, and died rejoicing in the hope of the glory of God. His last words were—"Glory! glory! glory!"

It deserves to be remarked, that he and several other distinguished ministers, although they had no liberty to accept of the indulgence themselves, yet did not deem it a reason why they should withdraw their affection from those who had, or throw any obstacle in the way of those they considered messengers of the gospel; for these worthies thought preaching salvation to sinners so paramount a duty, that they would have ventured upon every thing but sin to achieve it themselves or promote it by others.

Charles and his advisers in attempting to introduce despotism, had as little consulted their own peace as that of his kingdom. He was harassed by his English parliament; and Lauderdale having been voted a public grievance, was glad to seek refuge in Scotand, where, in the month of December, he came down to hold a fourth session of the parliament. Suspecting no opposition, if he secured the support of the clergy, he told the estates that the most effectual course would be taken for curbing and suppressing the insolent field conventicles, and other seditious practices, which had so much abounded—that if fairness would not, force must compel the refractory to be peaceable and to obey the laws. But instead of his declarations being met with the submissive adulation they were wont, the Duke of Hamilton, supported by a strong party, presented their grievances; and when the Commissioner with his usual haughty roughness interposed to silence complaint, Sir Patrick Home of Polwart demanded to know, whether it was not a free parliament? And after a short tumultuous session, in which, amid the dissensions of the statesmen, the Presbyterians escaped for the time any severer enactment, the meeting was adjourned, and the parties sought each to justify the strife to the king. Hamilton repaired to London and laid a statement of the enormous abuses before his majesty, but only received fair promises that were never performed, and incurred a resentment that never was appeased. Lauderdale retained his situation and rather increased in favour with the king.

[1674.] It is a melancholy and an appalling consideration for those who stand forward as reformers and patriots, that, in struggles for religion, for liberty, or for any good principle, those who sincerely strive to gain such objects are usually found in a minority at last; and when they have been the means of conferring the most essential benefits upon the country, they are generally left losers themselves. Amid the conflicts of the statesmen, and their loud complaints about the oppression and ruin of the country, no mention had been made of the primary and most palpable of all its distresses, the religious grievances of the Presbyterians:—those which in fact had been the origin of all the calamities of Scotland, and the triumph of which was to secure the cause of freedom, were utterly lost sight of in their miserable squabbling about the monopoly of salt and the smuggling of brandy.

Both Hamilton and Lauderdale were supposed friendly to the persecuted; and while the nation was convulsed with their political contentions, and their attention was sufficiently employed elsewhere, the pious, resolute, and consistent part of the persecuted ministers improved the respite for proclaiming peace upon the mountains, bringing good tidings of good, publishing salvation, and saying to Zion, "Thy God reigneth!" Conventicles increased both in number and frequency. They began early in the year, and the indefatigable Mr. Blackader beat up the primate's quarters upon the 2d day of January.* On that day he collected at Kinkel, within a mile of St. Andrews, a large auditory, which filled the long gallery and two chambers, besides a great number standing without doors. He lectured on the second Psalm, a portion of Scripture remarkably applicable, and preached from Jer. xiii. 18. The primate's wife hearing of the assembly, sent for the militia, who were fully prepared in warlike array, under a Lieutenant Doig, accompanied by a great number of the rascality, with many of the worst set of scholars from the college and some noblemen's sons. They drew up at a distance from the gate, before which stood the laird, his brother, and the minister's eldest son; but they caused no interruption till the lecture was finished and the psalm sung, when some people called out that there was an alarm; on which the service stopped and the men ranged outside the gate with the laird. Meanwhile, some of the rabble had got into the stable and were carrying off the laird's horse, which he observing, aimed a blow at the fellow who had him; but some of the "ill-set scholars" laying hold on his cane, a struggle ensued, and

* About the same time, the precise date is uncertain, Crail, where Sharpe had been a Presbyterian minister, was visited by Mr. John Dickson; and the unhappy apostate was tormented by the sound of the gospel on his right hand and on his left, while he vainly strove by military force to destroy the faith which once he preached.

the laird fell. Mr. Welsh, who was also there, and Kinkel's brother, instantly drew; and the Lieutenant and his men seeing them so resolute, and supposing that they were well supported, fell back, nor dared approach sufficiently near the gate to discover their error. Mrs. Murray then went up to the Lieutenant and asked him why he came in that hostile manner to trouble their house on the Lord's day? He said he had an order, which she requesting to see, he told her he would show it to the laird; and, attended by a sergeant, was drawing near the gate, when Mr. Murray called, as he approached—"How is it, Lieutenant, that you come to disturb us on the Sabbath day?" In great trepidation he delivered the laird an order which had been subscribed by the Chancellor about a year before for apprehending him and his brother. When Kinkel had read it, "I see," said he, "you have an old order from the Chancellor to that effect, which was extorted from him by the prelate. If you mind to execute it now, you may, but you shall see the faces of men." The Lieutenant, grievously alarmed, cursed himself if he had a mind to execute it. After which the lady caused bring forth some ale for the Lieutenant and his men; but one of them, whose companion had been a little hurt, said he would drink none of her drink; he would rather drink her heart's blood. The rest partook of the refreshments and went away. Composure being restored, the minister proceeded with his sermon, and the whole closed in peace.

Some time after this, Mr. Blackader had another meeting at Kinkel, where vast numbers from St. Andrews attended as hearers, and even some of the militia. Sharpe, who was that Sabbath day at home, hearing of it, sent for the provost and commanded him to order out the military, disperse the conventicle, and apprehend the minister. "My lord," replied the provost, to the prelate's dismay, "the militia are gone there already to hear the preaching, and we have none to send." And among them was the soldier that had refused drink from Lady Kinkel, who was especially marked to be moved, and wept beyond the rest; so wonderfully did the Lord countenance the persecuted gospel, even bloody enemies being overcome with conviction.

Exasperated at the multiplication of these meetings, the Episcopalian clergy added the foulest and the falsest calumnies to their other modes of opposition, and the synod of Glasgow, October 22, had the unblushing effrontery to charge these assemblies with crimes of which they themselves could never have believed them guilty—"incest, bestiality, murder of children, besides frequent adulteries, and other acts of wickedness;" after which, it is little that they should have been accused of fanaticism, disloyalty, and cursing the king. Towards the end of March, before Lauderdale left Scotland, he published an indemnity, which, although like many others with which the nation was insulted during this reign, almost only so in name, was received by the people as a license for frequenting conventicles, which continued to multiply in consequence, and especially as a report was assiduously circulated of his having secretly promised that an ample liberty would be granted to Presbyterian ministers soon after his arrival at court. Few were held in the west where the indulged ministers were settled, but on the borders, in the Merse, Lothians, Stirlingshire, and Fife, they greatly abounded, in houses, fields, and vacant churches. The more private worshippers in houses were overlooked, the vast assemblages in the mountains, and mosses, and muirs chiefly attracting the attention of government; and "at these great meetings," says Kirkton, "many a soul was converted to Jesus Christ, but far more turned from the bishops to profess themselves Presbyterians."

Mr. Welsh was among the most diligent and successful of the labourers, particularly in Fife, where many thousands were wont to assemble. His preaching was attended with a visible blessing in the conversion of many to the Lord; and among them were some in the higher ranks, especially ladies; for it is somewhat remarkable that in these days of peril and danger, the weaker sex were distinguished for their intrepid zeal; and there is reason to believe that not a few, conspicuous for their piety, were brought to the obedience of faith at these assemblies. The Countess of Crawford, daughter of the Earl of Annandale, was one of the number, and dated her first impressions from a sermon preached by Mr. Welsh at Duraquhair, near Cupar, where about eight thousand persons were present, and the power of God was manifested to the checking of the conscience and the awakening of the hearts of many. On the same Sabbath three other conventicles were held, and it was computed not less than sixteen thousand persons heard the gospel plainly and earnestly preached by Mr. Robert Lockhart at Path-head, near Kirkcaldy; Mr. Blackader, near Dunfermline; and Mr. Welwood on the Lomond Hills. This last meeting was fired upon by the soldiers, but although their bullets lighted among a crowd of men, women, and children, and brake the ground beside them, not one was wounded. They, however, took about eighteen prisoners, and then marched for Duraquhair to attack Mr. Welsh; but the people got notice and hurried him away, a great body escorting him as far as Largo, where they procured a boat, and he and his wife, with some others, crossed the Frith under night safely, and landed at Aberlady Bay, whence he got undiscovered to Edinburgh. Even the capital itself and the neighbourhood were sorely infested with these noxious meetings. Kirkton had long had regular house-preaching in the city, but this year, emboldened like others by the expectation of favour, he, along with Mr. Johnston, again ventured upon sacred ground, and Cramond Kirk being vacant, they had both been repeatedly guilty of declaring the truth from that pulpit to large and attentive auditories.

Against these there were many grievous complaints by the prelates, of which Lauderdale took advantage to lower the credit of the Duke of Hamilton and his party with the king, and in this he was so successful, that, about the end of May, the privy council was remodelled, and those only who were entirely devoted to his interest permitted to remain. On the 4th of June, when they first assembled, they were assailed in rather an unusual manner.

Reports of increased severities being about to be resorted to against conventicles having reached Edinburgh, as men durst not appear with any petition under pain of being fined or imprisoned, fifteen women, chiefly ministers' widows, resolved to present as many copies of "a humble supplication for liberty to the honest ministers throughout the land to exercise their holy function without molestation," to fifteen of the principal lords of council. Attended by a crowd of females, who filled the Parliament Close, they awaited the arrival of the counsellors. Sharpe came along with the Chancellor, and when he saw the ladies, in great bodily fear he kept close by his lordship, who seemed to enjoy the primate's terrors, and complacently allowed Mr. John Livingstone's widow to accompany him to the Council-Chamber door, conversing as they went along, while others very unceremoniously saluted Sharpe with the epithets of Judas and traitor; and one of them more forward than the rest, laid her hand upon his neck, and told him "that neck behoved to pay for it before all was done." The whole of the lords to whom the papers were presented, received them civilly, except Stair, who threw his scornfully upon the ground, which drew upon him a sarcastic remark—"that he had not so treated the remonstrance against the king which he helped to pen." When the council met, the petition was voted a libel, and about a dozen of the subscribers were called and examined. They declared severally that no man had had any hand in the matter, and that their sole motive was a sense of their perishing condition for want of the gospel, having no preachers except ignorant and profane persons whom they could not hear; upon which they were ordered into confinement, and the Lord Provost and the guard sent to disperse the ladies at the door;

but they refused to depart without their representatives, who were in consequence politely liberated, and the tumult ended. Next day, however, they were again summoned, when three were sent to prison—Margaret, a daughter of Lord Warriston's; a Mrs. Cleland; and a Lilias Campbell. The former, with Lady Mersington and some others, were banished the town and liberties of Edinburgh; and so ended this affair.

The fears of the ladies were not unfounded. A letter from the king to the council was read at the same meeting, requiring them "to use their utmost endeavours for apprehending preachers at field conventicles, invaders of pulpits, and ringleading heritors, and to make use of the militia and standing force for that end, leaving the punishment of the other transgressors to the ordinary magistrates according to law." In obedience to which a committee was appointed with full powers to meet when and where they should think convenient, to make the necessary inquiries, apprehend whom they should think proper, and the standing force and militia were placed under their immediate direction. At the head was the Archbishop of St. Andrews, the Lord Chancellor, and other servants of the crown, assisted by the Earls of Argyle, Linlithgow, Kinghorn, Wigton, and Dundonald. The Duke of Hamilton was named; but in present circumstances possessed little power and seldom attended. Orders were at the same time issued for apprehending the following ministers:—John Welsh, Gabriel Semple, Robert Ross, Samuel Arnot, Gabriel Cunningham, Archibald Riddel, John Mosman, John Blackader, William Wiseheart, David Hume, John Dickson, John Rae, Henry Forsyth, Thomas Hogg, Robert Law, George Johnstone, Thomas Forrester, Fraser of Brea, John Law, Robert Gillespie. And to encourage the parties sent out on this duty, for the two first, as the most notorious offenders, a reward of four hundred pounds sterling each was offered; for the others, one thousand merks; and the soldiers and others who might assist in their seizure, were previously pardoned for any bloodshed that might occur—such was the inveteracy the rulers of Scotland betrayed against men whose only crime was preaching the gospel. They then proceeded to show nearly equal abhorrence for those who heard it, by punishing with fines or imprisonment the most obstinate of the heritors. The town of Edinburgh was amerced in one hundred pounds sterling for conventicles in the Magdalene Chapel, to be exacted from the chief citizens present; Mr. John Inglis, of Cramond, for hearing sermon six times in his parish church, a thousand and thirty-six pounds Scots; a gentleman in Fife, for allowing Mr. Welsh to lodge in his house one night, was fined two thousand merks; and eleven heritors, upwards of five thousand five hundred for attending field-preachings—all which moneys were ordered to be summarily levied, and the offenders kept in prison till the same should be paid. Nor were persons, even of high rank, and against whom no charges of very intrusive piety are known to have existed, exempt from being harassed by any vile, petty, clerical informer. Lord Balmerino and Sir John Young of Leny, neither of whom had been present at any such preaching, were brought before the council; and when they denied the fact, were insultingly tendered the oath of allegiance, which both must have already repeatedly sworn before they were dismissed.

Two rigorous proclamations followed. By the first, all masters were required to prevent their servants from being present at any house or field conventicle, and to retain none in their employment for whose conduct they would not be answerable; heritors were ordered to require their tenants to subscribe a bond, obliging themselves, wives, cottars, or servants, to abstain from all such meetings, which, if they refused, they were to be put to the horn, and their escheat given to their landlords; but masters and landlords were responsible for the conduct of their inferiors to the extent of the fines their disobedience might incur; and all magistrates were empowered to oblige such as they chose to suspect, to give bond for their good behaviour. The second was directed against ministers, in terms of the orders already issued for their apprehension. Still further to stimulate the magistrates, another letter was procured from the king, informing them that his majesty had heard of the alarming increase of conventicles, for repressing which, together with the other seditious movements in Scotland, he had ordered his troops in Ireland and at Berwick to hold themselves in readiness, to march on the first alarm; and, in the meantime, required them to bring to punishment the authors of these insolent and seditious practices. But the difficulty of obtaining proof forming some small impediment in the way of conviction, the council therefore proposed that, when a suspected person was apprehended, against whom they had not sufficient evidence, he should be interrogated to answer upon oath, and if he refused to answer, he should be held as confessed, and proceeded against accordingly, only the punishment should be restricted to fining, imprisonment, exile, or the loss of a limb—most merciful judges!—to which his majesty was graciously pleased to consent, and the counsel proceeded to act.

They summoned a number of the "outted" ministers to appear, not in the usual mode by leaving written copies at their dwelling-places, but at the market-crosses of Edinburgh, Lanark, Stirling, and Perth, and that within such a time, that, had they been willing, they could not have complied. As the latter knew, however, that if they appeared, they were certain of being sent either to the Bass or into banishment, they declined, and were in consequence denounced as rebels.* When the council rose, on

* The names of these worthies who deserve, and who will be had in everlasting remembrance, when those of their persecutors must rot, are thus given by one of themselves:—Alexander Lennox, David Williamsone, Alexander Moncrieff, John Rae, David Hume, Edward Jamieson, James Fraser, William Wiseheart, Thomas Hogg in Ross, Robert Lockhart, John Wilkie, George Johnstone, Patrick Gillespie, James Kirkton, John Weir, Nathaniel Martin, Andrew Morton, Andrew Donaldsone, John Crichton, William

the last day of July, they reported to the secretary, that forty "outted" ministers had been cited before them, none of whom having appeared, they were all ordered to be denounced; and that eighty persons, for hearing sermon in the fields of Fife, had also been delated, of whom all that answered had been found guilty and imprisoned, the remainder declared fugitives, and their escheats appointed to be taken for his majesty's use.* The magistrates of Glasgow, also, had been fined one hundred pounds sterling; and the magistrates of burghs, south of the Tay, had been ordered to press upon the citizens the bond against keeping conventicles.

While the primate was urging the persecution of these excellent men, he was not without trouble from his own underlings. In the beginning of the year, some of the bishops, as well as curates, began to complain of the arbitrary measures of Sharpe, who managed all ecclesiastical affairs without consulting them upon any occasion, and had even the audacity to stamp upon him the opprobrious epithet of Pope. His friends repelled the accusations as the unfounded aspersions of the Hamilton or country party, who, having failed to overturn the Duke of Lauderdale by means of the Presbyterians, now wished to do it by means of the Episcopalians. The others declared they only wished what the act of Parliament allowed, to assemble in a National Synod, and regulate what they considered wrong in the church—the best

Row, Thomas Urquhart, Thomas Hogg in Larbore, [Larbert] William Arskine, James Donaldson, Robert Gillespie, John Gray, James Wedderburn, John Wardlaw, Thomas Douglas, George Campbell, Francis Irvine, John Wallace, Andrew Anderson, John Munniman, George Hamilton, Donald Cargill, Alexander Bertram, James Wilson, Robert Maxwell—in all thirty-nine. These were the stock of the preaching church that was driven into the wilderness—their ministry was a sort of outlawry—and, by the bishop's activity, these, with the ministers formerly forfaulted, and those who afterwards joined that body of people, who first caused the separation from bishops and their curates, thereafter overthrew their party, and wrought the Reformation.

* "One day a paper was fixt upon the Parliament House door, containing upwards of one hundred persons, whose escheats were to be sold to any who would purchase them."—*Wodrow*, vol. i p. 384,

method of securing its stability. But Sharpe, who, of all things, dreaded the least interference with his power, wrote to the Archbishop of Canterbury, entreating him—in a most impious appropriation of Scripture language—to interfere and assist him against those who wished "to break his bands, and cast his cords from them;" and his application was so successful, that the most active of the suffragans were silenced, and Ramsay, bishop of Dunblane, was removed to the Isles—a kind of honourable banishment, which effectually put an end to all attempts for the future at interfering with the supremacy of his Grace of St. Andrews. The only other bishop (Leighton) who had ever given him real vexation, but against whom his wiles had been useless, voluntarily withdrawing from the scene of contention, Burnet was restored to Glasgow, and henceforth was content to play second to Sharpe, only rivalling his oppression within the boundaries of his own archiepiscopal territories.

BOOK IX.

A. D. 1674—1676.

Divisions among the ministers respecting the church and self-defence—Armed meetings—Severities increase—Lord Cardross—Religious revivals in the North—Mr. M'Gilligan—Civil oppression—Home of Polwart—Finings—Durham of Largo—Magistrates of Edinburgh—Sufferers sent to France as recruits—Proclamation to expel the families of gospel-hearers from the Burghs, and enforce the conventicle act—Instructions for the indulged—Progress of the gospel—Rage of the prelates—Mitchell tortured.

Unhappily the seeds of division which the indulgence had sown among the Presbyterian ministers, were beginning to take root; and the different opinions that afterwards reached so great and ruinous a height, showed themselves in the discussions which took place during this year upon that important question—How the Presbyterian church was to be continued and supplied? The documents preserved are very scanty; only it appears that the propriety of ordaining a minister, except to a settled charge—of preaching within the nominal bounds of an unsettled presbytery—and the authoritative right of synodical meetings, were among the questions about which differences had sprung up among the brethren. And from the care with which they endeavour to provide against one minister noticing the conduct of another "in their preaching, and warning the people of the evils of the times," it seems pretty evident that this baneful practice had already commenced.

At the close of the year, the state of feeling and anticipation among the suffering Presbyterians was extremely dissimilar, as we find by the writings both of public men and private Christians which have been preserved. Numbers rejoiced in the bright and sunny side of the cloud, in the increase of faithful preachers of the gospel—in the desire for hearing that seemed to be abroad—and in the delightful and not rare instances of the power of the Spirit that accompanied the publication of the word; and they anticipated a speedy and a glorious renovating morn for the church. Those that studied the signs of the times, saw in the apostasy of some, and in the falling away of others who had been esteemed pillars; in the mournful waxing cold of the love of many; in the bitter dissensions of professors; and in the general abounding iniquity—the dark and dismal tokens of a deserted church; and, although they knew and believed that the cause of Christ could never fall, and hoped and rejoiced in the hope that a glorious day would yet arise upon Scotland, wept and made mournful supplication for the sins of the people among whom they dwelt, and anticipated heavier judgments for unimproved mercies, until a returning to Him against whom they had offended should again draw down the blessing.

The increasing severities which now began to be used towards the conventicles likewise occasioned a difference of opinion among the godly ministers and people as to the right of self-defence in hearing the gospel. The injunction of Christ as to individuals is clear, when persecuted in one city, flee into another; but in Scotland, where the throne of iniquity framed mischief by a law, and where the whole Presbyterians, who formed a large majority, were at once deprived of their civil rights, as well as their religious privileges—and where a constitution as solemnly ratified, and as sacredly sworn to, as any mutual agreement between rulers and people ever was, or ever can be, had been wantonly destroyed by a wretched minority of riotous unprincipled sycophants, and place-hunting apostates—the question involved, in the opinion of many, not only their duty as Christians, but as citizens. Paul had taught them that these were not incompatible, and their fathers had vindicated both in the field. The young men were generally of this opinion, and began to come armed to sermons about the commencement of this year [1675], and talked of imitating the example of the days of the congregation. The elder and most esteemed among the ministers were divided; while, in general, they allowed the soundness of the principle, they differed as to the propriety of the time. Among these appear to have been Mr. Welsh, Mr. Blackader, and Gabriel Semple; others, at the head of whom stood Fraser of Brea and Kirkton, were entirely averse to any resort to arms. The former thus states his views of the subject:—

"A violent persecution had broken out; and then there began to be fining, imprisoning, taking, and summoning of persons, disturbing of conventicles with soldiers. But yet the gospel prevailed more and more, and we were like the Israelites in Egypt, the more we were afflicted, the more we grew and multiplied. Some hot heads were for taking the sword and redeeming of themselves from the hands of the oppressors; at least I had ground to fear it. But I opposed rising in arms all I could, and preached against it, and exhorted them to patience, and courageous using of the sword of the Spirit; and I did not see they had any call to the sword, and their strength was to sit still; and if they did stir and take the sword, they would therewith perish; but if they patiently suffered and endured, God would himself either incline to pity, or some other way support and deliver them. I had influence with the people, being popular, and whilst I was at liberty I did what I could to keep the people peaceable. The truth is, there were great provocations given, so that we concluded it was the design of some rulers to stir us up that we might fall. Ministers still preached and laboured among the people; conventicles increased; many were brought in; the work of God in the midst of persecution, did always prosper, until we destroyed ourselves, first by needless divisions and difference of opinion, happening by reason of the indulgence; and thereafter by rash and unwarrantable taking up of arms."

Gentlemen in Scotland at this time, it requires to be remembered, always wore arms as a part of dress; and the substantial heritors and yeomen were in general accustomed to be accoutred when they went from home, so that part of the meetings at field-preachings had always consisted of armed men, who, before this, had offered upon several occasions to defend their ministers at the risk of their lives, but had been refused, and who now thought that in protecting their assemblies from robbery and dispersion, and themselves from imprisonment, fining, or slavery —the inevitable consequence of being seized upon these occasions—they were doing no more than was required by the law of God, and authorized by the law of their country, of which the prelatic party, and not they, were the invaders and violators.

Many contests had already ensued. The Episcopalian myrmidons in Linlithgowshire, and even in Fife, had repeatedly drawn blood, while the patient hearers of the gospel had only fled before them. The rough borderers were not equally submissive.* At Lilliesleaf, and throughout some of these districts, they had stood upon the defensive and beaten off their assailants; and affairs were in this situation during the greater part of this year. Upon the complaints of the prelates, troops were ordered to scour the country in different directions. Edinburgh and Glasgow were again fined each in the sum of one hundred pounds sterling; and in addition, a detachment both of horse and foot were quartered in the latter city. Mr. John Greg, for preaching at Leith

* Let it be always borne in mind, that the whole crowd who attended field-preaching, were not influenced by gospel principles, nor could be considered godly men, any more than that able disputers and fierce contenders for the pure faith, are always themselves believers. It is an awful consideration, that the most strenuous fighters for the purity of God's word—the Jews—were infidels, and thus addressed by our Saviour—"Ye have one that condemns you, even Moses, in whom ye trust;" and the best written "Plea for the Divinity of Christ," was written by a man who turned a Socinian. Beware of zealots!

mills, was sent to the Bass; and a Mr. John Sandilands, for hearing a sermon near Bathgate, was fined three hundred merks. Nor were the nobility themselves spared. One of the most cruelly oppressive cases was that of Lord Cardross.

His lordship being confined in Edinburgh in the month of May, his lady, who was far advanced in pregnancy, remained at home, with only a few attendants. Sir Mungo Murray, taking advantage of this circumstance, under cloud of night, accompanied by a posse of retainers, went to his residence, and outrageously demanded that the gates should be opened to him, else he would force his way and set fire to the house. Situated near the borders of the Highlands, the inmates naturally supposing them banditti, refused admission and demanded who they were. To this no answer could be obtained, but "Scottishmen," which increased their alarm; yet fearing the worst, as there were no means of defence, and no defenders, the gates were opened, when the ruffians rushed in; and, after searching the whole apartments in the most tumultuous and indelicate manner—forcing Lady Cardross to rise from her bed that they might search her chamber—and ransacking his lordship's private closet, they seized Mr. John King, his chaplain, and Mr. Robert Langlands, governor to his brother, afterwards Colonel John Erskine, and carried them off. Langlands was dismissed after being marched ten miles; Mr. John King was rescued by some countrymen who had profited by his ministry. For this proceeding they had no warrant; and Lord Cardross, immediately upon being informed of the outrage, presented a complaint and petition to the privy council; but, instead of receiving any satisfaction for the gross violation, not only of his privileges as a nobleman, but his rights as a subject, he was charged with having been guilty, art and part, in the rescue of Mr. John King, although he was sixty miles distant; for harbouring him in his house, and for his lady's having been present at many conventicles: and for these complicated crimes, he was sentenced to be imprisoned during his majesty's pleasure in Edinburgh Castle, to pay a fine of one thousand pounds sterling, besides various sums for the delinquencies of his tenants.

Fining, imprisonment, and exile being found inadequate to the suppression of conventicles, other and more rigorous methods were resorted to. The houses of some of the principal gentlemen in the most infected counties were seized, and garrisoned by parties of horse and foot, that the least appearance of any gathering for hearing sermon might at once be put down, with as much care and celerity as the gathering of a civil, or the landing of a foreign enemy; and a number of the most faithful, diligent, and able ministers this country was ever favoured with, were "intercommuned," their presence declared infectious as the plague, and every loyal person prohibited from conversing with or doing them any office, not of kindness, but of common humanity, under the pain of being placed themselves without the pale of society.*

But one of the persecuted themselves remarks—"Although this seemed to be the first storm of persecution that yet had fallen upon us, and that now the adversaries had boasted of an effectual mean for suppressing conventicles, and establishing prelacy and uniformity, and the good people feared it; yet the Lord did wonderfully disappoint them, and made and turned their witty councils into folly—for this great noise harmed not at all, it was powder without ball. For, as for myself, never one that cared for

* The names of these were—"David Williamson, Alexander Moncrief, William Wiseheart, Thomas Hogg in Ross, George Johnstone, Robert Gillespie, John McGilligan, John Ross, Thomas Hogg, Stirlingshire, William Erskine, James Donaldson, Andrew Anderson, Andrew Morton, Donald Cargill, Robert Maxwell, elder and younger, James Fraser of Brea, John King; and with these a good many ladies and gentlemen were joined, besides many of lower rank, altogether upwards of one hundred persons." *Wodrow*, vol. i. p. 394. This revival of a dormant and iniquitous law was peculiarly oppressive, as all who conversed with the intercommuned being liable to the same punishment, thousands might be unwittingly implicated, and laid at the mercy of their rapacious rulers.

me shunned my company; yea, a great many mere carnal relations and acquaintances did entertain me as freely as ever they did; yea, so far did the goodness of the Lord turn this to my good, that I observed it was at that time I got most of my civil business expede. And as the Lord preserved myself in this storm, so I did not hear of any intercommuned, or conversers with intercommuned persons, that were in the least prejudiced thereby; nay, this matter of the intercommuning of so many good and peaceable men did but exasperate the people against the bishops the more, and procured to them, as the authors of such rigid courses, a greater and more universal hatred; so that the whole land groaned to be delivered from them."

Danger, indeed, seemed to endear the ministers to the people; and the risks they ran, and the many providential occurrences which attended their meetings, produced a high degree of excitement, that tended in no small measure to secure large and attentive audiences, and prepared their minds for a solemn reception of the doctrines they heard, at the peril of their lives.

North of the Tay there were but few Presbyterian ministers, and they had not hitherto been very closely pursued; but among them were some of the most excellent, and these of course were included in the act of intercommuning—for their labours had been equally abundant with the rest. Mr. John M'Gilligan of Alness, was one of not the least conspicuous, either for success or for suffering. In September, the very month following his being denounced, he dispensed the ordinance of the Lord's Supper at Obsdale, in the house of Lady Dowager Fowlis, assisted by Mr. Hugh Anderson, minister of Cromarty, and Mr. Alexander Fraser, minister of Teviot. According to the account preserved of it, it seems to have been one of those heart-enlivening seasons which the Lord sometimes vouchsafes to his church in the day of her visitation. "There were," says the narrator "so sensible and glorious discoveries made of the

Son of Man, and such evident presence of the Master of assemblies, that the people seemed to breathe the very atmosphere of heaven; and some were so transportingly elevated, that they could almost use the language of the apostle—'whether in the body or out of the body, I cannot tell.' The eldest Christians there, declared they had not been witnesses to the like. They also remarked that the Lord wonderfully preserved them in peace."

Some rumours of an intended communion having got abroad, the sheriff-depute was ordered by the bishop to prevent or disperse the meeting. He accordingly sent a party to apprehend the minister; but he not knowing the spot, directed them to proceed to his house at Alness, naturally supposing the meeting would be there. The soldiers, upon finding the nest empty, attacked the orchard—a much more pleasant amusement, that detained them till the forenoon's service was over at Obsdale, where, before they arrived, Mr. M'Gilligan had got notice, and was under hiding, which, when they found, they retired without disturbing the congregation; and the sacred solemnities proceeded without any further interruption. Mr. M'Gilligan, however, was obliged to abscond; and one of his neighbours, Mr. Thomas Ross, being apprehended at Tain for a similar offence, was sent to the Bass.

Civil tyranny is always so interwoven with ecclesiastical persecutions, that it is seldom we are able to separate the two. But the sufferings of Sir Patrick Home of Polwart, although they undoubtedly originated from his religion, were ultimately effected through the medium of his patriotism: he legally, by a bill of suspension before the Court of Session, resisted a wanton stretch of power in the privy council, and endeavoured to rouse the opposition of the gentry of Berwickshire towards an oppressive unjust tax for planting garrisons among them in time of peace; and for this undoubted exercise of his right, was committed, by order of the king, prisoner to Stirling Castle, and declared incapable of holding any place of trust; and the heritors succumbed, although the other fines extorted from the shire this year amounted to nearly twenty-seven thousand pounds Scots.

Nor were the indulged suffered to enjoy their limited and precarious pardon quietly; their stipends were withheld or tardily paid, and that only upon their producing certificates from the sheriffs that they had kept no conventicles for the last twelve-month; but their most vexatious trials were the natural consequences of their acknowledging the power of the civil magistrate in ecclesiastical affairs, and owning his warrant, rather than the authority of Christ, as the rule in their ministerial labours. Complaints were brought against them, and they were summoned before the council for not celebrating the communion on the same day in all their parishes—for irregular baptisms—and for having preached in churchyards and other places than the kirks; but, above all, for having presumed to authorize young men to preach the gospel, and ordained others to the work of the ministry; and, at a time when a long tract of unseasonable weather seemed to threaten a famine, they had usurped a power which belonged to majesty alone, or his delegates, and had appointed a fast in their several congregations! Through the interest of Lord Stair, however, these grievances were not pushed to extremities this year.

[1676.] Whatever circumstances might induce any occasional relaxation in the severity of the persecution, the spirit remained the same; and no opportunity was suffered to escape by which the preaching of the gospel might be put down by men calling themselves Christian bishops. The soldiers in the garrisons were their willing instruments, and as they shared in the plunder, were active in the pursuit; yet meetings for hearing the word continued to increase, and the ordinances of religion were administered with a solemnity and power, often at midnight, which rendered them the general topics of interest and conversation among the people, and still more the objects of aversion to the prelates. Finings for "conventicles" were therefore inflicted by the council with unmitigated rigour. Durham of Largo, for offences of this nature, and harbouring that "notour traitor," John Welsh, was early in the year mulcted for nearly four thousand pounds Scots; Colonel Kerr, several ladies, and some citizens of Edinburgh, were legally plundered in various sums each, of five hundred merks, two hundred pounds, and one hundred pounds Scots, for being at house conventicles within the city; but the magistrates having also suffered for these "enormities," being soused for not preventing what they had never previously heard of, were allowed to reimburse themselves by fining the culprits, who were thus punished twice for one crime.

A more revolting case of wanton cruelty was, about the same time, exercised toward some poor men who had been guilty of attending sermon in the fields near Stirling. Towards the end of 1674, they had been seized in the act and carried to jail; eight, by some means or other, had got out—and the remaining seven sent the following affecting petition to the council in the month of February:—"The petitioners, being prisoners in the tolbooth of Stirling, these fifteen months bypast, some of us being poor decrepit bodies, and all of us poor creatures with wives and families, we have been many times at the point of starving, and had long ere now died for want, if we had not been supplied with the charity of other people: The truth whereof is notour to all who live near Stirling, and which the magistrates have testified by a report under their hands: Wherefore, it is humbly desired that your lordships would compassionate our pitiful and deplorable condition, and that of our poor starving wives and children, and order us liberty, we being willing to enact ourselves to compear and answer before your lordships whenever we should be called." Of those who signed, one, Charles Campbell, was upwards of sixty, and one, John Adam, near seventy years of age; the others were labouring under severe bodily indisposition.

Yet, instead of being moved by the pitiful tale of these harmless, aged, and sickly prisoners, the council, with an inhumanity which it would not be easy to designate properly, ordered them to be turned over as recruits, to one of Lauderdale's minions, a Captain Maitland, then an officer in the French service; and on Friday, February 18, at midnight they were delivered to a party of soldiers, fettered and tied together, and marched off without any previous warning. But they went cheerfully away, although they knew not whither; for they knew the Master whom they served would never leave them naked to their enemies in their old age.

These severities were followed up by a fresh proclamation against conventicles, in which, with the most hypocritical falsehood, after lauding the king's princely care and zeal for the interests of the Protestant reformed religion and the church, and lamenting the sad and sensible decay religion had suffered, and the great and dangerous increase of profaneness, through the most unreasonable and schismatical separation of many from the public and established worship, and the frequent and open conventicles, both in houses and fields—magistrates were required rigorously to apprehend all who were intercommuned, and to expel their families from the burghs, together with such preachers and their families as did not regularly attend public worship—to enforce the acts against conventicles and separation, under a penalty of five hundred merks if they did not annually report their proceedings, and five hundred or upwards additional, for every conventicle that shall have been held within their jurisdictions, besides whatever other fine the council might choose to inflict. All noblemen, gentlemen, and burgesses were forbid to entertain any chaplain, tutor, or schoolmaster, under penalties proportioned to their rank, from six hundred to three thousand merks; and informers were, according to the system of the times, by the same proclamation, encouraged and rewarded by a share of the fines. Committees were also appointed to investigate and punish transgressors, who fined and imprisoned many of the most respectable heritors and gentlemen, particularly in the west, and outlawed others who had declined answering their summons.

Enemies to the gospel of Christ, the prelatic rulers did not confine their opposition to the preaching of the "outted" ministers, the indulged were at the same time subjected to greater burdens. It was evidently one of their main objects to produce division among the Presbyterian ministers; and as we have seen the indulgence was admirably calculated to effect this, yet the breach being neither so wide nor so violent as they wished, "instructions" were issued to them by the council. Assuming that they had accepted of liberty to preach under conditions, the council accused them of violating their engagements by baptizing without the necessary certificates, and preaching in other places than their own kirk, without any license from the bishop; and they added this injunction, that they should not employ or allow any of their brethren to preach for them who had not also obtained similar liberty. The indulged eluded the charges, by alleging that they accepted of the indulgence as a boon from government, not upon conditions, but as a favour granted; and the instructions they considered as orders upon which they were to act at their peril. But this neither satisfied the council nor their brethren, both of whom concurred in thinking it an evasion rather than an honest justification of their conduct. With the injunction they appear to have complied also—a very unsatisfactory procedure—which induced some, particularly of the younger unindulged preachers, to visit the boundaries of their parishes, and led to heart-burnings and mutual accusations between those who thought they might yield a little to the pressure of the times, and those who in nothing would recede from their avouched principles. These differences, which afterwards unhappily led to coldness and estrangement among the friends of "the good cause," did not produce their most mischievous effects till the oldest, stanch, tried worthies were removed from the field. Meanwhile, the dispersion of the ministers, who, when they were scattered abroad, went every where preaching the word, was eminently blessed to promote that gospel it was intended to destroy, and conventicles multiplied on every side both in houses and fields.

Of the period from 1673 to 1679, Shiels gave this animating picture on reviewing it many years after, when the holy excitement had subsided, and temporal prosperity had begun to diffuse its seductive influence over the revolution-church:—"When by persecution many ministers had been chased away by illegal law sentences, many had been banished away, and, by their ensnaring indulgences, many had been drawn away from their duty; and others were now sentenced with confinements and restraints if they should not choose and fix their residences where they could not keep their quiet and conscience both—they were forced to wander and disperse through the country; and the people being tired of the cold and dead *curates*, and wanting long the ministry of their old *pastors*, so longed and hungered after the *word*, that they behoved to have it at any rate, cost what it would; which made them entertain the dispersed ministers more earnestly, and encouraged them more to their duty; by whose endeavours—through the mighty power and presence of God, and the light of his countenance now shining through the cloud, after so fatal and fearful a darkness that had overclouded the land for a while, that it made their enemies gnash their teeth for pain, and dazzled the eyes of all onlookers—the word of God grew exceedingly, and went through at least the southern borders like lightning; or, like the sun in its meridian beauty, discovering so the wonders of God's law, the mysteries of his gospel, and the secrets of his covenant, and the sins and duties of that day, that a numerous issue was begotten to Christ, and his conquest was glorious, captivating poor slaves of Satan and bringing them from his power unto God, and from darkness to light.

"Oh! who can remember the glory of that day, without a melting heart in reflecting upon what we have lost, and let go, and sinned away by our misimprovement—a day of such power that it made the people, even the bulk and body of the people, willing to come out and venture upon the greatest of hardships, and the greatest of hazards, in pursuing after the gospel, through mosses, and muirs, and inaccessible mountains, summer and winter, through excess of heat and extremity of cold, many days' and nights' journeys, even when they could not have a probable expectation of escaping the sword of the wilderness. But this was a day of such power, that nothing could daunt them from their duty that had tasted once the sweetness of the Lord's presence at these persecuted meetings.

"Then we had such *humiliation-days* for personal and public defections, such *communion-days* even in the open fields, and such *Sabbath-solemnities*, that the places where they were kept might have been called *Bethel*, or *Peniel*, or *Bochim*, and all of them *Jehovah-Shammah*, wherein many were truly converted, more convinced, and generally all reformed from their former immoralities; that even robbers, thieves, and profane men, were some of them brought to a saving subjection to Christ, and generally under such restraint, that all the severities of heading and hanging in a great many years could not make such a civil reformation as a few days of the gospel in these formerly the devil's territories, now Christ's quarters, where his kingly standard was displayed. I have not language to lay out the inexpressible glory of that day; but I doubt if ever there were greater days of the Son of Man upon the earth, than we enjoyed for the space of seven years at that time.*

The border districts, so notorious in our earlier history as the fields of constant plundering and murder,

* *Hind let Loose*, p. 132.

exhibited now amid their wild scenery a warfare of a very different description. "What wonderful success," says Veitch, "the preaching of the word has had by ministers retiring thither, under persecution, in order to the repressing, yea almost extinguishing, these feuds, thefts, and robberies, that were then so natural to that place and people, is worth a singular and serious observation. These news ought to be matter of joy and thanksgiving to all the truly godly in Britain, that, though the ark, the glory, and goings of our God be, alas! too much removed from Shiloh-Ephratah, the ingrounds, the places of greater outward plenty and pleasure, yet that he is to be found in the borders of those lands, in the mountains and fields of the woods. Some of the gentry on both sides of the borders have been forced both to see and say that the gospel has done that which their execution of the laws could never accomplish. And is not such a change worthy of remark? to see a people who used to ride unweariedly through the long winter nights to steal and drive away the prize, now, upon the report of a sermon, come from far, travelling all night, to hear the gospel; yea, some bringing their children along with them to the ordinance of baptism, although the landlord threaten to eject the tenant, and the master the servant, for so doing."* Mr. Gabriel Semple gives a similar statement. "These borderers were looked upon to be ignorant, barbarous, and debauched with all sort of wickedness, that none thought it worth their consideration to look after them, thinking that they could not be brought to any reformation. Yet, in the Lord's infinite mercy, the preaching to these borderers had more fruit than in many places that were more civilized."†

What ought to have filled the breast of every right-hearted minister of the gospel with joy, excited the fellest passions in the bosoms of the prelates, who

* Memoirs of William Veitch, written by himself, published by Dr. McCrie, p. 118.

† Semple's Life, MSS., in Dr. Lee's possession, quoted by Dr. McCrie, as above.

evinced their filiation by doing the deeds of their father, (John viii. 44,) furiously seeking to destroy those who declared the truth; because, wherever a Presbyterian preacher came, the Episcopalian churches were forsaken, and the curates were left to harangue to empty pews. Political squabbling for power between Hamilton and Lauderdale, had diverted the attention of the two parties for a while from Scottish ecclesiastical affairs, which the ministers eagerly took advantage of to pursue their sacred vocation, judging wisely that the respite which they enjoyed would be at best precarious. When Lauderdale gained the ascendency, they anticipated a longer continuance of the "blink;"* but the clouds soon gathered thicker and darker. He knew he could only maintain his own elevation by exalting Episcopacy; and he quickly showed that his repeated declarations were not empty bravadoes. More correct in their calculations, the bishops improved the opportunity; and the council, his and their ready tool, issued fresh proclamations against conventicles, increasing in severity as they increased in number.

Averting their eyes from the loveliness of these bright prospects that shone around them, they mourned withal "the sad and sensible decays religion had of late suffered, and the great and dangerous increase of profaneness through the most unreasonable and schismatical separation of many from the public and established worship, and the frequent and open conventicles, both in houses and fields, by such as thereby discover their disaffection to the established religion, and their aversion to his majesty's authority and government, endangering the peace of the kingdom, and dividing the church under pretence of scruple:" therefore, to manifest their zeal for the glory of Almighty God, the interests of the Protestant reformed religion, and of the church—to secure the same by unity in worship, and procuring all due reverence to archbishops, bishops, and all subordinate clerical officers—the magistrates of the several burghs

* "Blink"—a glimpse of sunshine in foul weather.

were specially required to seize upon all persons who were, or should be, intercommuned, and to remove the families of such from all places under their jurisdiction, together with all preachers and their families who did not attend the public worship! All noblemen, gentlemen, and others, were strictly forbid to afford shelter or aid to any intercommuned person, upon pain of being themselves intercommuned; and whosoever should discover those that transgressed, were to receive five hundred merks reward immediately. Magistrates were also rendered liable to severe fining, if they did not rigorously fulfil the imperative duty of searching out and punishing all such as worshipped God after the manner they chose to call heresy.

What means they thought lawful for obtaining information from suspected persons, is evinced in their treatment of James Mitchell, who made the unsuccessful attempt upon Sharpe. He had left the country at the time, and did not return till he supposed the affair was forgotten, when he married a woman who kept a small shop not far from the primate's town residence. In passing this way, his Grace observed a person eye him keenly, which rather alarmed him, as he thought he recognized his foiled assassin; and he caused him to be arrested. A pistol, loaded with three bullets, being found in his pocket, increased his terror, and he became extremely anxious to know the extent of his danger. Accordingly, before the prisoner was examined, he swore by the living God, if he would confess the act, he would obtain his pardon; and a committee of the privy council, consisting of Rothes, Lord Chancellor; Primrose, Lord Register; Nisbet, Lord Advocate; and Hatton, Treasurer-depute, authorized by the Commissioner, gave him a similar assurance. Disappointed, however, by his confession, as they expected to discover a conspiracy, on finding he had no accomplice, and unwilling that he should thus escape, they remitted him to the Justiciary Court, evading their solemn engagement by a jesuitical quibble, that the promise of securing his life did not guarantee the safety of his limbs. Having received a hint, as he was passing to trial, he disclaimed his confession at the bar; and there being no other proof, the judicial proceedings were abandoned, or, in Scottish law-phrase, the "diet" was deserted, and he was remanded to prison, where he remained till January this year, when the spirit of cruelty which appeared to actuate the then rulers against all who were rigid Presbyterians, especially preachers, urged them to subject their unhappy victim to the torture.

About six o'clock in the evening of January 18th, Mitchell was brought before a meeting of Justiciary, where the Earl of Linlithgow sat president, and questioned whether he would adhere to his former confession. He replied, that the Lord Advocate having deserted the diet against him, he ought to have been, agreeably both to the law of the nation and the practice of the court, set at liberty, and therefore knew no reason why he was that night brought before their lordships. Without any attention being paid to this strictly legal objection, he was again asked, if he would adhere to his former confession? He refused to own any confession; and Hatton most outrageously exclaimed, "that pannel is one of the most arrogant cheats, liars, and rogues I have ever known!" Mr. Mitchell retorted, My lord, if there were fewer of those persons you have been speaking of in the nation, I would not have been standing at this bar. The President said, "We will cause a sharper thing make you confess." "I hope, my lord, you are Christians and not Pagans," was the prisoner's response, with which the business of that evening closed.

Upon the 22d, he was brought before them in the lower Council-Chamber, and the question repeated, the President at the same time pointing to the boots, said, "You see, sir, what is upon the table; I will see if that will make you confess." "My lord," answered Mitchell intrepidly, "I confess by torture you may make me blaspheme God, as Saul did compel the saints; you may compel me to call myself a thief, a murderer, a warlock, or any thing, and then pannel me upon it; but if you shall, my lord, put me to it, I here protest before God and your lordships, that nothing extorted from me by torture shall be made use of against me in judgment, nor have any force in law against me or any person whatsomever. But to be plain with you, my lords, I am so much of a Christian, that whatever your lordships shall legally prove against me, if it be a truth, I shall not deny it; but, on the contrary, I am so much of a man, and a Scottishman, that I never hold myself obliged by the law of God, nature, or the nation, to become my own accuser." Hatton rudely answered—"He hath the devil's logic, and sophisticates like him; ask him whether that be his subscription." "I acknowledge no such thing," said the pannel, and was remanded to jail.

Two days after, the judges, in formal pomp, arrayed in their robes, and attended by the executioner with the instruments of torture, like true inquisitors, first attempted to terrify their prisoner, before they literally put him to the question. It was in vain. They could not shake him. Had they not been dead to every nobler feeling of our nature, they must have quailed when he thus addressed them:—"My lords, I have now been these two full years in prison, and more than one of them in bolts and fetters—more intolerable than many deaths. Some in a shorter time have been tempted to make away with themselves; but, in obedience to the express command of God, I have endured all these hardships, and I hope to endure this torture also with patience, on purpose to preserve my own life, and that of others also, as far as lies in my power, and to keep the guilt of innocent blood off your lordships and your families, which you doubtless would incur by shedding mine. I repeat my protest. When you please, call for the men you have appointed to their work." The executioner being in attendance, immediately tied Mr. Mitchell in an arm-chair, and asked which of the legs he should take. The lords said, "Any of them." The executioner laid in the left; but Mr. Mitchell taking it out, said, "Since the judges have not determined, take the best of the two; I bestow it freely in the cause." He was interrogated about his being at the battle of Pentland, his meeting with Wallace or with Captain Arnot—all of which he could veritably answer in the negative. The tormentor then began to drive the wedges, asking at every stroke if he had any more to say? To this he generally replied "No." After a while, when the pain began to be excruciating, he exclaimed, again addressing his inquisitors—"My lords, not knowing but this torture may end my life, I beseech you to remember, that 'he who showeth no mercy, shall have judgment without mercy;' for my own part, my lords, I do freely and from my heart forgive you who are judges, and the men who are appointed to go about this horrid work, and those who are satiating their eyes in beholding. I do entreat that God may never lay it to the charge of any of you, as I beg that God, for his Son Christ's sake, may be pleased to blot out my sin and mine iniquity." At the ninth, the sufferer fainted through the extremity of pain. "Alas! my lords," said the executioner, "he is gone!" The unfeeling wretches told him "he might stop," and coolly walked off. When Mitchell recovered, he was carried in the same chair back to his prison. Here he continued till January 1677, when he was sent to the Bass.

BOOK X

A. D. 1676—1677

Remarkable sacramental solemnities occasion harsher measures—Council new modelled—Committee for public affairs—Kerr of Kersland—Kirkton—The expatriated pursued to Holland—Colonel Wallace.

POLITICAL power combined with ecclesiastical, essentially forms a broad basis for the most excruciating tyranny, especially in spiritual matters, which admits of no medium between implicit obedience or cruel constraint. Accordingly, we always find, after some of those hallowed seasons in which the persecuted had been able to elude the vigilance of their oppressors, and had experienced them to be indeed times of refreshing from on high, that immediately some new and more violent proclamation followed, attempting, had it been possible, to have interdicted their sacred intercourse with heaven. Thus, the sacrament of the Lord's Supper having been longed for by many of those in the west who could not receive it at the hands of the incumbents of their parishes, several ministers resolved to celebrate it at diferent places, which was accordingly done with peculiar solemnity, under the covert of night, to numerous assemblages in the parish of Kippen, Stirlingshire; at the House of Haggs, near Glasgow; and in a barn at Kennyshead, parish of Eastwood; and it was remarked that the Lord very much owned these communions as sweet sealing ordinances; but no sooner were these doings whispered abroad, than a former proclamation against conventicles was repeated, of more extensive comprehension, and imposing a heavier penalty on every heritor in the land on whose estate they should be held. Several council-committees were appointed to perambulate the country, in order to enforce a vigorous execution of the extra-legal mandates. This they did by requiring a number of respectable gentlemen and ministers, whom they called before them, to declare upon oath what conventicles they had attended since the year 1674, what number of children they had seen baptized, and whether they had reset or harboured any intercommuned persons. Those who appeared were fined in various sums, according to their circumstances from fifty merks to a thousand pounds Scots. In this iniquitous inquisition, silence was construed into contempt; and to refuse, what no human law has a right to require, becoming one's own accuser, was punished even more severely than an acknowledgment of default.

At the same time, the council was new modelled. The primate was appointed president in absence of the Chancellor, and the two archbishops with any third creature of their own, formed a quorum of "the committee for public affairs," who assumed the entire management of ecclesiastical matters, then the chief if not the whole of public business. Perhaps the most detestable feature in the proceedings of this execrable committee was the system of espionage they carried into private life. An example will best illustrate the remark. Robert Kerr of Kersland having been forced to go abroad with his family, his lady returned to Scotland to arrange some little private business. He followed secretly, and to his great grief found her sick of a fever when he arrived, yet durst not lodge in the same house, but was wont to visit her stealthily in the evenings. Robert Cannon of Madrogat, a base spy, who hypocritically attended the secret meetings of the persecuted, at a time when he knew Kersland would be waiting on his sick lady, made application to Lauderdale for a warrant to apprehend Mr. John Welsh, represented as then keeping a conventicle in her chamber. A friend of her's who was with the Commissioner when he received the information, assured him that it was false, as she knew that Lady Kersland was very unwell. The warrant, however, was granted, but with express instructions from Lauderdale that the sick lady should not be disturbed if no conventicle appeared in the house.

A party came—there was no conventicle—and they were departing; but the reptile informer had told one of them that when any strangers came into the room, Kersland was wont to secrete himself behind the bed. He, accordingly, stepped direct to the place, and drawing the gentleman from his concealment, ordered him to surrender his arms. Kersland told him he had no arms but the Bible—the sword of the Spirit—which he presented to him. He was immediately made prisoner. When led away, his wife displayed great composure, and besought him to do nothing that might wound his conscience out of regard for her or her children, repeating earnestly as he left her—"No man having put his hand to the plough, and looking back, is fit for the kingdom of God."

Before the council, he undauntedly defended the patriotic "rising" at Pentland, as a lawful effort in defence of their liberties; on which he was immediately ordered to prison. When being carried off, the Chancellor sneeringly asked him what it was his lady said to him at parting? He replied "he did not exactly remember." "Then I will refresh your memory—she exhorted you to cleave to the good old cause;—ye are a sweet pack!" He was after this imprisoned in different jails for several years, till at last, being ordered into close confinement in Glasgow tolbooth, to be kept there during the archbishop's pleasure, who had a personal dislike at him, a dreadful fire most opportunely broke out in the town, which threatening the prison, the populace with instinctive humanity released all the inmates; and Kersland among the rest regained his liberty.* He

* "Nov. 3, 1677. The fire brake up in Glasgow in the heid of the Salt-mercat, on the right, near the cross, which was kyndled

then went to Holland, the common asylum for Protestant sufferers, and died at Utrecht, in November, 1680.

Perhaps a more flagrant and vexatious example of the harassment to which honest individuals were then exposed can scarcely be given, than that of the venerable Kirkton the historian. He was walking along the High Street of Edinburgh at mid-day, in the month of June, when—but we shall let him tell his own tale—"he was very civilly accosted by a young gentleman, Captain Carstairs, attended by another gentleman and a lackey. Carstairs desyred to speak a word with him, to which he answered he would wait upon him; but because he knew not to whom he spake, he quietly asked the other gentleman (James Scott of Tushielaw) who this young gentleman might be; but Scott answered with silence and staring. Then Mr. Kirkton perceived he was prisoner among his enemies, but was very glade they carried him to a private house, and not to the prison, which they were very near; but they carried him to Carstairs' chamber, ane ugly dark hole, in Robert Alexander, messenger, his house. As soon as ever he was brought into the house, Carstairs abused him with his

by a malicious boy, a smith's apprentice, who being threatened, or beatt and smittin by his master, in revenge whereof setts his work house on fyre in the night-tyme, being in the backsides of that fore-street, and flyes for it. It was kindled about one in the morning; and having brunt many in the backsyde, it breaks forth in the fore streets about three of the morning; and then it fyres the street over against it, and in a very short tyme burned down to more than the mids of the Salt-mercat; on both sydes fore and back houses were all consumed. It did burn also on that syde to the Tron Church, and two or three tenaments down on the heid of the Gallowgate. The heat was so great, that it fyred the horologe of the tolbooth (there being some prisoners in it at that tyme, amongst whom the Laird of Carsland was one, the people brake open the tolbooth-doors and sett them free); the people made it all their work to gett out their goods out of the houses; and there was little done to save houses till ten of the cloke, for it burnt till two hours afternoon. It was a great conflagration and nothing inferior to that which was in the yeir 1652. The wind changed several tymes. Great was the cry of the poor people, and lamentable to see their confusion. It was remarkable that a little before that tyme, there was seen a great fyre pass through these streets in the night-tyme, and strange voices heard in some parts of the city."—*Law's Memorials*, p. 135.

tongue, and pusht him till he got him into his own chamber, which made the people of the house weep. After he hade got him into his ugly chamber, he sent away Scott and Douglass, his lackey, (as Mr. Kirkton supposed) to fetch his companions; but as soon as they were alone, Mr. Kirkton askt him what he meant? what he would doe with him? Carstairs answered, sir, you owe me money. Mr. Kirkton askt him whom he took him to be, denying he owed him any thing. Carstaires answered, are not you John Wardlaw? Mr. Kirkton denied, telling him who he was indeed. Then Carstaires answered, if he were Mr. Kirkton he hade nothing to say to him. Mr. Kirkton askt him who he was. He answered he was Scott of Erkletone, whom indeed he did much resemble, but spoke things so inconsistent, Mr. Kirkton knew not what to think; for if Carstaires had designed to make him prisoner, he might easily have done it before. But after they hade stayed together about half an hour, Mr. Kirkton begane to think Carstaires desired money, and was just beginning to make his offer of money to Carstaires, when Jerviswood, Andrew Stevenson, and Patrick Johnston came to the chamber-door, and called in to Carstaires, asking what he did with a man in a dark dungeon, and all alone? Mr. Kirkton finding his friends come, tooke heart. 'Now,' sayes Mr. Kirkton to Carstaires, 'there be some honest gentlemen at your door, who will testifie what I am, and that I am not John Wardlaw; open the door to them.' 'That will I not,' sayes Carstaires, and with that layes his hand on his pocket-pistoll; which Mr. Kirkton perceiving, thought it high time to appear for himself, and so clapt Carstaires close in his armes; so mastering both his hands and his pistoll, they struggled awhile in the floor; but Carstaires being a feeble body, was borne back into a corner. The gentlemen without hearing the noise, and one crying out of murther, burst quickly the door open (for it hade neither key nor bolt,) and so entered, and quietly severed the strugglers, tho' without any violence or hurt done to Carstaires

"As soon as Mr. Kirkton and the gentlemen had left Carstaires alone, Scott, his companion, came to him, and they resolved not to let it goe so, but to turn their private violence into state service; and so to Hatton they goe with their complaint; and he upon the story calls all the Lords of the councill together, (tho' they were all at dinner,) as if all Edinburgh had been in armes to resist lawfull authority, for so they represented it to the councill: and he told the councill when they were conveened that their publick officers hade catcht a fanatick minister, and that he was rescued by a numerous tumult of the people of Edinburgh. The councill tryed what they could, and examined all they could find, and after all could discover nothing upon which they could fasten. Mr. Kirkton had informed his friends that it was only a reall robbery designed, and that indeed money would have freed him, if Carstaires and he hade finished what he begune to offer; and the council could find no more in it, and so some councillors were of opinion. But Bishop Sharpe told them that except Carstaires were encouraged, and Jerviswood made an example, they needed never think a man would follow the office of hunting fanaticks; and upon this all those who resolved to follow the time and please bishops, resolved to give Sharpe his will. So the next councill-day, after much high and hot debate in the councill, Jerviswood was fyned 9000 merks—[£562. 10s. sterling, a grievous sum in those days]—(3000 [£187. 10s.] of it to be given to Carstaires for a present reward;) Andrew Stevenson was fyned 1500 merks [£92. 15s.]; and Patrick Johnston in 1000 [£62. 10s.]; and all three condemned to ly in prison till Mr. Kirkton was brought to relieve them."

It would be difficult to find language to designate this transaction. Kirkton further informs us that it occasioned "great complaining," and "all the reason the councill gave of their severe sentence was, that they found Jerviswood guilty of resisting authority by Captain Carstaires' production of his warrand before the councill. But this did not satisfie men of reason; for, first, it was thought unaccountable that a lybell should be proven by the single testimony of ane infamous accuser against the declaration of three unquestionable men, and all the witnesses examined. Next, Carstaires' producing a warrand at the councill table, did not prove that he produced any warrand to Jerviswood, and, indeed, he produced none to him, because he had no warrand himself at that time; as for the warrand he produced, it was writ and subscribed by Bishop Sharpe after the deed was done, tho' the bishop gave it a false date long before the true day." What infuriated the council, was the deep interest the inhabitants of Edinburgh took in this foul business; when it came before them, the passages to the Council-chamber were crowded with anxious inquirers; and it was debated at the council-board, whether all who were in the lobby should be imprisoned or not;—it was decided not, only by one voice.

[1677.] Prelatic inveteracy was not, however, bounded by Scotland, it pursued into other countries those who found among foreign Protestants that freedom of conscience denied them at home. Messrs. Robert Macwaird and Mr. John Brown, two eminent ministers, who had sought refuge in Holland, having been requested by the other Scottish refugees to exercise their sacred function among them at Rotterdam, the states-general were instantly required by Charles to dismiss them from their territories; and, in order to escape a war with England, were forced to comply with the tyrant's demand, yet not till they had afforded their respected guests an opportunity of disposing of their effects to the best advantage, and looking out for another asylum.

The persevering rancour of Charles, and the reluctance of the states, occasioned a protracted discussion of two days in their senate; and Sir William Temple declared that it had been the hardest piece of negotiation he had ever entered upon. Its issue was productive of a nobler and more durable testimony to the worth of the persecuted exiles, than could otherwise have been procured, and will hand down to posterity the everlasting remembrance of these righteous men, while the memory of the worthless monarch shall rot. The states entered on their record a resolution, importing that "the foresaid three Scotsmen have not only not behaved and comported themselves otherwise than as became good and faithful citizens of these states, but have also given many indubitable proofs of their zeal and affection for the advancement of the truth, which their High Mightinesses have seen with pleasure, and could have wished that they could have continued to live here in peace and security." Besides which, each received a separate testimonial on their departure. The following is a copy of the one put into the hands of Colonel Wallace:—"The States-General of the United Netherlands, to all and every one who shall see or read these presents, health: Be it known and certified that James Wallace, gentleman, our subject, and for many years inhabitant of this state, lived among us highly esteemed for his probity, submission to the laws, and integrity of manners. And therefore we have resolved affectionately to request, and hereby do most earnestly request, the Emperor of the Romans, and all Kings, Republics, Princes, Dukes, States, Magistrates, or whomsoever else our friends, and all that shall see these presents, that they receive the said James Wallace in a friendly manner whenever he may come to them, or resolve to remain with them, and assist him with their counsel, help, and aid; testifying, that for any obliging, humane, or kindly offices done to him, we shall be ready and forward to return the favour to them and their subjects whensoever an opportunity offers. For the greater confirmation whereof, we have caused these presents to be sealed with our seal of office, and signed by the President of our Assembly, the sixth day of the month of February, in the year one thousand six hundred and seventy-seven."

Colonel Wallace was afterwards forced to lurk about the borders of France or the Netherlands, whence he addressed to "the Lady Caldwell, widow of William Mure of Caldwell," the following letter, which I give as a specimen of the seditious correspondence he was accused of holding with the fanatics:—

"ELECT LADY AND MY WORTHIE AND DEAR SISTER,—Your's is come to my hand in most acceptable tyme. It seems that all that devils or men these many years have done (and that has not been lytle) against yow, to dant your courage, or to make yow, in the avoweing of your master and his persecuted interests, to loore your sailes hes prevailed so lytle, that your fayth and courage is upon the groweing hand, ane evidence indeed to your persecuters of perdition, bot to yow of salvation, and that of God. It seems when yow at first by choyce tooke Christ by the hand to be your Lord and portion, that yow wist what yow did; and that notwithstandeing all the hardnesses yow have met with in bydeing by him, your heart seems to cleave the faster to him. This sayes yow have been admitted into much of his company and fellowship. My sowle blesses God on your behalf who hath so caryed to yow, that I think yow may take those words, amongst others, spoken to you—'Yow have continued with me in my aflictions; I appoint unto yow a kingdom.' It seems suffering for Christ, loseing any thing for him, is to yow your glory—is to yow your gayn. More and more of this spirit maye yow enjoye, that yow may be among the few (as it was said of Caleb and Joshua) that followed him fullie—among the overcomers, those noble overcomers, mentioned Revel. ii. and iii.—among those to whom only (as pickt out and chosen for that end) he is sayeing, 'Yow are my witnesses.' Lady and my dear sister, I am of your judgement; and I blesse his name that ever he counted me worthie to appear in that roll. It is now a good many years since the master was pleased to even me to this, and to call me forth to appear for him; and it is trew these fortie years bygone (as to what I have mett with from the world) I have been as the people in the wilderness; yet I maye saye it to this howre, I never repented my ingadgements to him, or any of my oneings of him; yea, these rebutes to say so I gott from men, wer to me my joye and crowne, because I know it was for his sake I was so dealt with; and this, it being for his sake, I was ready in that case (as Christ sayes) when men had taken me upon the one cheek for his sake, to turn to them the other also. Never was I admitted to more neerness, never was my table better covered, then since I left Rotterdam. Let us take courage and goe on as good soldiers of Jesus Christ, endureing hardnes. O for more fayth! O for more fayth among his people! As to this people, there is nothing to be seen in their waye that is promiseing of any good; bot on the contrar. O! I feare the Lord hes given them up unto their owne heart's lusts. They doe indeed walke in their owne counsels. That same spirit of persecution, and these same principles, that are among you, are heir; bot as God is faythfull, they shall be all brocken to pieces and turned backe with shame that hate Zion. Wayt but a lytle; they are diggeing the pit for themselves. The Lord hath founded Zion, and the poore of the people shall trust in it. Let us mynd one another. My love to all friends whom yow know I love in the Lord. God's grace be with yow, and his blessing upon your lytle ones whom he hath been a father to. In him I rest. Your's as formerly,

"JA. WALLACE."

END OF VOLUME I.

www.ingramcontent.com/pod-product-compliance
Lightning Source LLC
LaVergne TN
LVHW020231110826
845151LV00003B/893

* 9 7 8 1 4 2 5 5 3 0 8 7 7 *